MILLIONAIRE IN THE MILITARY

SHAWN WALSH

MILLIONAIRE IN THE MILITARY

A SERVICE MEMBER'S GUIDE TO SECURING FINANCIAL FREEDOM

WILEY

Published by John Wiley & Sons, Inc., Hoboken, New Jersey.

For general information on our other products and services or for technical support, please contact our Customer Care Department within the United States at (800) 762-2974, outside the United States at (317) 572-3993 or fax (317) 572-4002.

Wiley also publishes its books in a variety of electronic formats. Some content that appears in print may not be available in electronic formats. For more information about Wiley products, visit our website at www.wiley.com.

Library of Congress Cataloging-in-Publication Data is Available:

ISBN 9781394396443 (Cloth)
ISBN 9781394396450 (ePub)
ISBN 9781394396467 (ePDF)

Cover Design: Wiley
Cover Image: ekinyalgin/Getty Images
Author Photo: Courtesy of Katie Levine

SKY10162376_071426

To the men and women of the United States Military.

You swore an oath to a document—not a person, not a party, not a paycheck—and you have given this country 250 years of freedom. I am humbled to have stood among you.

I joined 22 years ago—a clueless kid from New Jersey with $50,000 of debt. I made mistakes—a lot of them. And somewhere in the middle of all of it, I figured it out. Enough to retire to the life I once only dreamed about.

This book is my way of giving back.

What if you were only 25 mistakes away from the life of your dreams?

Wouldn't you go out tomorrow and start making them?

You already took the hardest step. You raised your right hand.

Now go build something that matters.

Contents

Preface

I wrote this book after hundreds of "can I buy you a coffee and pick your brain?" conversations with friends and colleagues. Most commented, "I wish I knew this information sooner," and asked where I had learned. I could not direct them to a single source, and instead would give them a list of books, podcasts, people, and articles—collections of knowledge that I gathered over the years which grew in my mind like compound interest. These conversations made me realize that there was a financial information gap between our education system and the real world, and maybe I could put together a conglomeration of stuff I wish I knew when I joined the military 20 years ago.

The information within is from my direct personal experience. If I talk about any topic that I did not personally participate in, I will state that. I am not a certified financial planner. I'm not giving you personal financial advice. I'm giving you a playbook and the thinking that built it. This book is what I did, how I did it, the mistakes I made, and the eventual financial freedom that I achieved before my retirement.

Here is a guarantee that I want you to remember: *your life won't change toward the life you desire without action.* I will encourage you throughout this book to set it down and take action. That is all I can do; the decision to act is yours.

Part I

Getting Started

I am going to tell you a story. This is a true story, but I changed the names of most of the people, and where necessary—for classification, operational security, or to protect the innocent—I edited the details.

The moments before the start of a war, simulated or otherwise, are eerily quiet on the radio. The kind of quiet that makes you hear your own breathing in the mask. Broken only by the occasional check-in: "as fragged," "minus one," "on station." Short calls. Clean calls. Nobody wastes airtime. When fifty-plus airplanes share a frequency, every second matters.

I was the Mission Commander for this force package—coalition aircraft, multiple roles, multiple objectives, one timeline. I was being graded. This was my Mission Commander upgrade ride, and the war was Red Flag–Alaska: the most realistic air war in the world, fought annually with air assets from across the services and allied nations. We train like we fight, and Red Flag is the pinnacle of that training.

Statistically speaking, pilots in Vietnam who survived the first 10 missions had a much higher likelihood of surviving the entire war. Red Flag was built to simulate those first 10 missions in a high-stress environment—so young pilots could "pay the price" in training instead of in blood later. Iron sharpens iron.

By the time you step to the jet, everything has already been decided. Not emotionally—mathematically. We had an all-day mission planned, a solid 14-hour day of intense planning for every possible outcome and contingency. We always target backward. Start with the objective: strike the priority targets inside the time window and get everyone home safely. Then work backward through the whole chain—where the package needs to be, when it needs fuel, how we deconflict jets in the same piece of sky, what contracts trigger a reset, who has authority to change the plan.

In a normal four-ship tactical flight, deconfliction is manageable. When you place dozens of aircraft into the same airspace, with "red air" aggressors also fighting for altitude and geometry, deconfliction becomes the mission. Simplicity is almost always the best policy. A complex plan might look brilliant on a whiteboard, but in the fog and friction of war, complexity kills.

Second only to deconfliction is communication. If two airplanes are on the wrong frequency and miss a single update, it can tank the plan. In the heat of the moment, communication is the first thing that breaks down. That's why we train our whole careers to speak clearly and concisely under stress—and why we build a framework that holds even when people are task saturated and the radios are on fire.

All that planning was for one reason: so when things stopped being clean lines on a white sheet of paper, we could still execute.

Because the enemy always gets a vote.

That's what this book is about. Not fighter aviation. Mission planning. You have an objective. You have resources. You have constraints. You have distractions. If you plan in fragments, you miss targets. If you target backward, build contracts, and debrief honestly, you get better—and you win over time.

That mission was about getting dozens of people, systems, and decisions to align under pressure. This first section of the book is about building that same alignment in your financial life—before the pressure hits.

Financial freedom is the objective. And you are the mission commander.

My Starting Line

I am not a trust fund kid, and neither is my spouse. We did not grow up with money. My dad was a carpenter; my mom ran the home. I was the second of seven kids. We stretched bills, stretched meals, and stretched our imaginations. My parents taught me gratitude over envy—a mindset that shaped me—because gratitude and unhappiness do not coexist. What we weren't taught was how to build wealth. No one in our world knew how. Two decades after commissioning in 2004—with plenty of missteps in those 20 years—I retired from the Air Force with financial freedom and a playbook worth sharing.

Growing up in rural New Jersey in the 1980s I knew little of the world. I heard stories of faraway places from my uncle who flew cargo jets in the Air Force. I was young when I first saw the movie *Top Gun* and it had a profound impact on me, as it did much of the country. As the son of an immigrant, I learned an immense sense of pride in being an American and that fed a desire within me to serve my country, to give back for the privilege of growing up in a country where I had freedoms guaranteed by our Constitution.

As a kid in the 1980s I also learned about poverty. The early part of the decade saw soaring interest rates, set to combat high inflation, which led to a multi-year recession and some seriously "hard times" for working-class Americans with high unemployment rates and the worst economic situation since the Great Depression. I grew up thinking that Thanksgiving turkeys were picked up from the basement of the church and it was normal to pay either the cable bill or the phone bill each month, so you alternated which service was turned off. My parents were the hardest working people I know, and I grew up not even realizing how hard times were. In my teens, when I became aware of the struggle, I vowed to myself that I would find another way.

The combined influences of patriotism, aviation, and wanting to escape poverty led me toward the military. In high school I learned that the military could pay for my college through the Reserve Officer Training Corps (ROTC). I couldn't have afforded college otherwise. I was accepted and offered a four-year scholarship to study Civil Engineering at Embry-Riddle Aeronautical University (ERAU) in Florida. My plan was coming together. I would be around aviation, palm trees, and have school paid for.

After college I commissioned as a Second Lieutenant in the US Air Force and set off for pilot training. Along the way I met an amazing woman whose passion for life and big visions for the future completely captured me. Sixteen months later Hillary and I were married, and with our new life off to a running start, I knew I had to get serious about our finances. I approached my financial life as I would a mission in the jet. I studied, prepared, planned, considered contingencies, ran through possible outcomes, and I defined objectives for what we wanted to accomplish. It was a slow process, and for many years I wasn't sure it was working. But a decade passed and we had a small nest egg. Then another five years passed and we had nearly doubled it. Then, in the last five years we used what we had learned and saved to add jet fuel to our portfolio and through investing, real estate, and business ownership, we were able to grow our portfolio exponentially—a precursor to our financial freedom.

"Financial freedom." It's a term that means different things to different people. To me it means being able to do whatever I want with my time without the constant stress of how I am going to pay my bills. Time is a resource that we cannot get more of no matter how much money we acquire, and I use it as my currency for life.

On the day I was commissioned into the Air Force, I had a net worth of negative $50,000. I had $30,000 in student loans and I had just taken a loan to buy a truck—my "Lieutenant-mobile"—for $20,000. But worse than being $50k in the hole, I had zero knowledge of how to get out of that hole, other than saving 10% of every paycheck because I saw that in a movie once.

Twenty years and three months later, I retired from the US Air Force with a net worth over eight figures, and more importantly, what I considered "financial freedom"—being able to do whatever I wanted with my time and live the life of my dreams.

How did I do it? Well, that's what I'm here to tell you; to share my story—both my time flying fighter jets (to keep things interesting) and the steps I took to achieve financial freedom by retirement.

I know a lot of people will begin from the stance, "of course he did, he was an officer and made more money" or "This won't work for me because I am enlisted." And if that is what you truly believe, you are right. Henry Ford said it best: "Whether you think you can or you think you can't, you're right." If you are unwilling to challenge your own belief system, and you've already decided this won't work for you, this book won't be able to help you. But if you're willing to challenge that story—even a little—keep reading.

If you want to experience a *change* in your life, then you can't keep doing the same things day after day—that feels obvious but is surprisingly not. In her book *Sudden Death,* Rita Mae Brown summed it up well: "Insanity is doing the same thing over and over again and expecting different results" (a quote often misattributed to Albert Einstein). Don't be insane in this way; instead, you must change your environment, your habits, and your view of the world. In doing this, you will change your outcomes.

I am also not here to tell you that there is a "right" way to achieve financial freedom. Many other military members have accomplished as much in different ways. While there is no one right way, there are lots of wrong ways to do it (*cough, sports betting, cough*). So hopefully this book helps you steer clear of those. And I am also not here to tell you that you *should* do anything, because I hate that word. If you DESIRE to retire financially free and live your life to its fullest potential then this is something you *want* to do, not *should* do. Change that one word in your life and you will already start to see things changing in the way you show up every day.

This book can be read all the way through, or one chapter at a time. I tried to write each chapter so it could stand alone while also flowing with the story. I want you to be able to put the book down, return to it, take notes, record your wins and failures, return to it a year later, again 10 years later, check your progress, and begin the next step of your journey.

I am going to treat much of this like a fighter pilot debrief, where the rank is off. We're here to cut through to the facts and do root-cause analysis on my financial journey. As a fighter pilot, we don't take things personally. We don't bring excuses. We put in the work, and we treat every mistake as a learning opportunity. We grow and we get better. We win or we learn; there is no failure if you do not quit. If you are not here for that, then this book probably isn't for you. For all the work I did in writing it, I hope I can ask you to do one thing in reading it: that is, approach it with a mindset that is open to change. Finally, I am going to share stories—*unclassified*, of course—of my 20 years as an Air Force officer and F-16 pilot.

Pre-Flight: What You Need to Know to Begin

When I attempt to describe flying a fighter jet to friends or family—telling a story, relaying a lesson learned, or just reliving an experience—I find that I often use pilot jargon that makes the whole story difficult to understand. There is a concept that discusses how the more a person becomes immersed in their field, the harder it is to explain their field to other people. This has been my experience when talking about flying and to a lesser degree, when talking about financial freedom. Sometimes the best person to walk you through a process is someone who has done it recently. But the trouble is that the person who has done something recently has not demonstrated success yet. So, this section is the starting point, the baseline for understanding, and if you have even an intermediate level of financial literacy you can likely skip this section. I will include some very basic concepts that I now take for granted; but I did not know these things when I was 18.

If you find yourself reading this section thinking "yeah, I already knew that" or "why did I pay for a book to tell me what a checking account is," then I want to congratulate you! You already have a basic understanding and can probably jump to the next section. But just because you already knew *some* of it, doesn't mean you know *all* of it. Even I am still learning in the process of writing this book. Approach it from a place of curiosity about what you could learn; a place of gratitude for already knowing this portion; and a place of understanding that there are some people reading this who were never told or shown how to open an investment account and start earning compound interest.

But, before we taxi, we need to get on the same page with a few definitions. If you already know this stuff, skip ahead. If you don't, good—this is your foundation. Either way, no one gets to take off without a quick brief.

What Is Money?

The most basic place that I can start, although maybe not the most widely understood, is with the question "What is money?" Money is a tool, nothing more. It has value because we assign value to it. It is a printed piece of paper or a stamped coin of some sort that transmits a value that we have all agreed upon. Some money is created with a product that has inherent value—such as gold or silver coins—but is not widely circulated in the 21st century. Money is a tool that allows you to trade some amount of time, talent, effort, or planning for someone else's time, talent, and effort.

Historically, people would barter and trade. The baker would trade loaves of bread to the smith for new horseshoes; the smith would trade a new hoe to the farmer for eggs. It was difficult to move large volumes of goods over long distances. If the farmer wanted to trade a wagonload of cucumbers or wool, they had to haul it to the city to trade it. Money was a way to trade value without carrying the goods with you. You could carry an entire pouch of coins, with a value equivalent to a wagonload of wool, and buy the items you needed. The government ensured the quality and weight of the coins, typically made of precious metals, and would guarantee the value of the money. Most of the world went away from the "gold standard," a set amount of gold in a vault for every dollar in circulation and moved to a "fiat" currency. A fiat currency is a currency that is guaranteed by the government but does not have any actual gold to back it up (or silver, or other valuable resource directly tied to the value of the money). The advantage is that governments can manipulate the value of the currency in relation to goods to benefit the economy; they can devalue the currency in times of economic crisis to incentivize spending for example. The downside to fiat currency is that the government can manipulate the value of the currency.

The takeaway is that money only has the value that we assign to it. The starting place for this book is to remove any emotional attachment that we might feel toward money and view it more like a hammer or a wrench. Money is a tool to be used to live the life that you desire.

Bank Accounts

Now that we covered the basics of what money is, let's move on to where we keep money and the various investment vehicles that we will discuss in this book. The most basic bank accounts that every person should have are a checking and a savings account.

- A checking account is a *very* low-interest-bearing account that is meant to be used for a high volume of transactions, your day-to-day expenses, your monthly bills, your paycheck, etc.
- A savings account is also a low-interest-bearing account and is meant to be a place to park some extra money for a rainy day. The total number of transactions per month are usually capped and they typically offer a larger interest rate than checking accounts but still far below other accounts.

It is often recommended to keep three to six months' worth of expenses in your savings account for emergencies. This is a safe practice and can be beneficial if you find yourself in a tough situation and need cash. However, the underlying reason for the three to six-month recommendation is almost always rooted in the idea that you could lose your job at any moment and need to float your lifestyle until you find another job. Or that you would have a sudden medical emergency requiring extensive hospital bills and possibly the inability to work and make more money.

As a military member I did not have those same concerns and so I did not subscribe to the "three to six months emergency fund in savings principle." I was not worried about losing my job—the military job security is about as good as it gets—and I was not worried about medical because the military provided full medical benefits for me and my family, even if I were incapacitated. Consult with your local financial planner on base for a recommendation, and with all things, make your own informed decision.

I preferred to keep my money in higher-interest-bearing accounts that gave me access to my money with a few days' notice. This technique is a bit riskier, and I am not advocating that you do or do not follow the three to six-month recommendation; everyone's situation is different—my wife and I were healthy, had no children at this point, and did not feel we needed many months of cash on hand. If your situation differs—your spouse is a civilian and you rely on their income, you are a family with a single income, you have specific medical needs, for example—keep the tried-and-true three to six months in your emergency fund. But you can still put that money in a higher-interest-bearing account.

When flying a fighter jet every pilot knows that they have the authority to deviate from the plan if they are prepared to justify the reason for the deviation in the debrief. This rule applies to your emergency fund as well. If you do not have a sound and justifiable reason to deviate, then stick with the tried-and-true recommendation. When you feel the need to deviate, have a good reason.

If you do not have a checking and savings account, go open one of each. You can use any bank but there are some like USAA and Navy Federal Credit Union that have specific benefits offered to service members—I am not sponsored by any bank, but I have used these in the past.

Good, you have those accounts, now, what is interest? Interest is money you make on your money. More accurately, for checking and savings accounts, it is a small sliver of the money your bank is making on your money. If you deposit $10,000 into a bank, they do not lock it away in a vault with your name on it and save it for the day you may come knocking. Instead, they lend it out to other people who need loans for homes, cars, and other major expenses. To thank you for the fact that you keep "three to six months of emergency fund" in their bank, they are willing to give you a whopping 0.4% in your savings account—the same money they lent to Bob and charged him 6.5% interest for the loan. Now, there will also likely be bank fees associated with keeping these accounts open and maintaining them, so you are likely not making 0.4% on your money and instead are paying to keep your money there. This isn't necessarily a bad thing because you want the ability to write checks, use bank cards, and easily move money around. Your fees pay for that privilege.

You might be wondering what I do with my money? Well, I do keep some money in savings, just in case I ever need it for an emergency. But I do not keep the recommended three to six months, I keep about one month. I also have numerous other accounts where I can get money in a day or two. We will get into investment accounts next, index funds, mutual funds, stocks, and bonds—but I keep most of my money in investments making me around 10% per year over the last 20 years—in fact the S&P 500 (the "Standard & Poor's 500" is a list which tracks the 500 largest public companies in the USA) has averaged 10.4% per year over the last 30 years and 10.5% over the last 100 years![1] (This is a historical average and does not guarantee future performance.[2]) In other words, if I put $10,000 into an index fund (I'll explain these in a later chapter) and make 10%, I will have

$11,000 at the end of the year; that same money in a savings account and I will have $10,040 at year's end. And that will grow and net even more in future years—something which we will cover shortly. Pretty solid return, right? Yes, it is. But it also comes with risk, which we will also dive into later.

Now that you have finished the intro you have at a minimum, a checking account and a savings account. We will go further into investments and other types of accounts later. But it is futile to open investment accounts if you have no money to put in them. So first we must look at "how I spend my money." To start a journey toward financial freedom you must spend less than you earn. If you make one million dollars per year but you spend one million and one dollars per year, you will be broke. Conversely, if you make thirty thousand dollars per year and spend only twenty-five thousand, you are on your way to financial freedom.

Every chapter in this book will have Action Steps at the end meant to guide and remind you what the most important next steps are. Before going on to the next chapter, make sure to take these action steps.

Action Steps:

1. **Open a checking account at your preferred bank—I use USAA.**
2. **Open a savings account at your preferred bank—I use USAA.**
3. **Give yourself a high five for finishing a chapter.**

Chapter 1

How I Spend My Money

"Proper Prior Planning Prevents Piss Poor Performance."

—Military axiom

It was time to turn hot. Not eventually—now. In two seconds.

"Elvis hot left," I called on the intraflight radio.

A "hot turn" is a full-afterburner, max-rate turn that gets the pointy end of the jet pointed back into the fight. In this case, my weapon was a Block 40 F-16 in a loaded combat configuration. A machine built for speed and violence—if you respect it.

Years ago, going through flight lead upgrade, I had practiced hundreds of timing turns. The outbound leg. The clock. The turn so precise that you arrive on the exact second you planned. Not "close enough." Exact.

Because today, exact mattered.

Everything up until now had been clean lines on a white sheet of paper.

Then the fight started.

We were climbing fast, burners lit, radios beginning to fill. Picture calls, threat calls, updates stacking on top of each other. This is where plans stop being theoretical and start getting stress tested. This is also where pilots get into trouble—not because they're careless, but because they're saturated.

Task saturation is real. Every fighter pilot experiences it. When the workload spikes, your brain can only hold so much. You don't rise to your goals—you fall back to your habits. That's why we train the basics relentlessly. Aviate. Navigate. Communicate. Everything else waits.

Money works the same way.

Most financial mistakes don't happen because someone is bad with money. They happen when life gets loud. When you're tired. When you're busy. When decisions are made on autopilot. That's when small, unconscious choices—coffee, delivery, "just this once"—start stacking up quietly in the background.

We counter this through preparation, planning, and situational awareness.

Your financial life requires preparation and planning as well. Before you think about investing, retirement, or getting fancy, you need situational awareness. Where is your money actually going? Not where you think it goes—where it goes when you're stressed, distracted, or moving fast.

In aviation, we don't wait until we're out of gas to wonder what happened. We plan before we move. We give the jet orders before takeoff, so timing works even when the radios are loud.

This chapter is your pre-flight. Every dollar gets orders before the month starts. Awareness first. Control second. Everything else builds on that.

I walked into the office one morning and greeted Airman Jones behind the operations desk. I was the Director of Operations at the 309th Fighter Squadron at Luke Air Force Base in Arizona. Like most DOs in the fighter community, my desk was right next to the ops desk where our pilots received their daily briefing before going out to the flightline and the jets for the day's mission. Airman Jones and I were the first two in the building this morning and I asked him how his weekend had been. He replied with a sighing response about going out with friends to the bar and how expensive everything was. Before I knew it, we were into a full-blown conversation on how we each spent our money.

There is no right way to spend your money—but I would argue that there are several wrong ways. And, in my experience, discussions around spending money inevitably led to conversations about "budgeting," which we tend to approach with a mindset of "there is never enough." I prefer to reframe the budgeting conversation as "How I Spend My Money" rather than "what is my budget." This is a more proactive mindset, and you become an active participant in your monthly expenses rather than waiting for the bills to hit and then dividing up the pie into smaller and smaller slivers to cover your "budget."

Why do you think one of the first chapters of this book is about how you spend your money? Because if you earn $1,000,000 a year but spend $1,000,001, you are broke. By the same token, if you make $30,000 a year and spend only $25,000, you are on your way to financial freedom. Today you will give every dollar in your account a job to do at the start of each month. I put equal weight on the mindset of becoming financially free versus the steps and habit patterns that will get you there. And without understanding how and where you spend your money, achieving financial freedom isn't possible.

Every dollar has a job to do when the month begins. When people hear the word "budget," it elicits feelings of depriving themselves, of never having enough, pinching pennies and worrying about next month's bills. Let's start here by flipping the script on that "mindset of lack."

Mindset check:

- Scarcity Mindset = I don't make enough money.
- Abundance Mindset = I choose where my money goes; every dollar has "orders," and I can always make more.

From now on, refer to your budget as your "How I Spend My Money Plan." This is a powerful and proactive formation of the same thought. This is taking ownership of the money that you earn, not passively allowing it to slip through your fingers to the tax man or bill collector.

While we are at it, let's reframe our attitude toward paying bills. This is going to sound strange but stay with me—I love paying my electric bill. Yep, I do. Why? Because I love walking into my room, flipping on the light switch, and having electricity immediately. I love turning on my air conditioner in the Phoenix summers and keeping the house at a nice, cool temp while everything melts. And because I love my access to electricity, I love paying my electric bill. I am grateful for the privilege of electricity and my cell phone bill and my internet bill and my gas bill—you get the point.

So, we are no longer stretching our money in our "budget" to pay the evil bill collectors. We have ownership of our finances and our lives, and we proudly state "This Is How I Spend My Money and I am grateful." Well, maybe we aren't quite there yet, but even baby steps move you forward in life.

Back to my conversation with Airman Jones:

"We just don't make enough money as enlisted to be able to afford anything," he lamented. I listened, without interrupting, understanding that as an officer I did have a higher salary and any advice I passed along might not be received how I intended it. When he was finished complaining about his lack of money, he asked me what I thought—an opening, if only a slight one. I actually think

I could help here, but I proceeded with caution and care. I was not there to rescue him or tell him the "right" way to spend his money. Instead, maybe I could be a sounding board to let him find his own way.

"Well, what do your current bills consist of?" I asked, genuinely curious.

"I have a cell phone bill, my car payment, my insurance, gas, food, and there really isn't enough to cover everything," he said.

"That sucks," I really meant it. I have been in his shoes, getting to the end of the month and using my credit card for the last few things that I needed (or thought I needed).

"Do you want to write it out while we sit at the ops desk today in between flying go's?" I was the Squadron's Top-3 this day, the person on the ground who was always available via radio for pilots to call back for any reason they couldn't handle airborne, you name it, the Top-3 was there for it. But, while waiting for the jets to call in their maintenance codes or call in with a request, you often spent hours working on paperwork. And while I had plenty of paperwork as the DO, I much preferred a conversation about finances with a young airman who I might just be able to help a little.

"Really? You would do that? Yes please, I would appreciate it!" he said eagerly.

I had already had many of these conversations with other members of the squadron, and even other members from around the base. Somehow word had gotten around that I was proficient in investing, taxes, "how I spend my money planning," etc.—and many people had offered to buy me a coffee and pick my brain, from an Airman Basic, E-1, all the way up to a full-bird Colonel, O-6. I am not sure if I helped all of them, but I gave them plenty to think about.

Most importantly, I shared openly and freely about all the times that I screwed up—and there were many. I found over the years that one of the fastest ways to build trust with people and an organization is through vulnerability. An idea that was later reinforced in one of my favorite books for team building, Daniel Coyle's *The Culture Code*: build trust first and then results will follow. Brene Brown hits the nail on the head when she highlights the paradox: vulnerability is something we view as a strength in others and value, but for some reason we view it as a weakness in ourselves. Maybe it was because I was a member of the pretty macho-seeming community of fighter pilots. But being vulnerable always caught people off guard and usually led to deeper conversations and trust between us.

As the last of 12 pilots stepped out the door to the crew van for the short drive to where the jets were parked, Airman Jones already had out his paper and pen, writing line after line of things he needed to pay for every month. Just the simple act of writing things down can have a profound impact on how we view our situation. If you ever find yourself struggling with something, get a paper and pen and start writing. Write about the problem, all the reasons it is unsolvable, all the negative things about the situation; and then write one positive. Then ask yourself, "how did I contribute to this" and answer that question in writing. Then ask, "how would ____ solve this?" and insert whomever you think would be the best person, living or dead, to solve this problem. While the perfect solution may not always appear, the act of writing it out brings clarity and purpose to what you are attempting to achieve. This book will have notes pages and an accompanying PDF for you to take plenty of your own notes and write it down. And you don't need to take my word for it. Check out the book *Write It Down, Make It Happen* for the science behind why it works and a deeper understanding of the power of writing.

When Jones finished his writing, he paused and stared at the list. I could see the wheels turning. He added everything up a second time to double-check his math. I could see that something was off, and I had a suspicion of what it was.

"Well, I wrote everything but it's actually less than my pay; but I run out of money every month before the next payday; is it because I am not considering taxes?"

"Perhaps," I lied. "Why don't you pull up your pay stub on MyPay and write those numbers down as well over on the right side of the paper?"

He logged in and dutifully scribbled his income on the right side across from his expenses.

"No, I see the taxes here on my pay stub," he said. "Man, taxes are high. But that isn't it. I guess I just have more expenses that I am forgetting."

"I do that all the time," I didn't lie this time, I really do that. "Why don't you pull up your last three months of bank and credit card statements and look for expenses that you didn't already list?"

Twenty minutes later Jones looked up at me and said, "Wow, I didn't realize how much I was spending on other stuff."

"Like what?" I asked. Although, I had a pretty good idea already as I lobster-eyed his Big-Dumb-Coffee-Cup on the desk next to his paper. As a parent I have learned that if I tell my kids something there is only about a 20% chance they will hear it and internalize it; but if I bring them to the edge of the problem and let them have their own eureka moment, they remember the lesson nearly 100% of the time.

"Well, I am kinda surprised by how much all these food charges add up to," Jones said. "There are like 15 charges to 'coffee shop' for $9.23 each. But hey, you know, gotta have my venti cold brew with caramel."

"Okay," I respond slowly, starting to realize that maybe the lesson was not readily apparent.

"Oh man, food delivery destroyed me last month! That is like half my paycheck!"

I can see the realization kicking in; and it's time to look for solutions.

"Okay cool," I say, bringing him back from his state of shock. "Now we know *where* your money went last month; so, we can decide where you *choose* to spend your money this month."

"Umm, is it really that simple?"

"Yep." He stares for a minute, wheels turning in his mind, so I continue. "If we make a list of everything that you *want* to spend your money on, then we can determine if there really isn't enough money or if we just need to develop habit patterns to spend our money consciously on things we choose."

"Okay, I'm game, let's do it. Well, we gotta start with the car. I can't get rid of that even if I wanted to, not for another 30 months." More on car loans in a later section, for now, yep, he was stuck with it. "And that means I need to include insurance and gas as well, so I guess those stay."

"What about housing?" I ask. I know the answer but am hoping to lead him to another realization.

"I live in the dorms, so it doesn't cost anything."

"That's great," I add, "and what about your meals?"

"Well, I eat mostly at the chow hall and that is covered as well. Okay, well, except when I order delivery in the evenings—did you know they can come on base now? I can get cheesecake at 2 in the morning!" Ah, to have the metabolism of a 20-year-old.

"That's also great, so if you absolutely had to, you could spend almost nothing on food each month. . .you know, like if you absolutely had to." I don't want it to seem like I am accusing him of blowing his budget on late-night cheesecake; and frankly, if that is the one thing he loves more than anything in the world, then go for it! But maybe buy a whole cheesecake from the grocery store and keep it in the fridge for a fraction of the price.

"Yeah, true, I could probably cut back on food delivery," he says with a sigh. "I think I see where this is going. . ."

"Really? What are you thinking?"

"Well, when I write it down, I actually *do* have enough money, but I spend it on lots of random stuff that I don't have to buy." Bingo, the moment of recognition, now where to go from here?

"Yep, we all do that, I totally get it—did I ever tell you that with my first Air Force paycheck I bought a kayak that I only used once? What a ridiculous purchase. I've come a long way from that point, but it wasn't easy and often it still isn't easy."

"So then, what do I do next?"

"Well, my recommendation would be to make a list called 'How I Spend My Money'—I hate the word 'budget'—and then start making choices on how you spend rather than being a passive observer as you fall back into habit patterns like stopping by a coffee shop three to four times a week. . .no judgment, but I do see you with one of those Big-Dumb-Coffee-Cups in your hand almost every day."

"They are just so good! I don't think I could make this at home. . ."

"Have you tried?"

"No."

"Maybe that could be a place to start?"

"Okay, let's do it!"

The pages following this chapter have worksheets for you to take these steps on your own. Not because you need rules or restrictions, but because we all need clarity. Where are you spending money mindlessly because of habit patterns or poor planning? Where is money leaving your account without you noticing?

That moment with Jones wasn't unique. I've had some version of that same conversation dozens of times—across ranks, across units, across years. The details change, but the pattern is always the same. When you slow down long enough to actually look at where your money is going, clarity shows up almost immediately. Not shame. Not judgment. Just awareness. And awareness is powerful, because once you can see what's happening, you get to choose what happens next.

That's all we're doing here. We're not punishing past decisions or pretending you can't enjoy your life. We're simply pulling the jet out of autopilot and putting your hands back on the controls.

A lot of people assume they have a discipline problem. In reality, most people have a visibility problem. This is what I call unconscious spending—money leaving your account in small, quiet ways that you barely notice. Subscriptions you forgot about. Habits that feel harmless in the moment. Purchases you've made so many times they no longer register as decisions.

I've been doing this exercise for more than 20 years, and I still find things I didn't realize I was buying. That's not because I'm careless—it's because human brains are really good at automating behavior. Once something becomes routine, we stop thinking about it. And when spending happens without thought, it happens without intention.

There is a reason this happens. The part of your brain responsible for filtering information and bringing things to your attention is called the Reticular Activating System, or RAS. You've experienced it before. When you start shopping for a certain car, suddenly you see that car everywhere. They were always there—you just weren't looking for them. When you start tracking your spending, the same thing happens. Purchases that used to fly under the radar suddenly stand out.

Maybe last month you spent $100 on coffee and didn't even realize it. Once you see that number on paper, your awareness changes. The next morning, you start to pull into the coffee shop like you always do—except this time you notice the turn. And instead of giving in to the habit, you keep driving and grab the free coffee at work. Same morning. Different choice.

The easiest way to see unconscious spending is to do the math on something you barely think about.

The Big-Dumb-Coffee-Cup Math

- $9 per cup, 3 times a week.
- $27 Weekly = Annual: $1,404.
- $1 at 20 years old ≈ $72 at age 65 when compounded at 10% annually for 45 years. This is not a guaranteed rate of return, it is just compounding math.
- That first year's $1,404 of coffee could be $101,088 at retirement age of 65.
- If you invest that $27 weekly for 20 years, then stop contributing and let it sit another 25 years, at age 65 you will have more than $900,000!
- Small incremental steps can have huge impacts over time.

What's your version of the Big-Dumb-Coffee-Cup? Maybe it's something totally different—Magic the Gathering cards, sports betting, drinking on the weekends, food delivery, impulse Amazon purchases, or subscriptions you forgot existed. Look for the places where you don't even realize how much you're spending. You'll almost certainly find one. And you will likely find your own Big-Dumb-Coffee-Cup.

This is where the worksheets come in. Their purpose isn't to restrict you—it's to surface these patterns. To turn unconscious spending into conscious choice. Take control of your purchases and only buy what you want for your life. For the record, I don't care what it is that you want for your life. That's your life, not mine. You do you. Live your best life. Just do it with a plan.

The next time you're at work, walk around and see how many people are carrying one of those big dumb coffee cups. Do the math in your head. Then compare it to the cost of making it at home. Even after I retired from the military with a full pension, I still make my coffee at home every morning. Mostly because it's part of my habit pattern—but also because I don't see the value in regularly paying nine dollars for something I can make better myself.

Implementing the Plan

Now that we understand what's happening, the rules get very simple. Step one is spending less than you make. Period. Nothing else in this book will work if you don't get this right. This is the first action step. Everything else builds on it.

"But I've never made a How I Spend My Money Plan before—what's the right way?"

There isn't a single right way. But a principle that has stood the test of time is the 50-30-20 rule:

- 50% for needs
- 30% for wants
- 20% for savings and investing

Before you say this is impossible, know that almost everyone says the same thing. Remember what Henry Ford taught us: "whether you think you can, or you think you can't, you're right." We all have reasons why something won't work. This book isn't about excuses—it's about finding reasons it will.

Category	Percent of After-Tax Income	Example Expenses
Needs	50%	Rent or mortgage; utilities; groceries; transportation; insurance; minimum debt payments
Wants	30%	Dining out; entertainment; hobbies; alcohol; streaming services; non-essential purchases
Savings	20%	TSP, IRA, emergency savings fund; extra debt payments above the minimum if required

Maybe you can't get there overnight. Maybe your rent or car payment is too high right now and requires a longer-term decision. That's okay. The goal is direction, not perfection.

Start your How I Spend My Money Plan with necessities—what I call the Big Five: housing, utilities, insurance, transportation, and food. If you're living in base housing or have meals provided, you get to write zero in those columns. That matters.

One of the most overlooked advantages military members have is how early we start the money race ahead of our peers. Most civilians spend their early careers building emergency funds, paying for medical insurance, food, housing, and saving for a down payment. While they graduate and go get a job, they spend their first months just trying to save an emergency fund of three to six months' worth of expenses in case they get laid off—a concern that most military members do not have. They also must pay for their own medical insurance, which is costly each month.

Many of those expenses are partially or fully covered for us early on.

They must pay for housing, food, and clothes, necessities the military often provides in the beginning and then gives a stipend through Basic Allowance for Housing (BAH) and Basic Allowance for Subsistence (BAS). And when it is time to buy their first house, our peers must save for decades for the down payment, which is not necessary when utilizing a VA loan. There are many military benefits that give us a leg-up when first starting out, so learn how to capitalize on them. That creates something powerful: disposable income.

What I didn't realize as a young Airman living in the dorms was just how much disposable income I had. Housing, food, utilities, insurance: covered or subsidized. Transportation was optional. If I had chosen to, I could have invested the majority of my paycheck before I had real responsibilities. As a young Airman making around $35,000 per year, you likely have close to $30,000 of disposable income. The next time you'll have that much *disposable* income is probably after retirement.

Most military members get married around the eight-year mark, have kids and buy a house around year ten, and money tightens quickly.[1,2] That's when I usually met them—credit card debt creeping up, stress rising, and retirement suddenly feeling urgent.

> *"The best time to plant a tree was twenty years ago. The second-best time is now."*
>
> —Folk Proverb

I could not go backward for these folks, but I could help them with a way forward. However, if you are reading this and just starting out in the military then you are at a great advantage. Start now, invest and save, and if you must back off later how much you put away, you will still be better off.

The final—and hardest—part of the How I Spend My Money Plan process is sticking with it. The military ingrains discipline into everything we do, yet a lot of service members completely disengage when it comes to personal finances. As a fighter pilot, discipline is not only a requirement of the job, it means life or death for you, your wingman, your peers, and the people on the ground. We spend countless hours training to checklist-discipline because it is what saves us when things are difficult and we are stressed out. By reverting to our training and our checklist, we can calmly handle any situation that the jet, the environment, or the enemy might throw at us. Treat your spending plan like a checklist. Update it when necessary but always refer back to it. That's how we stay alive in jets, and it's how you stay on track with money.

In aviation, real learning happens in the debrief. We dissect missions unemotionally to determine whether mistakes were execution errors or game-plan errors. Do the same with your finances. At the end of each month, pull up your bank statement and your plan. If you went over, don't beat yourself up. Figure out why.

Execution error? You had a plan but gave in to the moment. A stop at the coffee shop because your friends were grabbing coffees.

Game-plan error? You didn't set yourself up to succeed. You didn't have a plan for morning coffee and were forced to buy one because otherwise you would have fallen asleep at your post.

By conducting your debrief on the last day of the month you start the next month with learning and momentum. Make small adjustments. Build systems. Turn systems into habits. When life gets stressful, you won't rise to the level of your goals—you'll fall to the level of your habits.

You are developing habit patterns here. When faced with adversity we do not rise to the level of our dreams and goals, we fall back to the level of our habits and our systems.[3] Create systems in your life for financial freedom; and develop those into habits that you will fall back on. Research shows that it takes approximately 66 days for a habit to stick. Print a paper calendar, tape it to your wall. Then, mark your calendar for 66 days from now; when you get up every morning, put a red X on your calendar for mornings that your coffee was ready to go, and you did not buy one on the way to work. Those red Xs will start to accumulate, and you will gain momentum from your own success. Before you know it, you will look back and chuckle at the old version of yourself who used to spend $45 per week on big dumb coffee cups.

If you think printing paper calendars and writing things down is too old school or too bad for the environment, no worries, I see you. There are several apps and online resources that you can use to help you build a How I Spend My Money Plan and stick to it. But, before you do, ask yourself (and answer honestly), has this worked for you before? Have you downloaded six other gym, fitness, or calorie tracker apps but never actually used them? I've done that. I know myself and I know that if I get an app, I likely won't do it. But, if I put a piece of paper on my kitchen wall next to my coffee maker with a red marker pinned to the wall next to it, I will almost certainly do it. And bonus, I will tell my family what I am doing, and they will encourage and remind me. This accountability partner concept can be life-changing, and finding the right person to help you with accountability can be the difference between success and failure.

When you track your spending like this, you'll start noticing purchases before they happen. That's the whole game. Awareness first. Then choice. And when you start having small victories, celebrate them. When you skip the coffee, move the money. When you cancel the subscription, reallocate that $12 per month automatically. Every dollar needs orders. And once you've got your personal leaks under control, you'll start seeing the bigger ones.

Hidden Costs

Once you start seeing the obvious leaks, you'll notice something else: the world is engineered to drain your money quietly. So, what are the things that you are spending your money on that are holding you back—consciously or unconsciously. I did not grow up in an age of cell phones—my kids now plan to have a phone and a monthly cell plan for the rest of their lives starting from the time they are teenagers. My parents owned one or two pairs of shoes their entire lives, because they didn't need more. I now have a closet with more pairs of Jordans than I care to admit.

Young people today spend their money in many different places and are constantly inundated with far more marketing than when I was growing up—because I did not have a cell phone in my hand advertising to me 24/7. It's not hard to see where the money goes: dining out, food delivery, entertainment, trends, fashion, electronics, and whatever the algorithm is selling this week.

Young military members tend to spend their money on expensive vehicles, partying (alcohol), sports betting, eating out, video games, tobacco, and impulsive purchases, among other things.[4] I am not here to lecture you on how you should live your life. Frankly, I don't care. But I say that in the best of ways, the same way I used to explain it to young military members who worked for me.

I would tell them, "I do not care what you want to do with your career because it is YOUR career. I will help you and support you, and if you want guidance or suggestions, please ask. But I am not going to try to push you in one direction or another, because it is your life and career, not mine."

The same applies here. I am not trying to push you one way or another; it's your life, go live it. Instead, I want to help you see where your money is being spent so that you can choose for yourself. The key is to make a conscious decision about where your money goes and not blindly spend.

Here are some truths; if you feel "activated" by this list, then I encourage you to go deeper and figure out why this bothers you. First, sports betting is for suckers. You WILL lose. Sports betting is one of the largest and fastest growing industries in the world.

Guess what? The largest and fastest growing industries do not become that by losing money. They are large and fast growing because of the number of young people willing to spend their money on a chance to win. But the house always wins in the end. Period. It is also a highly addictive behavior because the dopamine hit you get when you occasionally win. Sports bettors notoriously underreport their losses and overreport their winnings, it is human nature. You are being fed a story by a very large industry that this is fun, and you will win money. I promise you; you will lose money and that will not be fun in the end. Make your own decision, just know that you will always lose in the end. That is how they stay in business.

The second hard truth, alcohol is likely ruining your life, or at least not contributing to you achieving your goals. If you want to learn a cool and interesting skill that you probably won't learn in the military, study sales and marketing—how they market alcohol to you. As you study it, you will start to see it everywhere around you. It was mind-blowing to me the more I learned about sales and marketing because I became acutely aware of all the areas of my life where I was blindly buying things because a clever sales or marketing person had convinced me of it. This is very evident in the alcohol industry. If I had to choose one single moment that had the biggest positive impact on my life, it would probably be the moment I quit alcohol. I drank for years and have no judgment for anyone who chooses to partake. I am just letting you know that the moment I quit, everything turned around for me. My life took off like a fighter jet in the best of ways. There are entire books written on the topic, such as *This Naked Mind* or *Sober Curious*. Not only is it eating through your brain cells, your relationships, and your health (alcohol has been linked to cancer in every reputable study ever done), it is eating through your wallet at an insane rate.[5] The Bureau of Labor Statistics determined that in 2023 the average American spent $637 per year on alcohol. In my experience with the military, it was far more than that.

Third, cars are not as cool as you think they are—this is a tricky one. We all want to drive the cool car. I cringed every time I saw the new E-3 in the squadron pull up in his Corvette—but I also empathize. It feels good. For a little while. In a later chapter I explain "the marshmallow test"—how having the discipline to delay gratification can lead to much bigger gains in the future. The urge to buy a flashy car that eats up half your paycheck is a real thing. Again, you do you. But, if instead you took a hard and sober look at your NEEDS right now you would probably find that you don't "need" a car at all. Once you are well established and on your way to financial freedom, go for it. When you are just starting out, I would approach car purchases with caution. For example, if you live on base and work close by, can walk to the commissary and base exchange, you likely do not even need a car.

"But I go out on the weekends," you might argue.

Do a cost comparison of catching a ride, taking public transport, or owning a car. Don't forget to factor in insurance, gas, and incidentals. If you determine you need a car, go for it. But define your mission—to and from work, taking kids to school, etc.—and then find a car that meets your needs for a reasonable price. Now that I have poo-pooed on all the fun stuff—gambling, booze, and cars, let me backtrack a little. I am not suggesting that you will *cut* your way to millionaire status. To reach a millionaire state you will need to *grow* into being a millionaire. Instead, I want you to make conscious choices about how you spend your money so that you will be living in alignment with your vision for your life.

So, set aside your 5% to TSP and gradually increase your monthly investments. Create and *stick to* your How I Spend My Money Plan; that will, in turn, ensure you live within your means. Every incremental raise you get in pay, go increase your investments. Look for opportunities to add value in your life and your portfolio. These are the basic principles that will start you down a path toward financial freedom. When you feel comfortable, investigate other investments. But most young people today give in to consumerism; they are bombarded by social media and what they "should" have—the cars, the clothes, the jewelry, etc. A generation ago, no one even had a cellphone; now every 16-year-old has a thousand-dollar device in their pocket that they make monthly payments on just to have cell service.

Spend less than you make. Give every dollar orders. Debrief monthly. Repeat until this becomes who you are. Put as much, or more, effort into your financial preparedness as you do time spent learning your job or playing video games.

- Conduct thorough financial reconnaissance by gathering all account statements, debts, and income sources
- Analyze enemy forces (debt, expenses, financial obstacles) and friendly forces (income, assets, opportunities)
- Assess terrain (economic environment, interest rates, market conditions) that will affect your financial mission
- Evaluate time and weather factors (career timeline, family changes, economic cycles) impacting your strategy

Action Steps:

1. **First, spend less than you make. Period.**
2. **Second, create a "How I Spend My Money Plan."**
3. **Third, stick to it.**
    a. **Develop systems for success.**
    b. **Use those systems to build habit patterns.**
    c. **More on this in the goal-setting chapter.**

HOW I SPEND MY MONEY PLAN

WORKSHEET

Mission Checklist:

- Download the last three months of statements.
- List your fixed obligations (rent, insurance, debt, etc.).
- List your variable habits (coffee, delivery, bars).
- Assign every dollar a job.
- Automate: pay yourself first (savings and investments), bills next, spending last.
- Schedule a monthly **Debrief** (last day of month): Game-plan error or execution error?

Debrief Outcomes:

- Savings rate: % of your monthly pay going into a *future* account
- Debt reduction: amount your debt *principal* is being reduced each month. Broken out separate from the debt interest being paid
- Leaky spending list
- Habits completed, habits in progress, & habits to build

Mindset Check:

Scarcity Mindset = "I don't make enough money."

Abundance Mindset = "I choose where my money goes. Every dollar has orders, and I can make more."

Mission Planning Phase

Monthly Income

Income Source	Monthly Amount
Base Pay/Salary	
Allowances/Stipends	
Side Income	
Other	
Total After-Tax Monthly Income	

Fixed Obligations

Expense	Monthly Amount

Variable Habits

Category	Monthly Amount

Savings & Investing: Paying Yourself First

Category	Monthly Amount

Execution Phase

Assign Every Dollar a Job

Category	Monthly Amount
Total Monthly Income:	
Total Fixed Expenses:	
Total Variable Spending:	
Total Savings & Investing:	
Money Left Unassigned (Should be $0)	

Where am I spending money unconsciously?

Where am I going to focus this month?

Debrief Phase

Monthly Debrief Form:

Was this month a success: Yes No Mixed

Explain:

Savings/Investing Rate (%): ____________________

Debt Reduction (Principal Only): ________________

What went well?

What did not go as planned?

Was it an Execution Error or a Gameplan Error? Explain.

Next month, in order to improve, I will. . .:

THE 50/30/20 RULE

A simplified framework for aligning your spending with your goal of financial freedom.

What is the 50/30/20 rule?

This rule is not a rigid framework; it is a guiding principle. You are deliberately choosing how to allocate your after-tax income across three broad categories: Needs, Wants, and Savings. The goal here is not perfection but awareness of where your money is going and intention with how you spend your money.

Mindset Check: This is not about restriction. It is not about judgment. It is simply about alignment. Aligning your spending habits with your stated goals. If your numbers today are not perfect, treat it as a piece of information to be used later, not failure.

Step 1: Reference your Mission Planning Phase table from the previous worksheet.

Income Source	Monthly Amount
Base Pay/Salary	
Allowances/Stipends	
Side Income	
Other	
Total After-Tax Monthly Income	

Step 2: Allocate your money.

Category	Target %	Target $
Needs	50%	
Wants	30%	
Savings	20%	
Total	100%	

This is your *PLAN* not your actual percentages

To calculate your Target $, multiply Total After-Tax Income × Category Percentage

Step 3: Calculate your ACTUAL expense ratios. Reference your Execution Phase table from the previous worksheet. Group your expenses into the three main categories and enter them into the table below.

NEEDS: Non-Negotiables

Expense	Monthly Amount
Housing	
Utilities	
Groceries	
Transportation	
Insurance	
Minimum Debt Payments	
Other:	
TOTAL	

WANTS: Lifestyle Choices

Expense	Monthly Amount
Eating Out	
Entertainment	
Hobbies	
Alcohol/Tobacco	
Subscriptions	
Travel	
Video Games	
Other	
TOTAL	

SAVINGS: Future You

Expense	Monthly Amount
Retirement Accounts	
Emergency Fund	
Investments	
Extra Debt Payments	
Other	
TOTAL	

Step 4: Analyze *PLANNED* versus *ACTUAL*

Category	Target %	Target $	Actual $	Actual %
Needs	50%			
Wants	30%			
Savings	20%			
Total	100%			

To calculate your Target $, multiply Total After-Tax Income × Category Percentage

Step 5: Reflection

Where am I currently out of alignment?

What is one adjustment I can make this month?

If I cannot hit these percentages today, what is one step I can take to move closer?

Reminder: The goal is progress, not perfection. Awareness precedes change. Analyze where you over- or under-allocated your money and adjust.

HABIT TRACKER

Habit I am building: ______________________.

Day	Completed (✓ X)	Notes
1		
2		
3		
4		
5		
6		
7		
8		
9		
10		
11		
12		
13		
14		
15		
16		
17		
18		
19		
20		
21		
22		
23		
24		
25		
26		
27		
28		
29		
30		
31		
32		
33		

Day	Completed (✓ X)	Notes
34		
35		
36		
37		
38		
39		
40		
41		
42		
43		
44		
45		
46		
47		
48		
49		
50		
51		
52		
53		
54		
55		
56		
57		
58		
59		
60		
61		
62		
63		
64		
65		
66		

Chapter 2

Retirement Planning

"Someone's sitting in the shade today because someone planted a tree a long time ago."

—Warren Buffett

By the time we stepped to the jets that morning, the mission was already decided.

Not emotionally. Mathematically.

When people hear "retirement," they think it's one decision—one big move—one moment where it all clicks. In my world, nothing important works that way.

A mission like Red Flag is not one aircraft and one target. It's a package: timing, fuel, contingencies, recovery, deconfliction, communication, and a whole team executing different roles at the same time. If one piece is late, the whole thing bends. If one piece fails, the package has to flex.

That day I wasn't just flying my jet. I was responsible for timing, fuel, packages, contingencies, and recovery. And I felt it. Maybe the only comparable feeling I've had was buckling my newborn twins into car seats for the first time and driving them home from the hospital. Same weight. Same thought: I can't afford to screw this up.

But here's the part that matters: no mission ever fully rests on one person. We are a team. We brief contracts so the team can function under pressure. We assign roles so success doesn't depend on one perfect human making one perfect decision.

Retirement is the same. If you prepare in fragments, you miss targets. If you "target backward" and assign roles—TSP, IRA, cash buffer, debt plan—you build a package that hits on time even when life gets loud. Automation becomes your timing turn. Your contributions become your push point. Your system keeps working on the days you don't feel like it.

Most people don't fail retirement because they don't care. They fail because they never built the package. They never assigned the roles. They never set the timing.

This chapter is where we fence in for your future. We're going to turn retirement from a vague hope into a plan with a structure—so it keeps working even when you're tired, distracted, deployed, or just human.

"I don't really need to worry about retirement planning," Sergeant Smith proudly states. "I'm going to make a career out of the military, so I will be set for life."

"That's great," I say, trying not to let my skepticism show and alienate him right off the bat. "How much will you make in retirement?" I ask, genuinely curious if he had already done the math—as his confidence seemed unshakeable.

"I don't really know, but one of my buddies said the military retirement is like a million dollars."

"Wow, that sounds like a lot, very interesting. Would you be interested in figuring it out while we sit here, just to feed my curiosity?"

"Sure, although I don't really know where to even look." This was a great inroad to the discussion. I often made assumptions about a future outcome because of my preconceived notions—maybe I heard someone mention it around the water cooler, or maybe I picked it up somewhere outside of work—but my perceptions were shaped by assumptions rather than reality.

As a fighter pilot I learned early on never to make assumptions when real data exists. Making assumptions in the absence of information can lead to catastrophic results when traveling 600 miles per hour and flying just feet off the wingtip of another fighter jet. We spend years training and standardizing our actions so that all our "assumptions" in the air are Contracts that we made with each other. For instance, if I direct my wingman to Line-Abreast formation, we have a contract that they will be two miles off my wing within 10 degrees of a line extending perpendicular from the nose of my jet. If my wingman cannot comply for some reason—maybe they are stuck in a four-mile trail position after aggressive maneuvers, and it will take a few minutes to catch me at 450 knots—the Contract is that they will let me know they are unable and working on it.

Our financial readiness can take on the same format as mission planning for a complex fighter mission. We begin with everything that we know. Then we identify what we do not know. We take stock of what we have available to us. And then we start at the target we need to strike and plan backward through the mission to the starting point. We call it "targeting backward" and it is synonymous with goal setting, which we will get into in section two.

"Sure, but I don't even know where to begin, I guess with a google search?" he asks hesitantly.

"Okay, let's start by researching the Blended Retirement System (BRS), since you will fall under that program." Signed into law in 2015, the BRS took effect on 1 January 2018 and is the system that all members of the military now fall under unless they were grandfathered into the old system as I was. Blended Retirement gives you 80% retirement from the old system and replaces the other 20% with a 401(k) retirement plan called the TSP.

What We Know: The Shift from Legacy Retirement to BRS Changed Everything for Military Wealth Building

As a reminder, under the pre-2018 system, known as "High-3," a military member would receive 50% of the average of their last 3 years of base pay in retirement plus 2.5% for each year they served past 20. A benefit of the new BRS is that members are eligible to receive retirement benefits even if they do not stay for 20 years—the 20-year "cliff" was a common complaint under the old system. Additionally, the BRS added the option for an employer match in the service-members Thrift Savings Plan (TSP), making it more like the 401(k) plans that so many civilian employers offer. While this created some positive opportunities for proactive service members, it also created a problem for those who did not know or did not contribute.

The trade-off in the BRS was that service members would now receive 20% less than their counterparts on the High-3 plan, which was meant to be covered by the service members contributions to their TSP. Putting more flexibility and responsibility into the hands of the member. However, at the end of the day, the government was shifting risk from the Department of Defense (DoD) to the members, and perhaps even saving a few dollars on the backs of our service members.

"The BRS seems pretty good, why doesn't everyone love it?" Smith asked after reading through the literature.

"In 2024 service members in the DoD left more than $2.5 billion on the table in unmatched contributions," I replied. "That money is now gone, and they can never go backward and claim it. So, this system is only great if everyone maxes out their employer-matched contributions. And as you can see, many fall short of that goal."

Federal data shows that 56% of eligible service members do not contribute to a TSP and even more contribute less than the 5% required for maximum matching.[1] This represents billions in unclaimed government matching funds annually across all services. And, when broken out, individual service members are leaving an average of $1,800 per year in free matching money on the table. Extrapolated over a 20-year career, this missed matching compounds to more than $98,000 in lost retirement wealth per person.

"Dang, billions of dollars? That's insane, why can't they just claim it this year?" he said.

"The DoD employer-match contribution is set up so that for every percent of your base pay you put into TSP, the DoD will *match* that amount—up to 5%," I told him. "There are finer details of how they match but for now, make it 5% so we can focus on getting you your money."

Numerous studies of behavioral economics have shown that when an employer, like the government, makes retirement savings an *Opt-Out* program rather than an *Opt-In* program, people save exponentially more money.[2] One oft-cited study showed that employees of a large company increased their savings for new hires from 37% to 86%.[3] That is a huge difference when you consider the millions of service members who will be affected over the years. Fortunately for service members, the BRS now automatically enrolls you in the program and sets your contributions at 3% of your base salary. You can always opt out or change it, but if you dip below 3% the system will re-enroll you every January. A good change that was made to help service members not miss out on those matching contributions. But, to fully maximize the match you need to go in and make your contribution 5% of your base pay.

Since this is a text concerned with accuracy, I should add some of the nuances of the program. The TSP contribution on your behalf technically starts on day 61 of your service at 1% of your base salary whether you contribute anything or not. Then, at the start of your third year it increases to match your contribution up to a maximum of 4% contributed if you are putting in 5%—reference Table 2.1. This is also subject to change so check the most recent program specifics at your government resource center. The simplified, bumper-sticker version is this: as soon as you join the military set your TSP to 5% of your base salary and then never reduce it. TSP management is done in two places: myPay and the TSP website. Use myPay for your allocations out of your paycheck, and use the TSP website for determining what investments your money goes into.

You contribute 5%, the military matches you 5%, and this nets you a 10% savings of your base pay for the price of 5% out of your pocket.[4] The "match" does not come out of your paycheck. It comes out of a pot of money set aside for this purpose. If you don't claim it, you don't get it, and it doesn't cost you anything other than the discipline to save for your retirement.

If everyone took this one simple step, we could put billions into the retirement accounts of service members over the coming years. And the kicker about the DoD-matching contributions is this: if you do not contribute this year, you can never go back in time and claim that contribution. Once the year is over, the matching for that year is gone. In flying terms: it is as useless as runway behind you when you need to abort or altitude above you when you lose your engine.

If you contribute 0%, you still get an automatic 1% from the government after a short period of service—but you miss the full match. Contribute 5% and you effectively save ~10% of base pay with help.

If you don't turn it on this year, you can't claim the missed match later. Set it now and never turn it off.

"Okay," Smith says. "All this info is neat, but what would my actual *number* look like?"

"Let's check our math."

We pulled his Leave and Earnings Statement (LES), the pay stub for military members, and in 60 seconds had the number: 5% of his base pay was about $212 per month. The government would drop the same amount on top—free. That is $424 in monthly contributions, more than $5,000 annually. If Smith starts now and never turns it off, that single decision is worth about $85,000 by military retirement; and then with compounding it will be worth about $940,000 by age 65.[5]

After seeing it put like this, Smith set it to 5% before we left the ops desk.

You can project your income with incredible accuracy. If you want to see what a full 20-year career actually produces in compensation, see Appendix.

The final step of setting up your TSP for success is the idea of "being healthy in the future." People often make better choices for their future self than their present self. This applies to eating habits, workout habits, and financial habits. So, treat your future self to a healthy habit and set your TSP to increase every time you get a raise.

- Day 1: Set Roth TSP to 5% of Base Pay.
- Each January, when you receive a pay increase—typically around 2% per year—increase your retirement investments by another +1%.
- Every two years when you receive your time in grade raise, increase your retirement investment by a small portion of that raise.

- For example: An E-5 with 8 years of service will receive about $100 extra per month when they reach 10 years of service. So, increase your retirement contributions by $10.

- Each promotion to the next rank comes with a pay raise. Increase your retirement contributions by a small 1–2%.
- After 5% in Roth TSP, all these increases should go to your Roth IRA. And then stop at your max for the year. If you max out your Roth IRA, then return to increasing your Roth TSP until that is also maxed out.

By pre-planning your increases, it removes individual decisions in the moment and replaces them with a single decision, made once, that you are "someone who is going to live financially free." Your contribution climbs while your lifestyle doesn't feel the hit.

Table 2.1 Blended Retirement Contribution Schedule[a]

Your Contribution	Automatic 1% Contribution (%)	Agency Matching Contribution (%)	Total Contributions
0%	1	0	1%
1%	1	1	3%
2%	1	2	5%
3%	1	3	7%
4%	1	3.5	8.5%
5%	1	4	10%
5% +	1	4	Your % + 5%

[a] https://www.tsp.gov/making-contributions/contribution-types/#:~:text=Agency/Service%20automatic%20(1%25),50%20cents%20on%20the%20dollar

BRS Summary

Here are some of the BRS criteria that you should know and understand. As a service member you can contribute 1–100% of your incentive pay, special pay, or bonus pay, *if you contribute at least 1% from your basic pay*. You may not contribute from your BAH or BAS—housing or subsistence allowances. If you are receiving tax-exempt pay, in a combat zone for instance, your contributions will also be tax-exempt. You must stay under the annual IRS elective deferral limit—$24,500 in 2026.

As a Blended Retirement System participant, the Department of Defense will contribute 1% of your basic pay each pay period into your TSP account starting on day 61. This is the Agency Automatic Contribution column in the BRS chart. You do not need to do anything to make these happen; they are automatic. This 1% does not come out of your pay, does not reduce your pay for tax purposes, and it goes to you whether you set up your TSP or not. Further, since 2020, the system will automatically set up a contribution of 3% of your base pay every January if you have taken no action. So, if you are eight years in and just realizing that you should set up your TSP, there has already been 1% of your basic pay being contributed from day 61 until today, plus 3% of your base pay with a match since 2020. When you begin contributing to your TSP, the DoD will match your contributions in accordance with the table; they will match you dollar-for-dollar on the first 3%, then fifty cents on the dollar for the next 2%. At full match, they will put in 5% for the 5% that you contribute. You may contribute more than 5% but they will not match it. After age 50 you become eligible for catch-up contributions where you can contribute more than the IRS limit. While it can seem confusing and overwhelming, the bottom line is this: contribute 5% of your base salary to TSP as soon as you possibly can to get the full match from the DoD.

Overall, in the world of military retirements, the change to BRS created winners and losers based on individual financial decisions rather than just years of service. Service members now must understand investment principles, asset allocation, and compound interest to maximize their retirement. The system requires active participation and regular monitoring rather than passive accumulation. Financial literacy became a mission-critical skill for military members under the new system. Poor decisions early in career now have dramatically larger consequences due to compound interest effects. The wealth gap between informed and uninformed military members is growing exponentially under the new system. Do not be part of the uninformed group.

TSP (Roth Versus Traditional), IRA (Roth Versus Traditional), 401(k)

I've already mentioned the Thrift Savings Plan and 401(k) accounts, but what *are* they exactly?

Years ago, the government recognized a need for tax-advantaged accounts that allow people to set aside money for their retirement years without paying heavy tax penalties. Most accounts grow tax-free, and you only pay taxes when you withdraw the money in your retirement years. Some accounts, specifically Roth accounts, allow you to pay tax on the money in the year you put it in and then pay no tax when you take it out. Since we all plan to make more money later in life, and because historically taxes have gone up and not down, we can assume that we will pay more taxes later. Because of this, it is usually better to invest in Roth accounts first.

Why Roth first? Because you are early in your career, likely in lower tax brackets now versus later, and Roth buys you tax-free growth and tax-free withdrawals in your retirement years when your taxes are higher.

The TSP is basically a 401(k) for the military. And, fortunately, they now offer a Roth TSP which I highly recommend. The annual contribution limit for the Roth TSP is much higher than the IRA; as of this writing the contribution limit is $24,500 per year, which I do not expect you to jump right into but can offer you a tax-advantaged investment opportunity later. As I outlined earlier, *the first step is to contribute 5% of your base pay into a Roth TSP*. The second step is to open an IRA because it gives you more flexibility with how you invest that money.

In addition to the TSP and 401(k), the most common Individual Retirement Account (IRA) is the Traditional and the Roth. Traditional IRAs allow you to deduct the amount you put into the account from your taxable income. So, if you made $45,000 and put $5,000 into an IRA, you would only be taxed on $40,000 of income—that is called a tax deduction, more on that in the tax section. That money will grow inside of the IRA from whatever you choose to invest in—stocks, bonds, funds, real estate, etc.—and when you withdraw it to use it for retirement you pay taxes at that time.

In this same example, a Roth IRA would have you put in $5,000 and you still pay taxes on your full income of $45,000. But when you withdraw the money, it is tax-free. You must make this annotation on your taxes each year.

These accounts come with several restrictions, so make sure to do your homework and consult with your local financial planner before committing funds. For instance, if you withdraw your money early from an IRA, you may face penalties that are greater than what you will pay in taxes. Roth IRA earnings are tax- and penalty-free if five tax years have passed and you're 59½ (or meet another qualifier). Contributions can be withdrawn anytime. Traditional IRA withdrawals are taxable and may incur a 10% penalty before 59½.

Additionally, you are limited to contributing $7,500 per year, as of January 2026, and you may not go over that amount. After age 50, you may contribute the annual catch-up for the current year (TSP/401(k) and IRA), subject to IRS limits. So, the key is to start early, contribute what you can afford without putting yourself in financial risk, and then keep contributing so your money compounds tax-free or tax-deferred until retirement. To be clear: do not do this at the risk of meeting your basic needs—instead, plan your spending and be disciplined about your investing.

Contribution limits, matching rules, and auto-enrollment percentages change. As of 2025, the elective deferral limit for TSP/401(k) plans is in the low-20Ks, with an additional catch-up allowance for age 50+. IRA limits are lower. Always check the current IRS/TSP numbers before you set your targets.

Once you are comfortable contributing 5% of your base pay to your Roth TSP, you will next grow your Roth IRA contributions to $7,500 per year (or the maximum for the year and age when you are reading this), then you can return to investing more into your Roth TSP until you have maxed it out at $24,500. I know it seems daunting right now; it was for me as well in the beginning. But through incremental gains and discipline, I was maxing out all of my eligible retirement accounts for both my wife and me before I retired from the military.

Lastly, if you and your spouse make over a certain amount of money each year ($150,000 individually and $236,000 as a couple in 2025—check the annual IRS limits for your situation) then you are prohibited from contributing to a Roth IRA. Not to fear, Congress wrote in a loophole for you—you can contribute to a Traditional IRA, and then once the money is in there you can do a "Roth Conversion" sometimes called a "Backdoor Roth Contribution," which is perfectly legal, and allows you to pay tax on it when you convert to the Roth IRA and get that money tax-free later. Your financial institution can assist with these transactions; they are not complex and are routine for most banks. Gotta love those loopholes.

TSP Funds Explained: Where Your Money Gets Invested

Congratulations, you've waited 60 days, and now the DoD will begin contributing the automatic 1% of your base pay, and you decide to contribute 5% of your base pay immediately. You set up your online account at TSP.gov and then go to myPay to set your allotments. So, what happens when you deposit money into a TSP? The default location for TSP dollars is the L Fund, or Lifecycle Fund, based upon the year that you were born.[6] If you do nothing else, your money will stay in the L Fund until you withdraw it. Once you log into TSP.gov and change your allocation, the change will supersede this allocation.

At the time of this change—through a TSP bulletin in 2020—anyone born after the year 2000 will have their money invested in an L Fund based on their year of birth. For instance, if you were born in 2000, you will be invested in L 2065. The number, 2065, next to the L designation denotes the approximate year that you will be withdrawing money—in this case, 65 years after the year 2000, so when you reach retirement age. TSP uses the age that the participant will turn 63 and then rounds up or down as necessary. The 11 Lifecycle Funds are allocated in 5-year increments. At the time of this writing TSP has an L Fund out through L 2075.

Lifecycle Funds are based on the principle of taking more risk when you are young and less risk as you approach retirement—a common financial strategy. The Fund is a varied blend of the five funds described in Table 2.2. The L Fund is updated every quarter to create a blend of risk to match the time remaining until you need the money. Think of it like a countdown clock to your withdrawal date with less-and-less risk as you approach withdrawal age. When the L Fund reaches the target date, the funds from it will roll into the L Income Fund.

The L Income Fund returned 9.33% in 2024 and has an allocation of:

- 67.29% G Fund
- 5.46% F Fund
- 14.17% C Fund
- 3.54% S Fund
- 9.54% I Fund

By comparison, in 2024, the L 2065 fund returned 21.92% with the following allocation:

- 0.43% G Fund
- 0.57% F Fund
- 51.48% C Fund
- 12.87% S Fund
- 34.65% I Fund

The L Income Fund is considered lower risk and is heavily invested in Special US Treasuries (G Fund) whereas the L 2065 fund is heavily invested in the C & I Funds—large US stocks and developed international stocks ("developed international stocks" are stocks from well established, economically advanced countries outside of the US). This information is always available on the TSP website and should be reviewed regularly to make sure that your retirement investment is aligned with your retirement goals.[7]

I recommend spending time learning about investing before self-managing or creating your own blend of funds. There is no shortage of people on social media touting their perfect blend of TSP funds for maximum gains; I advise exercising extreme caution. No one, not even the greatest investors in history, can predict what will happen in the future. The "perfect" blend of funds from last year might be the biggest losers this year. The L Funds are not randomly chosen or allocated. There is a team of financial professionals who study this for a living, allocating funds and making quarterly updates. I recommend staying with your designated Lifestyle fund until you have a deeper understanding and might want to go at it on your own.

When you are ready to reallocate yourself, simply go to the TSP website, go to the Investments tab, and select Change Investments. That will take you to 3 options: Change Your Investment Mix, Move Money Between Funds, and Set Up a Mutual Fund Window Account. If you want to change the way all your future money gets allocated, then select the first option—Change Your Investment Mix. If you want to simply move around some of the money already in the account, then select the second option—Move Money Between Funds. Simply follow the steps for each of these, choose the money to move, then choose the new allocation; it is a simple process.

The third option is a way to have more flexibility with your investments by moving a portion of your TSP (up to 25%) into a Mutual Fund Window (MFW) account. The MFW Account allows you to choose from thousands of mutual funds and give you more flexibility with your money. I do not recommend this option currently. There will be more on mutual funds in the investing section, but the fees are very high compared to the relatively small advantage that you may get—currently $132 per year plus whatever hidden fees there are in the mutual funds. The minimum amount to start an MFW is $10,000, and because you can only move 25%, you must have a TSP balance of at least $40,000 to begin.

Below is a description of the 5 core funds that make up the Thrift Savings Plan. For more information visit TSP.gov.

Table 2.2 Core Funds

Fund	What It Holds	Risk/ Volatility	When It Can Help	When It Can Hurt	Notes
G	Special US Treasury securities (principal guaranteed)	Low	Capital preservation; emergency runway; near-term goals	Long-run returns may trail inflation	No market price risk; still has inflation risk over time
F	US investment-grade bonds (Bloomberg US Aggregate)	Low-to-Moderate	Diversifier versus stocks; ballast in downturns	Sensitive to rising interest rates	Bond prices fall when rates rise
C	Large US stocks (S&P 500)	High	Growth engine for long horizons	Big drawdowns in bear markets	Broad US large-cap exposure
S	US mid/small not in S&P 500 (DJ US Completion)	High	Adds smaller company growth	Higher volatility, tracking error	Complements C for total US market
I	Developed international stocks (MSCI EAFE)	High	Diversifies beyond US	Currency swings; different sector mix	No emerging markets exposure

Self-Managed Retirement Accounts

It took me almost a decade to learn that I didn't have to leave the management of my individual retirement accounts to big banks and other people. To be fair, it was probably in better hands during that time. But, nonetheless, you can choose to "self-manage" your IRAs at any time—it's your money after all! When you self-manage, you can choose to invest that money wherever you want (within guidelines of course). This includes real estate.

Yes, you read that correctly. You can take some, or all, of your IRA, move it into a self-managed account, use that money for the down payment on a multifamily investment, and then start receiving income from that property into your IRA for the next few decades before you are ready to retire. Your property will continue to grow equity from the property value, and when you sell, those proceeds will go back into your Roth account and be eligible for another purchase or a tax-free withdrawal in retirement.

You can also buy stocks, bonds, mutual funds, gold, crypto, and all sorts of other assets using your retirement account. Just keep in mind that this is your future nest egg, and many investments have higher risk than a traditional approach. For me, I like the idea of making rental income for 20 years while my retirement investment grows tax-free.

The IRS has a list of prohibited investments so do your homework, talk with your financial planner, and double-check that list before trying to invest your IRA in Pokémon cards (yep, prohibited).

Every good pilot checklist has what we call "Notes, Warnings, and Cautions," which is the information that is good to know (notes), the information that will keep you alive (warnings), and the information that will keep you safe (cautions). I do not recommend going at this alone. I have done it for years now and still use a licensed professional for every real estate transaction. Here are a few Warnings & Cautions about self-managed IRAs and real estate:

- No personal use or renting to family (prohibited transactions).
- If you use a mortgage inside the IRA, part of the income/gain may be taxed (UDFI/UBIT).
- You'll need a specialized custodian and should expect extra fees and paperwork.
- TSP is **not** self-directed; this applies to IRAs only.

Okay, as promised, here is what I did and what worked for me.

1. I first maxed out my, and my wife's, Roth IRAs.
   a. I began contributions in my first year of active duty at $100 per month and grew my contributions annually until I maxed them out.
   b. I never stopped my contributions, even when times were hard.
   c. The trick to retirement accounts is that you can't go backward and make contributions for those years when times were tough and you stopped contributing, so create a plan and stick to it.

2. Once we were in a place where we could afford more, we then opened a TSP account and increased our contribution every year.
   a. This was before the Blended Retirement System and there was no match from the DoD.

   b. We contributed to Roth TSP (military version of 401(k)).
   c. We increased our annual contribution until we had maxed it out.
3. We moved some of our Roth IRA money into a self-managed account and invested in a multifamily real estate deal making us rental income every month.
4. We reserved a small portion of our income for personal investments and exploration.
   a. First into a Robinhood investment account that we used to explore the stock market, take some risk, and learn more about investing.
   b. I also contributed a small amount regularly to a crypto wallet, even when crypto was down.

If I were joining the military today in the age of the Blended Retirement System, I would immediately set my TSP contribution to 5% of my base pay into Roth TSP *minimum* and Never Turn It Off. That would ensure the maximum "match" or free, tax-free, money from the government. Next, I would contribute to my Roth IRA until I could max that out ($7,000 in 2025) and do the same for my spouse if was married. Once I could comfortably max out my Roth IRA, I would increase my Roth TSP until I hit the max on that ($24,500/year).

Action Steps:

1. **Open a TSP Account if you haven't already and set your contribution to 5% of your base salary into a Roth contribution.**
2. **Calculate what 5% of your base salary is so you can put it into your How I Spend My Money Plan.**

3. **Open a Roth IRA at your preferred institution and contribute what you can afford. I would start with that $27 per week you were spending on coffee.**
   a. **THIS IS KEY: Every single year when you get your annual inflation raise (~2%), increase your contribution to your Roth IRA until it is maxed out, and then increase your contribution to your Roth TSP.**
   b. **Bonus if you also do this step at every two-year pay raise from Table 2.1, even if only a few dollars per month.**
   c. **Double bonus if you also do this step at every promotion.**

Chapter 3

Debt and My Journey

"It is not the mountain we conquer, but ourselves."

—Sir Edmund Hillary

Not every sortie in my career went well. In fact, some of the most important lessons I learned came from the ones where I screwed it up. Where I missed something obvious. Where confidence outpaced discipline.

And, not all mistakes in a fighter jet announce themselves loudly.

Some are subtle. A heading that's a degree off. A fuel flow slightly higher than planned. A switch left in the wrong position—not enough to fail now, but enough to matter later. These are the ones that get you in trouble, because everything still looks okay. . .until it isn't.

As the mission unfolded, I felt that familiar tension: things were busy, but manageable. We were hitting our timelines. The radios were active but controlled. Nothing was on fire. From the outside, it would have looked like the plan was working.

But I knew better.

In large force missions, the most dangerous errors aren't usually the dramatic ones. They're the small deviations you rationalize because the jet is still flying and the timeline hasn't slipped yet. You tell yourself you'll fix it later. You tell yourself it's not a big deal. And then you stack another one on top of it.

That's how people end up out of position, out of gas, or out of options.

Debt works exactly the same way.

Very few people wake up one day and decide to wreck their finances. It starts with tolerating small deviations. A balance you carry because it's convenient. A purchase you justify because "I'll catch up next month." Nothing breaks immediately, so it feels manageable. And because nothing breaks, the behavior sticks.

Earlier in my career—both as a pilot and financially—I made these kinds of quiet errors. I didn't lack intelligence or work ethic. I lacked discipline in the unglamorous moments. The places where nobody was watching and the consequences were delayed.

In aviation, if you let deviation go unchecked long enough, it eventually becomes the plan. And once deviation becomes the plan, recovery gets expensive.

This chapter is about recognizing drift before it becomes a crisis. I'm going to walk you through my own journey with debt—not because my mistakes were unique, but because they were ordinary. And ordinary mistakes, left uncorrected, have extraordinary consequences.

Discipline isn't about never being wrong. It's about catching deviation early—and having the humility to correct it before it costs you the mission.

When things go wrong in flight, pilots set their priorities and "aviate, navigate, communicate" in that order. The first step is always to "aviate," fly the jet—in debt that is, stop new spending.

Then you can navigate the challenge, to rebuild your budget. Finally, you communicate; structure and automate your payoff plan.

Put another way, when you find yourself in a hole, the first thing you must do is stop digging. Put down the shovel (credit card), and plan. *You do not dig your way out of a hole, you climb out.*

I began my career with a net worth of about -$50,000. Between student loan debt and the truck, I had just bought myself, I had $50,000 in debt and no plan to get out of it. I just let the plan happen to me rather than being proactive about my plan. Later, in fighter training, we would spend a lot of time learning to be proactive and push the envelope—making your enemy react to you and not the other way around.

It is likely that at some point in your career you will find yourself in some debt. Not all debt is bad debt, some of the biggest fortunes in the world have been built on debt, but as a young military member it is likely that the debt you find yourself wrapped up in is not the wealth-building type. And just because you made a killer How I Spend My Money Plan in Chapter 1, I would be naïve to think that you will always stick to it and will not have credit card debt.

But let's pause for a moment and go over what debt is. Basically, for the purposes of this book, debt is the state of owing money. Many lenders are eager to lend to military members because there is an asterisk next to your name that you didn't know was there. You see, if you rack up high-interest debt and stop paying your bills, those delinquencies can lead to wage garnishment through legal process and may trigger command involvement/financial counseling. So, it can act as a safety net for certain lenders. And it can sometimes lead institutions to lend more than they really should. If one bank offers you a new credit card with a limit of $1,000 and another offers you a similar card with a limit of $3,000, which will you take? Probably the $3,000 one, you know, just in case. They are competing for your business, but their incentive is not to get you the best product for *you,* it is to sell you a product that makes them money. This is true for most of the consumer world.

So, you take your shiny new credit card and go out and buy that new game console you have been eyeing, or maybe a new luxury item from the exchange like a designer bag or shoes. No worries, you can pay it back later, right? Yes. And no. Typically on day 31 after the purchase, you start accruing interest—the charge the bank levies on you for the privilege of the card. If you do not pay the balance in full within the 30-day window, you will pay interest on the charge until it is fully paid off. That $100 pair of shoes could end up costing you a lot more if you don't pay it off in a timely manner. The "minimum payment" that the credit card requires will usually only cover the interest. So always pay your card in full every month. And any time you get even one month behind, put the card away in a drawer until you catch back up.

Fortunately, credit card fees and rates are capped for military members through the Military Lending Act (MLA). It sounds cool, and can be helpful, except that the cap is a whopping 36%! The MLA caps the Military Annual Percentage Rate (MAPR) at 36% on covered consumer credit, which includes fees. If you want a year to pay off that $100 purchase, you will pay $136 for it in the end, and it will be a year older. Additionally, the Servicemembers Civil Relief Act can also assist by limiting debt you incurred *before* joining the military to 6%. So, if you came in with existing debt, make sure to discuss that with your lender.

Responsible credit card use can be a good thing though. The difficulty is that word "responsible." By regularly using and paying off your card each month, you are demonstrating to the banking industry that you are a trustworthy credit partner, and they will be more likely to lend to you later when you want to buy a house or a car. They keep track of it through your credit score. In my career I was both a responsible and irresponsible user of credit card debt, and I learned many lessons along the way. Here are my recommendations and keys to success:

1. Never use your card for luxury items or splurges.
2. To build your history, choose one expense to pay on your card monthly and then set your bank to autopay it off every month. Something simple like a Netflix subscription.
3. Do not carry your card in your wallet. Leave it at home. This will limit your impulse purchasing. Do not store it in your phone wallet or use a digital pay service which encourages unconscious spending versus taking control of your finances.
4. If you ever have a month where you do not pay off the card completely, go back to Chapter 1, redo your How I Spend My Money Plan, and put the card away in a safe or a drawer until it is paid off for at least a full month.
5. As you build trust with yourself you can expand your use, always paying it off fully each month so you do not get hit with interest.

If you ever find yourself unable to pay off your card for two or more consecutive months, it is time to seek professional help. Think of it like going to the doctor when you have a bad cold or the flu—there is someone who can help you through this. There are trained professionals, eager to help you, at almost every base.

Your Credit Score

An important topic that most people know surprisingly little about is your credit score. This "score"—a number between 300 and 850—is like a grade in school. Banks, lenders, landlords, and other companies use it to determine how trustworthy you will be if they loan you money, rent you an apartment, give you a cell phone plan, or even hire you. Think of it as your report card for borrowed money. In the eyes of most lenders a good score is going to be in the high 600s or above, many banks say they look for a 670 or above for creditworthiness. For you, the goal should be to get your score above 700 so you can get the best rates available when it is time to borrow money.

Your score begins accumulating when you turn 18, although if your parents added you to their credit card as an authorized user before you turned 18, you could start building credit history earlier. This is something that we have done for our children to hopefully give them a slight head start in the credit world when they are adults. The credit score is composed of five categories with slightly different weighted values assigned to them: timeliness of payments, amount of credit used versus authorized, length of your credit history, new applications for credit, different types of credit.[1] There are three major credit bureaus in the United States that create your score: Experian, Equifax, and TransUnion. Because they collect their data independently your score will likely vary across the three platforms. Additionally, there are different standards for different industries: auto loans, credit cards, home mortgages, etc., where the scale may also vary. The score that you see may not be exactly what your lender is seeing, and they might only use one source, or an average of the three.

The most important factor in your credit score, which makes up about 35% of the total score, is whether you pay your bills on time.[2] Even one late payment can cause a drop in your score and stay with you for years. This is why I recommend starting with something simple like your Netflix subscription on autopay to build a history of on-time payments.

The second factor, and about 30% of your score, is the amount of credit you have used versus the amount you are authorized. As a good rule of thumb, keep your balances at less than 30% of your authorized limit. So, if you have a card with a $1,000 limit, keep it below $300 and pay it off monthly. And do not simply pay it by the due date. Instead, pay it before the "close of cycle" from your statement. Let's say you have $500 of expenses on your card with a $1,000 limit and you pay it off every month by the due date. Your credit card company reports to the Credit Bureaus that you keep a balance of 50% of your available credit every month—even though you pay it off monthly! So, go to your statement and you will see "statement close date" which is usually a few weeks before "payment due date"; then, set your monthly autopay to pay your card in full just before the "statement close date" so that every statement you show a $0 balance—or at least below the recommended 30%. This will help boost your credit score.

The third factor, which makes up about 15% of your score, is length of credit history. If you are just getting started there is nothing you can do to go backward; so start today and build a slow and steady history of on-time payments.

The fourth factor is new credit applications and can drop your score by as much as 10%. If you have recently made multiple requests for credit, banks view that as risky behavior. So, if you are shopping for rates, look for one of the sites that can do a single "credit pull" and give you multiple bank rate options.

The final component of your score is the variety of your credit and is also about 10% of the score. If you have 10 credit cards and no other forms of credit reported, lenders may frown on it, and your score will reflect it. A mix of loans and credit cards can help.

You may wonder, "But does having a steady job like the military impact my credit score?" And the short answer is no. Credit bureaus do not look directly at employment, but it can indirectly impact your score. The Credit Act of 2009 requires that banks ensure you can pay a loan back before giving you one—so showing the bank you have a job will allow you to get that credit card in the first place. Then, having a history of paying that card will impact your credit score. So, there is an indirect relationship, and the security of a military paycheck can help you get started on the road to creditworthiness, but how well the journey goes is up to you.

If you are interested in deliberately building your credit score, then you can take some steps now to set you up for years down the road when you are ready for your first real estate investment or home, car, or business loan. First, follow the steps from the previous section about small bills on your card and steady on-time payments, always paying the card off. Second, periodically request a credit line increase, even if you do not need it. I typically requested an increase every one to two years during my career even if I did not need it. This will gradually and slowly increase your available credit—which you are not going to use at this time—so your ratio will come down (item 2 in your score). This may also help when you plan to use your credit because you will not be asking for an increase at the time you plan or need to use it (item 4).

To diversify and grow your credit, consider looking into small unsecured or secured loans when you do not necessarily need them. For instance, if you are going to buy yourself a new mattress, because the one in the dorm is ruining your sleep, and you have the $250 you need to buy it. Rather than walking in the store and paying $250 cash for it, ask them if they offer a credit program. Many furniture stores will have specials like 6 or 12 months, no interest. Use this small loan and pay it back immediately, or within the no-interest period. Early in my career I did this several times with purchases I made, and it paid off by strengthening my credit score. Now, if you DON'T pay it off you will seriously impact your score—but you are not going to do that because you are disciplined and responsible.

If you are struggling to get approved for your first credit card, you may want to investigate the option of a Secured Credit Card. You give the bank a "security" that you will pay it back. This typically looks like: you pay $500 up front to get a credit card from the bank. As you build history and show you will pay it back monthly, they will eventually give you your $500 back.

Check your credit history annually. The Fair and Accurate Credit Transactions Act (FACT Act) authorizes everyone to be able to check their credit report once per year without fees and without your credit taking a hit. The act does not guarantee that the company will share your score, they may charge a fee for that, but they must disclose what they are using to determine your score. Check it annually to make sure it is accurate—check for places you have lived, names you have used, credit accounts you have opened or closed, late payments reported by creditors or billers, etc. If there are any inaccuracies, dispute them immediately, if you do this regularly you will keep your report clean and accurate, and it may help you determine how you are doing on your goal of a 700+ score. You can access this resource through AnnualCreditReport.com. Additionally, there may be other benefits for military members such as credit monitoring, fraud monitoring, dark web monitoring, and credit assistance—check with your local financial planner.

Building credit, like anything worthwhile, takes time, patience, discipline, and dedication. Start small, do not worry if your friend has a higher credit limit than you. Be responsible with the credit you do have and play the long game. Don't let your card balance build; pay it off every month, and you will be well on your way to that 700-credit score that will get you a killer loan percentage on your first property. Here is a handy credit score checklist for you:

1. Timeliness Rule: Pay off credit cards monthly and on time.
2. 30% Rule: Keep total balance less than 30% of your authorized limit.

3. Authorized User Strategy. Add your kids, or have your parents add you, as authorized users before age 18 to start building credit history.
4. Seven-Year Rule. A single late payment will typically stay on your report for seven years. So, one mistake is not forever, but it can have long-lasting effects. Pay your bills on time.
5. Credit Impacts. Credit scores don't just impact your ability to buy a house—they can impact your ability to rent an apartment, get a cell phone plan, your insurance rates, and even getting certain jobs. Keep it clean and you will be set.
6. Slow & Steady. Time is an important element of investing as well as credit. Let time work in your favor through on-time monthly payments and slow and steady growth.

Loans

No chapter on debt would be complete without a discussion on loans. There are many other types of loans like unsecured loans, secured loans, debt consolidation loans, medical loans, student loans, airplane loans, and boat loans, to name a few. We will focus on the two you are most likely to encounter in your career: auto and mortgage loans. A car loan is borrowed money you use to buy a car and then you pay it back, with interest, over a pre-determined time period known as the "term." The interest is usually referred to as Annual Percentage Rate, or APR. The APR should include any fees associated with the loan—if the lender just says the "interest rate" then will likely only include the *interest* you pay. This is important when comparing rates between lenders—to always compare apples-to-apples, or APR-to-APR.

A mortgage works similarly to a car loan but is typically spread out over a 30-year period. There are many different mortgage products on the market, too many to mention here, but the most common is a 30-year fixed mortgage. A "fixed" mortgage is when the interest rate is locked in for the entirety of the loan, versus an Adjustable-Rate Mortgage, or ARM, that will fluctuate as the interest rates change. Interest rates typically stem from the federal funds rate which is set by the Federal Reserve. Most banks will add an amount to the federal funds rate, usually 2.5–3%, which they will set it as their "prime rate" for lending. For example, if the Federal Reserve rate is 3% then you can expect mortgage rates to be around 6%.

As a military member we have a huge advantage when buying our first home because of the VA loan program, which allows us to buy a home with 0% down payment. This single benefit often means that military members buy their first home 10–20 years earlier than their civilian counterparts. Most lenders require a down payment of 20% of the purchase price. To buy a home for $433,000 (the average home price in the USA in early 2026), a civilian would need to set aside $87,000 for a down payment and still prove to the bank that they could cover the closing costs and the monthly payment. And a home often goes on to become an asset when it is time to sell. We will cover investment real estate assets in the investment chapter.

TSP Loans

One advantage of starting early and creating a nest egg in your TSP is that later in your career you can access these funds through a TSP loan that you pay back to yourself. You pay interest on the loan, but the best part is that the interest is paid back into your own account, not to a third-party lender.[3] And the interest rate is fixed at the rate of the G Fund at the time the loan is initiated, so it is a comparatively low-interest rate loan. Repayment is done through automatic deductions from your paycheck every month, and you can set the repayment terms—up to five years to pay it back if you use the loan for any general purpose, or up to 15 years if you use it for a primary residence. You can also make additional payments to pay off the loan faster if you choose.

I learned about this option and used it to buy my first commercial rental property with a $50,000 TSP loan. The TSP loan helped me get the required funds for the down payment and I was able to pay it back quickly with the monthly revenue from the property. When I took the TSP loan, I had an interest rate under 3%. Being able to use my own retirement account as my bank was very helpful in growing my real estate portfolio. As with all loans, do the math on how much will be held out of your paycheck every month *before* you take the loan and adjust your How I Spend My Money Plan.

The rules for the TSP loan include:

- You can borrow up to the lesser of 50% of your total contributions and earnings or $50,000—minus your highest outstanding loan balance in the last 12 months.
- There is a fee of $50 for a general-purpose loan and $100 for a primary residence loan.
- You must be currently employed as a federal civilian or uniformed service member in active pay status.
- You must have at least $1,000 of your own contributions and earnings in your account.
- No taxable loan distribution within the past 12 months unless related to separation.
- You have not repaid a TSP loan of any type in the past 30 business days.
- You do not have a court order placed against your account.
- The consequence of failing to repay the loan may cause the loan to be deemed a "taxable distribution" from your TSP and you may have to pay a 10% early withdrawal penalty. So always have a plan to pay back every loan that you sign up for.

Buying Your First Car

A typical auto loan requires 10–20% of the purchase price as a down payment, and then the rest of the loan is spread out over the term. A first-time car buyer with little credit history will face higher APR and possibly a higher down payment because you have not yet demonstrated your creditworthiness—trustworthiness with credit. In 2025, new car loans are usually around 6.5% while used car loans are around 11%. So, if you feel that you absolutely must buy that Corvette you've been eyeing (stop and re-read Chapter 1), the purchase price will be $75,000; the down payment $15,000, and the payment plan to be for $60,000 at 6.5% APR over 5 years, or $1,168.75 before insurance, registration, and gas. Many young military members have found themselves "car broke" when they rushed out to buy that car with their first paycheck—just because you *can* doesn't mean you *should*. Make informed decisions that align with your own personal goals and values, and you will be on your way to a successful financial career.

But, when it is time to buy that first car out of necessity, there are several steps you can take to set yourself up for success. First, do your research, lots of it. You can and should research and compare rates *before* going to the car dealership—including getting a preapproval from your primary bank. By having this preapproval letter in hand, you have a negotiating chip when it comes time to buy that car. Do this within a two-week window so that multiple "hard" credit pulls will show as the same event on your credit score. Then, know your budget before you go to a dealership. Your budget is *not* the maximum down payment you can afford today.

Your budget includes planning for the long-term costs of the vehicle and use your How I Spend My Money Plan to know what that is. Too many people look at "what can I afford today" rather than "what impact will this have on my monthly finances later?" Just because you can afford a 10% down payment on a $50,000 car doesn't mean that should be your purchase budget. Instead, start with your How I Spend My Money Plan to determine your monthly allotment for your transportation. Then, calculate insurance, registration, and gas and subtract it from that number. . .now you have your *actual* monthly car payment number. Take that number and reverse your way into a purchase price using an online loan calculator. Let's say your number is $400 per month and you are expecting a 6.5% interest rate. If you do a 5-year loan term, then your maximum loan amount will be $20,443. Divide that number by 0.8, if you plan to put 20% down, and your car purchase number is $25,553—with a $5,110 down payment.

Second, read the book *Never Split the Difference* and *Start with No* to learn a ton about how to effectively negotiate. Even if you aren't making a big purchase, those books will change your life. Go to the dealership armed with the knowledge of negotiating that you gained from these books; your preapproval letter as a negotiating chip; and your exact budget with down payment ready to go. You will also have to pay additional fees like tax, tag, and title, before you get to drive away in your car so make sure to include that in your negotiations—that $25,553 is my out-the-door number. The price tag that you see on the car is almost always negotiable. The best deals of my life have been when I went in fully prepared and unemotional.

Third, have a strategy. Most car dealerships run thin margins—that is they only make a 1–2% profit. However, there are many deals to be found if you are looking in the right place. First, used cars tend to have more room to negotiate over new cars. Second, most dealerships have quotas—monthly, quarterly, and annual sales numbers they need to hit—so try to catch them at a time when they are trying to make a quota or hit a sales goal and you might find more room to negotiate. The absolute best buying days are usually December 30 and 31, so if you can wait, do it. After that, look to go at the end of a quarter—March 29–31, June 28–30, or September 28–30. If you don't want to wait, shoot for the end of the month in the last two to three days. Although some dealerships count the first day or two of a new month toward the previous month so you might find good deals in the first two days as well. Monday to Wednesday are usually the slowest days, and if they align with the end of a quarter, you may have hit gold—take a day of leave and make a fun day of it. Dealerships also need to make room for new arrivals when the next year's models come out—typically August to November—and Black Friday, the day after Thanksgiving, is a particularly good day. Especially if you are wanting a new car and don't mind last year's model. If you do not want new and are going used, you might find good deals around tax refund time when dealerships usually run sales to attract consumers who just got a refund check.

Now, the age-old question of "should I buy new or used." And the answer, usually, is "It depends." It depends on many different factors that you will need to determine for yourself, but we will unpack some of the most common differences and questions when buying your first or even your twentieth car.

A new car is going to come with a lot of advantages over a used car, such as a manufacturer's warranty, new safety and technology features, lower financing (sometimes 0% if you catch the right special), no previous wear-and-tear that can lead to unforeseen and costly maintenance, better fuel efficiency, and almost no maintenance costs. They also come with several downsides: immediate depreciation when you drive it off the lot, higher price and higher monthly payment, and possibly higher insurance premiums. If you *need* to sell your car in the next three to five years, you likely will not recoup your costs and probably won't even break even in the sale. But that typically starts to turn around as you approach year five and the car is paid off.

A used car also has its advantages and disadvantages. On the plus side, the cost is usually lower, roughly half the cost of new, as well as a lower monthly payment. Maybe the biggest advantage, which is much lower depreciation after purchase. A new car will typically lose 30% of its value the minute you drive it off the lot whereas a used car may not lose any value. There are also many downsides and some unknowns when purchasing a used car, such as previous damage or wear and tear that is not immediately apparent on inspection, which can lead to reliability issues. Many used cars no longer have a warranty on major parts so if your transmission goes out you are stuck with a huge bill to pay. Additional drawbacks are typically fewer features to choose from—a minor issue if you aren't picky and looking for something specific—and they also come with higher interest rates when you finance them.

When buying used, you also have the option of buying from a dealer or direct from a seller. You typically pay less directly from a seller than a dealer. However, you really *should* get an independent inspection done by a certified mechanic if buying from a seller—the cost of which can often negate the savings over the dealership, especially if you end up looking at and inspecting multiple cars before finding the right one. If you are going to need financing, you can get it directly from your bank as we discussed, and this can be used to buy from either a dealer or a direct seller. Oftentimes in the military there will be a lot on base where people who are PCSing overseas can sell their cars—we always affectionately called it the "lemon lot." You can sometimes find great cars from reliable sellers and at a good price in these lots. But buyer beware: just because the seller is also military does not mean you should forgo the inspection. If you are looking for something specific, you can also look at nationwide searches and online sellers. Sometimes you will find exactly the car you want in a city with a lower cost of living, and the price will be much lower. Car prices vary dramatically across the United States, often differing by thousands of dollars between major cities and rural areas. Just know that you will likely need to pay local taxes when you bring the vehicle into the state—which is sometimes waived for the military members under certain conditions. Some of the best states to buy a car are New Hampshire, Oregon, Delaware, Montana, and South Dakota. Each has its own reasons, lower taxes, lower cost of living, some states have lower dealer fees, registration costs, and no sales tax at point of sale, so do your research and shop around. Keep in mind that taxes are charged based on where YOU live, not where you buy the car. As a military member there are often options for where you call home, so see the section on "choosing your residence" for more info.

My Roadmap

I've had many screw-ups in my debt journey. Despite having a college degree and officer commission, I started my career deeply in debt with no financial knowledge. So I began to seek out this knowledge by reading books that I found at the base library. One of the foundational books for me was the *7 Habits of Highly Effective People*, which helped reset my thoughts on habit building. Next, I read *Rich Dad, Poor Dad* by Robert Kiyosaki, which is still one of my favorite books on understanding wealth. But not much changed after reading these books, at least not at first.

Student loans, car payment, and lifestyle inflation left me living paycheck to paycheck on an officer's salary. Something had to change. I was going out with my friends to happy hour a few times a week and spending money like it was endless. As a recent college graduate, I had never really had a steady paycheck before. But I knew at least some basic principles, like saving 10%, living on less than you make, etc.

The military provided steady income but no financial education or wealth-building guidance. I assumed that having a "good job" meant I was financially successful, despite having a negative net worth. A turning point came for me when I learned about pre-paying principal on loans. Each month I would make my regular minimum student loan payment. Then two weeks later with my next paycheck, I would make an additional payment of principal only. The technique of bi-weekly payments or even doubling your monthly payments works for nearly all types of debt. You can either pay half your bill every two weeks; or just add a second payment during the same month. By switching to bi-weekly payments, you make one extra month's payment every year and reduce your payoff timeline by about one month for every year of the debt. If you pay your bill twice in a month you will pay the debt in half the time. In both cases you save considerably on interest. In my case described here, it allowed me to pay back my student loans in half the planned timeline and slash my interest by more than one third.

From Debt to Freedom: The Decisions That Changed My Trajectory

Getting out of debt didn't happen because I made more money or got lucky. It happened because I stopped making the same mistakes—and then made a series of disciplined decisions at key moments. What follows isn't a highlight reel. These were inflection points where I could have slid backward into debt or quietly moved forward toward freedom.

The first major decision that became a pillar of my future financial success was opening a Roth IRA in my first month on active duty. I didn't fully understand it, but I read what I could, booked a call with a financial planner, and took action. By the end of that call, I had opened the account with $100 and set up automatic contributions twice a month. As I adjusted to my new income, I built my first How I Spend My Money Plan and reeled in my spending—remember the kayak? Then I gradually increased my contributions until I hit the maximum, which was about $333 per month at the time.

I didn't have a crystal ball. I just figured that consistently investing early and never stopping was probably a good idea. Fifteen years later, that same Roth IRA became the vehicle I leveraged to buy my first commercial property—one I still own today. That young lieutenant with a kayak had no idea where this would lead. He just made a boring, disciplined choice and stuck with it.

The second major inflection point came with deployment savings. Combat pay, tax-free income, hazardous duty pay, family separation pay—money that could have easily disappeared into lifestyle upgrades. Instead, I invested it and later used it for real estate. Deployments come with financial incentives for a reason, and if you're heading into one, you should treat it like a financial opportunity, not a shopping spree. Have a plan before the money hits your account.

If you don't give money a job, it will find one on its own—and it won't be your future. Every major transition in your career is an opportunity for course correction: deployments, PCS moves, promotions, new responsibilities. At each one, make small increases to savings and investments. Time is the one factor you can't replace.

The third milestone was starting a side business using military skills and relationships while still serving. I am not encouraging anyone to violate the rules or take on outside employment without permission. I checked with legal often. But there are many compliant ways to earn additional income while on active duty, and we'll cover those in the Side Hustles chapter. This was the point where momentum really began to build.

The final phase was systematic wealth building: multiple income streams, disciplined investing, and fully leveraging military benefits.

There is no single right way to do this. Curiosity leads to learning, learning leads to opportunity, and opportunity compounds when paired with discipline.

When I took off the uniform for the last time—20 years and three months after taking the oath—my net worth had grown to more than eight figures. I don't share that to brag. I share it because none of this required extraordinary talent, luck, or a trust fund. It required consistency, planning, and a willingness to make boring decisions when exciting ones were available.

If a poor kid from New Jersey with no financial education could do this on a military salary, so can you.

Action Steps:

1. **Put down the shovel. You can't dig your way out of a hole—stop spending more than you make.**
2. **Build the ladder. Create your *How I Spend My Money Plan* and a week-by-week debt repayment strategy.**
3. **Climb consistently. Progress beats perfection. Stick to the plan.**

If you have significant debt, then you should take time to meet with your local readiness center financial planner to help with debt management and explore options for debt consolidation and refinance.

Chapter 4

Taxes, Setbacks, and Emergency Funds

"Most people over-estimate what they can accomplish in one year, but underestimate what they can accomplish in ten years."

—derived from *Amara's Law*, Roy Amara

No plan survives first contact with the enemy.

In fighter aviation, we don't pretend otherwise. We plan hard, then we build contracts for the moment the plan stops working. Because it will. The only question is whether you have a framework for what happens next.

We were approaching our transition point, and the air picture was not clean. Not the way we wanted it. Not the way we briefed it. But we had a contract.

If we didn't have the condition we needed to safely execute, we weren't going to force it. We were going to reset.

"Elvis, Spin."

Two words. And with that call, nearly a hundred airplanes executed a coordinated change—because we had targeted backward and briefed exactly what the reset looked like. We bought time. We reduced risk. We gave the team a chance to get the conditions back under control.

That's what a Spin is: a planned reset that keeps the mission intact.

Life throws you Spins. Taxes you didn't expect. Cars that break. Moves, kids, deployments, medical bills. Most people don't get taken out by the event itself—they get taken out because there's no buffer. No reset. No margin.

An emergency fund isn't pessimism. It's professionalism. It's your planned reset that keeps one surprise from cascading into panic, debt, and bad decisions.

This chapter is about building resilience into your financial system—so you stay in the fight long enough to win.

Taxes

"I'm proud to pay taxes in the United States; the only thing is, I could be just as proud for half the money."

—Arthur Godfrey

What are taxes and how do they work?

We all pay taxes. But, unfortunately, most of us did not learn the why, how, and what behind taxes while we were in school. Our first experience with taxes is usually our first paycheck—we are told we are going to get paid $20/h for 40 hours and we expect to get a check for $800. Much to our surprise, we get a check for closer to $600 and think we've been cheated or robbed! (Maybe we have. . .but that is a different book.) If you are like me, you probably learned about taxes through trial-and-error, through many rounds of Turbo-Tax, through *Taxes For Dummies*, through saving receipts all year only to learn that you are going to use the standard deduction, etc.

This section is going to give a brief overview of taxes, the basics of taxes, and then some info specific to the topics in this book—real estate, passive income, investment income, etc. So, to kick it off, what are taxes? Merriam-Webster dictionary tells us that taxes are a charge usually of money imposed by authority on persons or property for public purposes.

In basic terms taxes are charges levied by the government on its citizens in order to run the government. I chuckle every time I hear people say, "the government should pay for that!" I laugh because the government doesn't have any money and doesn't make any money, so how can it pay for something? Taxes. To fund our 2023 $6.3 trillion budget, the US government collected about $4.8 trillion in "federal revenues" and financed the rest. By "financed" I mean, they printed $1.5 trillion new dollars and added them to the global currency pool—often referred to as "quantitative easing," or for the rest of us, "inflation." When the government says "federal revenues" it means "taxes" with a few very small exceptions like national park admission fees and customs duties.

There is an important and often overlooked point on taxes: taxes are paid by citizens, not companies. Yes, I know, there are corporate taxes and payroll taxes and transaction privilege taxes and business taxes, and on and on, that *appear* to tax corporations and businesses. But they just tax their customers in additional ways. Consider a large fast-food chain. The government says, "we are going to levy a corporate beef tax on all restaurants serving hamburgers." Do the large fast-food chains shrug their shoulders and say, "Oh well, I guess that cuts into our profits?" No! They raise the price of the hamburger by the amount the government increased the tax. The same applies to all industries. Only people pay taxes. Remember these points when you are choosing your elected leaders, get out and vote, participate in government, and be informed on how the government is deciding to spend *your* money!

A very important part of taxes is documentation. Save your info throughout the year for retrieval rather than saving it for ease of saving. This is true for all record keeping. We tend to take the easiest path to saving information—maybe to a general folder or a location without a purpose. Instead, take an extra minute to organize your folders on your computer or cloud drive and deliberately save info so that when it is tax time you have everything in one location.

Types of Taxes

There are dozens of different types of taxes, but for this book we are going to focus on three: income tax, property tax, and capital gains tax.

Income taxes are taxes that are taken out of your wages—your income—that you pay *after* you have done the labor, and *before* you have been paid for that labor. Sounds less fair when written this way, doesn't it? Everyone pays federal income tax at a percentage based on your income tax bracket—even if you are a military member whose salary is paid by taxes. Tax brackets are adjusted periodically, at the time of publication, the tax brackets are listed in Table 4.1.

For most military members at the start of their career, you will fall into the 12% federal tax bracket. To simplify the math, let's say you earn $40,000 per year. The government does not wait until April to collect its money—it withholds taxes from every paycheck throughout the year.

In MyPay, you can influence how much is withheld from each paycheck by adjusting the number of exemptions you claim on your W-4. Exemptions are essentially your way of telling the government, "don't take quite as much now—I'll settle up later." The higher the number of exemptions you claim, the less tax is withheld from each paycheck, which means more cash in your pocket throughout the year. Fewer exemptions mean more is withheld each month.

Most people start with zero exemptions, which causes the government to withhold more than is strictly necessary. Then, at the end of the

Table 4.1 2026 US Tax Brackets[a]

Filing Status	10% Bracket	12% Bracket	22% Bracket	24% Bracket	32% Bracket	35% Bracket	37% Bracket
Single	Up to $12,400	$12,401 to $50,400	$50,401 to $105,700	$105,701 to $201,775	$201,776 to $256,225	$256,226 to $640,600	Over $640,600
Married Filing Jointly	Up to $24,800	$24,801 to $100,800	$100,801 to $211,400	$211,401 to $403,550	$403,550 to $512,450	$512,451 to $768,700	$768,701 and over

[a] https://www.irs.gov/newsroom/irs-releases-tax-inflation-adjustments-for-tax-year-2026-including-amendments-from-the-one-big-beautiful-bill

year, they get a tax refund. That refund is not free money—it is simply your own money being returned to you after the government held onto it interest-free all year. If you prefer to keep more of your money during the year instead of waiting for a refund, you can gradually adjust your exemptions until your withholding more closely matches what you actually owe. The goal isn't to game the system—it's to be intentional and avoid giving the government an unnecessary, interest-free loan.

But wait, I thought you said that I had to pay 12% of my income to taxes, how do I get a refund? Well, the government also gives you an opportunity to take a deduction from your taxes. Most people, in the early years, will use the standard deduction. This number is calculated by the government for the absolute bare minimum to live on, and the taxes that you likely paid for essentials; they then give you a "break" on your taxes by reducing your income by that number.

For 2026 the standard deductions are:

Filing Status	Standard Deduction
Single	$16,100
Married Filing Jointly	$32,200
Head of Household	$24,150

This means, that if you make $16,100 per year, the government will withhold 12% from your paycheck in taxes (unless you change the withholding); then at the end of the year when you file your taxes, you reduce your income by the standard deduction, in this case $16,100 income –$16,100 deduction = $0 taxable income. So, at this level you pay $0 in taxes, and you will get a refund of what you did pay.

If you made $40,000 this year and claim no deductions, the government would have withheld $4,800 from your paychecks over the

12 months. When you file taxes, you take the standard deduction, so your income becomes $40,000 – $16,100 = $23,900 taxable income. You still fall in the 12% tax bracket, but now you only owe 12% of $23,900 = $2,868. You will get a refund check for $4,800 – $2,868 = $1,932.

That refund that you get from the government is your money that they held onto all year in a free loan from you to the government, that they pay back with no interest to you. So, when I mentioned earlier the ***right ratio*** for you, you can start calculating your taxes for the future. Once you know what your annual raise will be, and you know any other tax-impacting activity (rental properties, family member exemptions, etc.) you can start doing your taxes for next year before the year begins. Then, once per quarter update your tax plan for the year and make sure that you are paying the appropriate amount and no more—and then invest that difference!

In this example, $40,000 income with the standard deduction, you would calculate your taxes ahead of time and see that you are going to be responsible for $2,868 in taxes. You can make sure that in every monthly Leave and Earnings Statement (LES) the government is withdrawing $239 (2,868/12) and no more. If they are withholding more than that, you can adjust your exemptions higher until your withholding is approximately $239 per month. When you submit your tax forms for the year, you'll come out to $0, nothing more to be paid and nothing to come as a refund.

As your portfolio grows and your taxes become more complicated you will likely want to seek professional advice and assistance with these calculations. The **big takeaway from this section is that we should all be doing our taxes *for the future*.** There is no reason we can't do this. And yet, for most of the country, people wait until April, then calculate what they owed *last year, then* hold their breath hoping that they paid enough and won't owe more or paid too much and will get a refund. This is how I used to do it for much of my life, and how probably 99% of the country does it.

However, this is NOT how the top 1% does it. This is not how the wealthy do their taxes. I did not learn this until I had a net worth more than eight figures and began working with a tax strategy attorney to do taxes looking forward into the future and begin planning our tax-impacting activities a year before they occurred.

A great example of future tax planning is outlined in detail in the real estate section. To summarize it here, if you do your taxes for the future, you can pre-plan how much to spend on a rental property and how much it will save you in taxes.

Effective Tax Rate

Often you will hear people discuss their "effective tax rate"—that is, the amount of taxes you pay in relation to your income *after* you have factored in all deductions, exemptions, credits, adjustments, depreciation, etc. The effective tax rate is a more accurate description of the taxes you pay. In our example above of an E-3 making $40,000 per year who takes the standard deduction, and pays $2,868 in taxes, on paper he was in the 12% tax bracket. But, after his deduction he only paid an *effective* tax rate of 7.17%.

It can be confusing when a person grows their income and moves into a higher tax bracket. A common misconception is that if you jump to the next tax bracket all your income is taxed at that higher rate, and you would be better off to keep your income below the next bracket; that is false. Table 4.1 shows the tax brackets, the amount of income in the bracket, and the amount of taxes that you will pay. If you are single and you made $105,701 of taxable income (after deductions) you would be in the 24% bracket. It seems like you would pay $25,368 in taxes which is 24% of your income. But you would actually pay 10% on the first $12,400; then 12% from 12,401 to 50,400; then 22% from 50,401 to 105,700; then 24% from 105,700 to 105,701.

It looks like this:

Bracket	Range	Taxable Amount	Tax You Pay
10%	$0 to $12,400	$12,400	$1,240
12%	$12,401 to $50,400	$37,999	$4,559.88
22%	$50,401 to $105,700	$55,299	$12,165.78
24%	$105,700 to $105,701	$1	$0.24
		TOTAL TAX PAID:	$17,965.90

So, on your single income of $105,701 you paid $17,965.90 in taxes which is an *effective tax rate* of 17%.

State Income Taxes

In addition to Federal Income Tax, most states charge some form of a State Income Tax. A later chapter outlines strategies around state income tax as a military member—i.e. changing your state of residency when you live in a state with a more advantageous tax structure. Very few people have the option to choose a state with a tax advantaged structure while living elsewhere—this is unique to the military and how our PCS structure works. Specifically, if you are from California, Hawaii, New York, or another state with very high state taxes, you may want to consider changing residency when you PCS to another state. While many states will offer tax breaks for active-duty military members, you also want to consider how they will tax your retirement after you leave the military. State taxes work much in the same way that federal taxes work, and you can also calculate your state taxes ahead of time and look for opportunities to minimize your taxes while maximizing what brings you joy and furthers your purpose and goals. For example, in Arizona, where I live, the state allows you to give to a qualifying charity of your choice up to $400 dollars per year and deduct it from your state taxes dollar-for-dollar. I love this option. I can either pay $400 to state taxes, or I can give it to a charity I want to support.

Most tax deductions are "deducted" from your income. So, a $10,000 deduction does not reduce your taxes by $10,000. It reduces your income by $10,000. And if you are in the 24% tax bracket, that means that a $10,000 deduction will *save* you $2,400. Keeping this in mind, sometimes deductions can cost you more if you do not calculate them ahead of time. This is why I love the Arizona rule that gives you dollar-for-dollar deductions on your first $400 to a qualified charity. You will need to do research for your own state and situation, but there are many ways to maximize and optimize your taxes—one of the largest expenses of your entire life.

Property Tax

This tax, as it sounds, is a tax against property you own. It is levied locally where your property is located and is based on an assessed value of the property from the county appraiser. This money usually goes to fund local schools, roads, police, and other essential local services. There are typically no exemptions or write-offs on property taxes unless after retirement the VA deems a person 100% disabled, in which case many states offer reduced or no property tax on a primary residence.

When you buy your first home your property tax will be paid from your escrow company. Escrow is a third-party company that keeps money in an account on behalf of two other parties—in this case the bank who owns your loan and you. There are many other types of escrows, but most mortgages are paid through an escrow account that withholds money for taxes and insurance. When talking about the price of a home we usually speak in PITI—principal, interest, taxes, insurance. When you buy your first home you can expect to make a monthly payment with a small portion going to property tax, then the company will make the annual property tax payments on your behalf.

When you are ready to start investing in rental properties you will need to plan for paying these taxes unless you set up an escrow payment for your rental properties. When talking about commercial property it is more common to only discuss principal and interest because the taxes and insurance are not usually in the same monthly payment and are instead paid separately.

Capital Gains Tax

This tax is simultaneously advantageous for some situations, and brutal to others. This tax applies to various categories where you make money in your life that you did not specifically get paid on a W-2 pay stub, i.e. you didn't trade your time for money; you made money while you slept. This applies to selling certain property, making money in the stock market, etc. It only applies (currently) when you claim that money—so if your stocks are up 20% this year, you only pay capital gains tax when you take that money out of your brokerage account.

Long-term capital gains can be leveraged for people later in life to receive income in a relatively low tax bracket. Capital gains tax has three brackets—0%, 15%, and 20%—that are also broken out by filing status and amount of gains (see Table 4.2).

If you are currently in the 12% tax bracket, you might be thinking "That doesn't make sense. If I make capital gains, I will pay higher taxes!" Well, consider this: we all plan to make more money later in life than we do right now. If you did not believe this, you would not be reading this book. With that in mind, we all secretly

Table 4.2 Capital Gains Tax Rates

Filing Status	0% Rate Income Threshold	15% Rate Income Threshold	20% Rate Income Threshold
Single	Up to $48,350	$48,351 to $533,400	Over $533,400
Married Filing Jointly	Up to $96,700	$96,701 to $600,050	Over $600,050
Married Filing Separately	Up to $48,350	$48,351 to $300,000	Over $300,000
Head of Household	Up to $64,750	$64,751 to $559,300	Over $559,300

want to be in the highest tax bracket. . .because it means we are making great money! But we also secretly don't want to *pay* the highest tax bracket rate because that is not fun. So, later in life, when you retire a millionaire from the military and are living the life of your dreams, you will likely be in one of those higher tax brackets.

If you make most of your income from a W-2 high-paying job—maybe, you and your spouse are both defense contractors making $250,000 each and you find yourself in the 35% bracket—you will typically have to pay very high taxes. In fact, the people who pay the most in taxes are typically high-wage earning professionals who get most of their income from a W-2 salary—like doctors, engineers, and other professionals.

When you can offset your income with capital gains from investments, you can often reduce your tax burden as a percentage of your income. There are also additional tax strategies that you can take advantage of when your income comes from sources other than a W-2 paycheck—for instance through real estate, business ownership, S-corporation exemptions, etc.

To determine capital gains tax, you must take the original purchase price of the asset and subtract it from the price you sold it for. For instance, if I had bought $10,000 worth of the VOO exchange traded fund in 2004 when I joined the Air Force, it would have been worth about $80,000 at my retirement 20 years later. If I then sold those shares, I would have to pay capital gains tax on $80,000 – $10,000 = $70,000. If I were married filing jointly, we would pay $0 in taxes. If I were single filing taxes, then I would pay $0 on the first $48,350; then 15% on the remainder ($70,000 – $48,350 = $21,650) so I would pay $3,247.50 in taxes. That is an effective tax rate of 4.6%. Not bad, right? Later in life you can begin using capital gains to supplement your income and reduce your effective tax rate.

It is also important to note that if you hold an asset for less than one year, you pay taxes at your tax bracket rate, not capital gains tax. So, if you bought some crypto currency that made you a million dollars overnight and you sold it immediately, you would pay 37% taxes on that because you would be in the highest tax bracket and it would not be considered long-term capital gains.

You can also use this to your advantage when you have losses. You can claim capital losses on your taxes if you have an asset that lost money and you sell it to reallocate that money elsewhere. I do not advocate trying to lose money but many of the top investment strategies include selling your "losers" and reinvesting in other assets then bundling those losses together to help offset your taxes. This strategy is known as "tax loss harvesting" and can be helpful to your tax burden later in your investment career. I recommend working with a financial professional, like a fiduciary, to discuss the pros and cons of various investment strategies.

Tax "Loopholes"

I really dislike the term "loophole" in this context because it makes it sound like you are taking advantage of something that they accidentally missed and any minute they will fix the "loophole" and you won't be able to use it anymore. That is false. The advantageous tax strategies that are available to people who are proactive about their taxes were placed there ON PURPOSE. The IRS knows about them. Many of them have been litigated in court and found to be legal. Congress has not changed them. They are there for anyone to take advantage of if they choose.

The amount you pay in taxes is, at least in part, a choice you make. There are legal ways to reduce your tax burden through smart investments that will continue to grow your wealth throughout your life. If you decide to follow the pack and blindly file your taxes every April hoping, with fingers crossed, for a refund, you will continue to live like the pack. And that is, not financially free.

Let me be clear. You must pay your taxes. And do not screw around with taxes. Always follow the applicable laws. But you absolutely SHOULD NOT pay more than you are required to pay. Ignorance of the tax code is not an excuse in court if you underpay your taxes. How then can you look your grandchildren in the eyes and tell them, "I would have had more for your inheritance if only I had learned the tax code earlier." Don't use ignorance as an excuse. Educate yourself, seek professional guidance, and use the legal tax code to your advantage.

But hey, don't take my word for it, ask the court:

> *"Anyone may so arrange his affairs so that his taxes shall be as low as possible; he is not bound to choose that pattern which will best pay the Treasury. There is not even a patriotic duty to increase one's taxes."*
>
> —Judge Learned Hand

Or this cool lady:

> *"It's not our job to overpay the government. No matter how you lean politically, it is not your duty to fund the government beyond what you legally must pay them. That is the entire point of the tax system. Not following it and allowing yourself to overpay because you feel guilty is not in line with why the system exists to begin with."*
>
> —often attributed to Margaret Thatcher

Setbacks

The chances of having a financial setback in your life and career are nearly 100%—it will happen to pretty much everyone. If you approach your financial journey knowing that it will happen, it can help soften the blow when it does. There is a downturn in the stock market almost every decade, sometimes catastrophically. But it has always recovered—at least so far. There have been sound institutions that were always great investments, but they ended up going out of business. And there are occasionally setbacks in life that lead to big financial burden.

It could be a divorce, a family emergency, a bad investment, a legal issue, or an honest but costly mistake. Whatever the cause, just know that you will likely have a setback in your journey to financial freedom. The best advice that I can give is this: seek professional advice. The military has a tremendous network of resources available to its members for advice—financial counselors, mental health counselors, etc. It takes courage to walk into the family life center and admit that you need help. I cannot stress this enough. The life of a military member is stressful and different from the life of a civilian in many ways. When you find yourself in a tough spot, I guarantee that you are not the first person who found themselves there. Go get advice.

I signed up for my first "coach" when I was well into my 30's. And to be honest, my wife kind of dragged me there kicking and screaming. I thought it was silly—like the Stuart Smalley comedy sketches from *Saturday Night Live*. What could a "coach" provide me in my life? Man, was I wrong. My first coach helped me see that no matter how good I thought I was doing, someone who is watching from the sidelines and helping me call plays is invaluable. He pointed out that Michael Jordan, the G.O.A.T., had a coach his entire career. He had numerous coaches, and he upleveled at each phase of his career. In fact, at his peak he had separate coaches for strength and conditioning, mindset, and basketball! If it's good enough for MJ, it's good enough for me.

I highly recommend going into the family life center, or whatever your base calls it, long before you ever need help. Go meet the financial planner when your finances are great. Go see a marriage counselor when your marriage is thriving. It will reduce the barriers to getting help when you truly need it—and someday you will, trust me. It will also help you to get ahead of problems before they develop.

Emergency Funds

This is a sensitive subject, so I begin with a caveat, that this is my opinion, I am not a certified financial planner, and this is not financial advice. Here is what I did about an emergency fund. When the same institutions that need your money sitting in their bank urge you to keep an emergency fund in their savings account, you should be at least a little skeptical. The three most often cited reasons for needing an emergency fund are (1) sudden job loss, (2) unforeseen medical expenses, and (3) unexpected expenses. The reason why banks recommend keeping it in savings is so you can quickly and easily access it, and you don't lose it in risky investments.

These are all valid reasons, and I do not intend to discredit the reasons. Instead, I offer a different opinion, specifically, as a military member. In my 20-year career I did not have a fear of sudden job loss. My job was guaranteed if I met the requirements. And, even for those who did not meet requirements and found themselves on the other side of a discharge, they always had many months of notice. In the civilian world it is true that you can lose your job at any time. In the military you and your family are provided good healthcare. If you make a career of it, you will have healthcare for life. It is possible that you may have unforeseen medical expenses in your life, but in the military, it is much less likely. The same applies to unexpected expenses—the military provides some "top cover" in life including base housing, various forms of assistance, and an all-around robust support network. It is my belief that an emergency fund is less critical while on active-duty military—I still believe it is a good thing, but I think it requires less emphasis.

Further, while banks recommend keeping savings accounts, those recommendations haven't changed for the last 50+ years. But, 50 years ago it was difficult to get your money out of an investment. In today's digital age I can perform a same-day wire and get my money from almost anywhere in the world to almost anywhere else; I can get it from almost all my investments; and I can do it all from my phone. In fact, I cannot think of any circumstance where I would absolutely need cash today that would require I have a savings account fully funded. Some may argue with me, but for my part an emergency fund is just as reachable sitting in an investment that makes me money.

So how do I do my emergency fund planning then? Well, I do my own personal and family risk assessment. I start with extreme "black swan"-type events and list them from least likely to most likely. Then, I add a column for how big an impact they would have. Then, I add a column for the financial cost or burden it would bring me if it happened. I do this exercise about once a year, and I treat it the same way

I would do contingency planning for a Large Force Employment in a fighter jet. Once I have my master list, I focus on items that are higher likelihood with higher impact. Then I look at the financial requirement to determine my own "emergency fund." Finally, I look at the time it would take for me to access the money and the impact that would have. Each time I do this exercise I find that I need a little less than I thought I did and I need it a little slower than the worst-case-scenario-talking-TV-personalities tell me that I need it. Table 4.3 shows some examples to give you an idea of planning your own emergency fund:

Table 4.3 Risk Assessment Matrix

Event	Likelihood (1–10)	Impact (1–10)	Cost	Timeline
Government Shutdown	9	1	$0 unless paychecks stopped	30+ days of notice
(another) Pandemic	4	7	$0 if prepared $1,000 for supplies	Immediate & unplanned
Natural Disaster (in AZ—maybe drought?)	2	5	$0 if prepared $1,000 for supplies	Immediate & unplanned
Job Loss	1	7	3 months of bills ($12,000)	3+ months of notice
Medical Emergency	3	8	$5,000 unplanned travel expenses because medical is covered	1 week
Vehicle Loss	4	2	$1,000 deductible	1 week

My table will typically have another 20–30 rows specific to me, and more data for the ones that are high likelihood and high impact. We see from Table 4.3 that the most I anticipate needing is $12,000, but the likelihood of losing my job in the military is a 1 on a scale of 1–10. I would also have many months to figure it out, find another job, cut expenses, etc. So, this one does not go into my bucket of Emergency Fund.

Losing a vehicle that I need to get to work and having to pay a deductible while it is getting fixed is much higher likelihood but only costs $1,000 based on the auto insurance I have. This would be my floor for the minimum in my emergency fund to start. I also have a week or so to gather the money, so I can easily keep that money invested somewhere if I can get to it within a week. Which currently is almost anywhere.

In sum, I think emergency funds can and should be part of your long-term financial freedom strategy. However, I put much less emphasis on it than traditional financial people who work at banks and have a financial incentive for people to keep their money tucked away making almost nothing in a savings account.

Chapter Takeaways

Now that you understand the basics of taxes you are well equipped to take more control of your money and your future. Here are key takeaways from this chapter:

- Everyone should do taxes FOR THE FUTURE rather than in the past, after the year is over.
  - You know how much the military will pay you, now figure out your tax burden.
- Using your tax burden, make sure that you are withholding the correct amount each month, no more, no less.
  - Invest the extra during the year once you make this change.

- Be proactive about taxes.
  - Taxes are one of the biggest bills of your entire life. Take action to reduce them where able.
- Everyone experiences setbacks at some point. Don't let a setback define you. Remember what Roy Amara said: "most people over-estimate what they can do in a year but underestimate what they can do in ten years."
- Use your own judgment and situation to determine your necessary emergency fund. Invest the extra.

Action Steps:

1. **Do your taxes for the future—this week.**

   Pull your last LES (or most recent pay stub), look up your filing status and standard deduction, and do a rough estimate of what you'll actually owe this year. Don't make it complicated-just get within striking distance. The goal is not perfection. The goal is to stop flying blind.

2. **Adjust your withholding so you stop giving the government an interest-free loan.**

   If you normally get a big refund, that's a clue your withholding is too high. Go into MyPay, update your W-4 settings, and move toward a "close to zero" outcome: no big check owed, no big refund coming. Then automate the difference into your investing or debt plan. Give those dollars orders.

3. **Build your "Spin" plan: one-page risk assessment + emergency fund target.**

   Make a simple table: (1) event, (2) likelihood, (3) impact, (4) estimated cost, (5) timeline to pay. Pick your top three most likely/high-impact risks and set an emergency fund floor based on the most likely cost, not the scariest headline. Decide where that money sits and how fast you can access it.

Part II

Purpose

By the time we were airborne, the plan was already wrong. Not fatally wrong—but wrong enough to matter.

We had briefed the mission the day prior: a large force package with multiple strike elements, escort, SEAD, tankers, and command and control layered across hundreds of miles of airspace. Timelines were tight. Weather was marginal but acceptable. Tanker tracks were placed precisely to make the math work. On paper, it was clean. But reality voted early.

Ten minutes after takeoff, the first wrinkle appeared. The weather at the target area was deteriorating faster than forecast. Ceilings were dropping and visibility was trending the wrong direction. Nothing unsafe yet—but trending. Then one of the tankers reported a delay. Maintenance issue. Not a showstopper, but it compressed everyone's margins. Shortly after that, a supporting package checked in late, then went quiet altogether. Radio issues. Lost comms.

This is usually where things unravel.

In complex missions, chaos doesn't show up all at once. It leaks in through the seams. One small deviation forces a workaround. The workaround steals time. The stolen time creates pressure. Pressure leads to rushed decisions. Rushed decisions lead to mistakes.

Except this time, something different happened.

No one asked, "What do we do now?"

Flights adjusted without being told. Tanker plans flexed. Altitudes shifted. Timelines slid, but in the same direction. Some aircraft pushed. Others held. A few turned cold briefly, then rejoined the flow. Calls were short. Calm. Intentional.

Everyone already knew what mattered.

The mission wasn't about hitting a specific second on the clock. It wasn't about flying the exact routing we had drawn the night before. It wasn't even about perfect execution. The objective was simple: accomplish the priority effects and bring everyone home safely.

That intent had been made clear long before we stepped to the jets.

So, when the plan broke—and it did—no one froze. No one waited for permission. No one tried to "win" their piece of the mission at the expense of the whole. Each flight made decisions that aligned with the same north star. Different actions. Same direction.

From the outside, it might have looked messy. From inside the cockpit, it felt controlled—because we had a shared mental model of why we were there.

Later, during the debrief, we talked through what changed. Weather. Timing. Assets. Deviations from the original plan. There were plenty. But no one was confused about whether the mission succeeded. It did—because success had been defined clearly before anything went sideways.

I've flown missions where the plan survived intact and missions where it didn't last five minutes. The difference between chaos and coherence has never been intelligence or talent. It's clarity.

When people know the intent, they don't need constant direction. They don't need micromanagement. They don't need perfect conditions. They can absorb friction and still move forward together.

Life works the same way.

Pressure doesn't wait for things to settle down. It shows up early. Unexpectedly. Often all at once. And when it does, you won't have time to figure out who you are or what matters to you.

You'll default to whatever is already clear.

That's what this section is about.

What made that mission work wasn't flexibility, talent, or even experience. It worked because the intent was clear long before the first problem showed up. Everyone knew what mattered most, so when the plan broke—as it always does—no one panicked. They adjusted. They acted. They stayed aligned. That clarity didn't appear in the air. It was built on the ground.

In fighter aviation, we call those agreements "contracts." Not legal contracts—mental ones. If this happens, we do that. If that fails, here is what still matters. Contracts remove hesitation when time and attention are limited. They let people act decisively without waiting for permission.

Most people don't have those contracts in their personal lives. So, when pressure hits—financial stress, career decisions, family obligations—they improvise in the moment. They react instead of executing. Not because they're incapable, but because they never defined their intent. That's where purpose comes in.

Your mission/vision/values become contracts with yourself—who does what by when—so your calendar and bank account align with your target. This part of the book will be a deep dive into your purpose. Maybe you have already done this for yourself—I truly did not do this exercise until I was almost 40 years old. I had been involved in sessions where we worked on the mission and vision of a military organization and aligned it with the guidance from our headquarters. But it wasn't until I was much older that I applied those principles to my personal life and laid out my own mission, vision, and values. You may be tempted to skim over this part of the book and skip the deep work that is required to understand your own personal Why. I highly encourage you to set aside the time for this work.

I used to tell my squadron, "Nobody loves you as much as you do." I always said it in the context of writing your annual report; invest the time into writing good bullets about the work you did that year, and your boss will be able to help you create an excellent report. This holds true for your personal values. Nobody can define your values for you. By the same token, there is no right or wrong answer, these are *your* values.

The process this part of the book uses is one that I have used many times, but it is not the only option out there. There are many different variants of these exercises, so if this one doesn't do it for you, find one that does. But the desired outcome at the end of this part of the book is that you have defined your personal Core Values in three to five words; you will have a personal Vision for your life; and you will have a personal Mission defined for your life.

These will be the foundation for your goal-setting exercises. Before you run out and get them tattooed on your neck, just know that they can change over time. So, if you feel like your core values are a 95% correct solution, use them and continue the exercises—eventually you will start to narrow down what is important to you even further and maybe next year when you do this exercise again your core values will have changed a bit. Mine certainly have, particularly after major life changes like getting married, having kids, retiring, etc.

The process is as follows:

1. Define your core values using the core values exercise
2. Define your personal Vision statement
3. Define your personal Mission statement
4. Use your mission, vision, and values to inform your long-term Big Hairy Audacious Goals (BHAGs)
5. Use your BHAG to work backward to small steps you can take today to be on your way toward your goal

Here is the thing about goal setting: a goal without small daily steps is unachievable. Every day when you wake up you get to decide if today will be a success or a failure toward your future goal—by whether you do the thing that you need to do. If every day is a success, it will be impossible not to succeed and hit your goal. Similarly, if every day is a failure, then you will not reach your goal.

What do Purpose, Core Value, Mission Statements, or your personal why have to do with financial freedom?

Understanding your own personal "why" is the guiding principle of your life. It is incredibly important to define; as well as super intimidating. And, for many, me included, it can lead to feelings of stress and anxiety when you don't feel like you "have it all figured out."

From the time I was a child I was continually asked, "What do you want to be when you grow up?" That question felt more pointed and dangerous the older I got. By the time I was in high school it seemed to have a tone all its own. Like when people asked that question, they were really saying, "You don't have your shit together, do you?" As someone who prided myself in having my shit together,

I didn't appreciate the frequency of that question. Nonetheless, I have decided to begin this part of the book with a discussion of my "why," and your "why," and our collective "why."

I've always thought of my life, opinions, and worldview as a pyramid.

At the very top—the sharp point—is my ***why***. There's no left or right, no forward or back. Just my why, standing alone at the top.

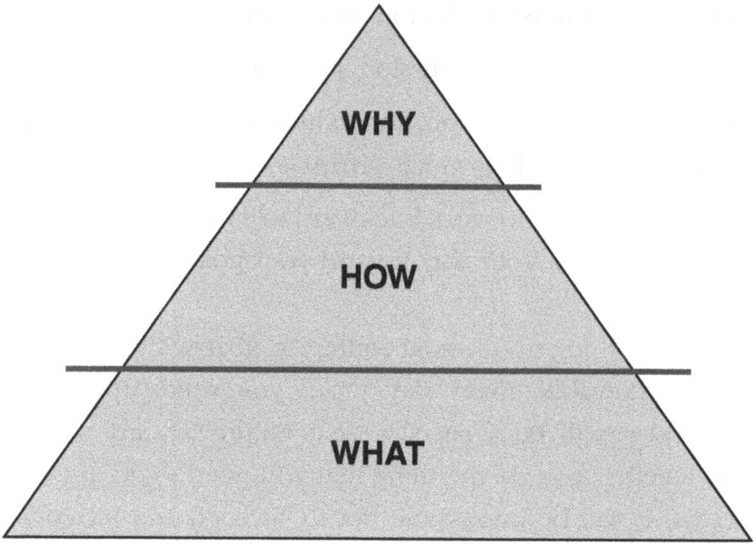

As I move down the pyramid, I reach my ***how***—the plan I'm constantly refining to move toward that why. Lower still, near the base, is my ***what***—the actual actions and tasks I execute.

In military terms, my why is the *strategic level*, my how is the *operational level*, and my what is the *tactical level*. Simon Sinek's *Start with Why* presents this idea as concentric circles with the why at the center. Whatever model resonates with you is fine—but I highly recommend reading his book to clarify your own why.

For me, the pyramid visualization works best. Here's why.

Imagine I put two people in a room who are completely opposed on a high-stakes, emotionally charged topic—politics. One far right, one far left. We start at the top of the pyramid—the ***why***.

I ask: "Do you believe we should act in the best interest of the United States of America?"

Both raise their hands. Agreement. At the top, ideology doesn't matter. We want what's best for the country. Now we move down to the ***how***.

I ask: "Should we raise taxes to make the country better?"

One hand goes up. One glare. We've started to move apart.

Then we reach the ***what***.

I ask: "Should we tax the wealthy based on net worth and redistribute that money?"

One enthusiastic hand shoots up. The other person accuses them of socialism—and the conversation unravels. The closer you get to the base of the pyramid, the farther apart people become.

Too often in life, we start with the what—our tasks, opinions, tactics—and are met with immediate resistance. That resistance can discourage people before they even begin.

Don't start with what.

Your why is bigger than you. It's a higher purpose, a just cause, a vision that contributes something meaningful to the world. When you start there, alignment becomes possible—and progress follows.

When your *why* is clear, your *how* becomes disciplined, your *what* becomes consistent—and that consistency is what creates long-term financial freedom. Money follows clarity—and clarity starts at the top of the pyramid.

Action Steps:

1. Schedule the work.

Block uninterrupted time on your calendar to complete the exercises in the next three chapters. This is not something you do between meetings or while scrolling your phone. Treat it like mission planning—because it is.

2. **Write it down, even if it's uncomfortable.**

   Don't try to "think" your way through your mission, vision, and values. Put pen to paper. Clarity comes from writing, not from having the perfect answer in your head.

3. **Commit to iteration, not perfection.**

   Your first pass does not need to be final. A 95% solution is more than enough to move forward. You can—and should—revisit this work as your life evolves. The only real failure here is skipping it.

Chapter 5

Mission | Vision | Values

"The ultimate measure of a man is not where he stands in moments of comfort and convenience, but where he stands at times of challenge and controversy."

—Martin Luther King Jr.

The call was technically correct.

That's the part that bothered me the most.

We were under time pressure, the kind that compresses your thinking and forces decisions before you feel ready. Multiple aircraft airborne, timelines slipping, weather beginning to creep in from the edges of the map.

I had an element struggling to get there on the left flank. Nothing dramatic. Nothing unsafe. Just enough friction to make every choice matter.

I had two options: cut the struggling element and execute the contingency plan—or slow the package and let them work through it.

One was clean, conservative, and well within the rules. It aligned with precedent. It would keep the timeline intact and avoid drawing attention. The other option carried more risk—not recklessness, but exposure. It would complicate coordination, require additional communication, and put me slightly outside the comfortable center of the decision space.

Both were defensible. I chose the first.

I made the call quickly, confidently, and without hesitation. It was the kind of decision no one would question. The radios stayed calm. The formation flowed. The mission continued. From the outside, it looked like exactly what a competent leader should do under pressure.

Nothing broke.

No safety issues. No missed objectives. No raised voices on the radio.

And yet, almost immediately, I felt it.

Not panic. Not regret. Just a quiet, internal signal that something was off.

I couldn't have articulated it in the moment, even if you had asked. The jet was flying. The mission was still unfolding. There was no room for introspection at 400 knots. So I did what pilots do—I logged it mentally and kept moving.

It wasn't until later, during the debrief, that it surfaced again.

We walked through the mission the way we always do. Facts first. Timeline. Decisions. Outcomes. The call came up. No one challenged it. No one suggested an alternative. On paper, it was solid.

But the feeling was still there.

Eventually, I realized what was bothering me: the decision wasn't wrong—it just wasn't aligned.

I hadn't violated any rules. I hadn't ignored guidance. But I also hadn't filtered the decision through anything deeper than procedure and expedience. I chose the option that was easiest to defend, not the one that best reflected who I wanted to be as a leader.

That distinction matters. Had I let that element continue, they likely would have learned valuable lessons—and collectively, we might have been a stronger fighting force down the road.

In aviation, we train extensively on procedures. Checklists. Rules of engagement. Contracts. They exist for a reason, and you ignore them at your peril. But there are moments—usually the important ones—where procedure alone is not enough. Where the manuals stop short and judgment takes over.

When that happens, something else fills the gap.

If you've defined it, your values step in. If you haven't, pressure does.

In that moment, under time and authority pressure, I defaulted to safety and precedent because I hadn't clearly defined my own internal filters. I wasn't acting against my values—I simply hadn't articulated them well enough to guide the decision.

That realization was uncomfortable.

I had prioritized short-term mission success over long-term growth as a community.

I had always assumed values were something you refined later. With more experience. More rank. More perspective. But that day made it clear: decisions don't wait for you to feel ready. They show up early, demand an answer, and move on.

And whatever is clearest in your mind at that moment—rules, fear, convenience, or purpose—is what will drive the call.

I flew the rest of that mission just fine. But that one decision stuck with me long after the jets were parked.

It wasn't a tactical miss.

It was a values gap.

That experience forced me to confront something uncomfortable: I had been making decisions without a clearly defined filter. Not because I didn't care—but because I hadn't taken the time to articulate what mattered most.

If you've ever made a decision you can defend. . . but don't feel proud of, you know exactly what I mean. This book will make a lot more sense if we, together, define your "why."

The first step in this process is to determine what you value. I will share my personal core values with you after you have done the exercise yourself so that you are not influenced by them—they are not right or wrong, they are just mine. Just like your core values are yours.

Don't put too much pressure on yourself. These are not permanent—even if you get them tattooed—and you can revisit this exercise later. I do this exercise at least once a year when my wife and I host our annual goal-setting retreat. I find that while they may vary slightly year-to-year, I have always been in the same family of values. This is your opportunity to determine what really matters to YOU—not your spouse, your parents, your friends, or what anyone else thinks you should focus on.

There are no right answers here. The goal is not to impress anyone—it's to notice patterns.

Start by reflecting on the following things from your life. Once you have answered these questions in the space provided you can move on to the next activity.

1. When do you feel joy? ______________________________

____

____

a. Who are you with? ______________________________

____

b. What were you doing? ______________________

____

c. Why did you enjoy it? ______________________

____

2. How do you currently spend your time? ______________________

____

____

a. List an average number of hours you spend in a week on the things you do: work, sleep, family, hobbies, etc.

____

____

____

____

____

____

b. Where do you want to spend more time? ______________________

____

c. Where do you want to spend less time? ______________________

____

d. Are you satisfied with your current time investments?

____

3. What do you value about where you are in life right now?

____

____

4. List 5 things that you are grateful for?

a. ______________________

b. ______________________

c. ____

d. ____

e. ____

5. What are the key relationships in your life?

a. Who are they with?

b. Why are they important to you?

c. List 1 way to improve each one.

The next exercise is best performed with a deck of Core Values cards. You can keep the cards and reference them every time you do this exercise as well as have your family join in! My kids started doing this exercise as young as seven and it has been fun to write down what they come up with each year and see how their lives evolve. I'll give you a hint, at seven you are far more likely to have core values like "Fun," "Laughter," or "Play"—we could all probably use some more of that in our lives.

Don't have cards? Print your own or use the list provided at the end of the chapter. If there is a word that you love but is not on the list or in the cards, add it!

STEP 1: Go through the cards, the list you printed out, or the list at the end of the chapter. Take two seconds per word. If it resonates with you, put it in the keep pile; if not, put it in the discard pile or cross it off the list. Don't overthink it, just do it.

> Note: You may be wondering if these words should be factual about yourself or aspirational to who you want to become—I always lean toward aspirational when doing my exercise, but it needs to be true to who you are. Words that resonate the most with me are a little of both—factual and aspirational.

Try not to hold any judgment of the words or judgment of your own reactions to the words. You might wonder, "Am I a bad person if family is not one of my values?" No, you are not a bad person. Just because a word is not your core value doesn't mean that you don't value it at all.

STEP 2: Take your pile of keepers and go through the list again. Spend two to three seconds per word and again make two piles, "keep" or "discard."

If using the list, underline or circle the words that stand out to you the most. I typically end up with a list of definite "no's," a bigger list of words that resonate, and a short list of "maybe" words. For step three, I go back through my "maybe" list to see if any are clearly "yes" or clearly "no" and need to be adjusted.

STEP 3: Transpose your list of "yes" words into a notebook or separate sheet of paper while saying them out loud.

This step is important, don't shortcut it. By writing out the words and saying them out loud, you are making a conscious connection with the word. I often end up cutting a handful of words as I write them because saying them out loud and writing them hits differently than reading them on paper. By this point you should have a much shorter list.

STEP 4: Group the words into similar categories.

Pick the categories based on your own interpretation of the words you kept. For instance, if I have "Creativity," "Innovation," "Curiosity," and "Uniqueness," I may put them all into a single category and pick the one that best represents the sentiment I feel when I read these words—in this case "Innovation."

I typically end up with five to seven categories with varying quantity of words in each one. The very first time I ever did this exercise I ended up putting 35 separate words under the heading "Legacy"—which remains a core value of mine to this day.

STEP 5: The final step is to whittle the categories down to just three words that best represent what you value in life.

When you know exactly what you value in life, you can shape and plan your life in accordance with those values. If you are feeling stuck, no worries. Just pick three from your narrowed down list and go with them!

Action > Inaction.

Chances are, as you move through the process of designing your great life of purpose, the values that are not truly core to your being will become apparent. Then you can do this exercise again with more insight. There is no right or wrong answer, only what you value.

My core values are ________________, ________________, and ________________.

These values answer the question: *What is most important to me in my life?* And now that I have identified them, I am ready to plan a life of greater fulfillment and meaning.

Core Value 1: ______________________ is important to my life because ____

____

____

I will live this value by: ____________________

____

Core Value 2: ____________ is important to my life because ____________________

____

____

I will live this value by: ____________________

____

Core Value 3: ____________ is important to my life because ____________________

____

____

I will live this value by: ____________________

____

____

____

Write these values down in prominent places—your bathroom mirror, hang them on the fridge, your daily planner, your phone, and computer background. When you are frequently reminded of what you value, you are less likely to violate your values.

A violation of core values leads to internal friction, stress, and eventually unhealthy patterns. You are more likely to stick to your values, avoid destructive habits and regressive behaviors, and live a life of purpose when your values are displayed prominently in your life.

My personal Core Values.

As promised, I will share my core values with you: Legacy, Innovation, Adventure. I live out my core values in these ways:

1. Legacy—I have a deep and meaningful life; I am important to my family and my family is important to me; I am a leader who has a positive impact on the people around me.
2. Innovation—I find elegant solutions to complex problems; I have credibility and trust with the people I help and work with.
3. Adventure—I am excited by the life that I live; I push my personal comfort zone to experience new things; I seek difficult challenges and dedicate myself to conquering them.

The first time I conducted this exercise I ended up with more than 70 words after going through the list twice, I started putting them into piles of words that had similar meanings for me and ended up with this list:

Legacy = Future Generations, Leadership, Success, Family, Connection, Pride, Altruism, Recognition, Ambition, Community, Tradition, Caring, Abundance, Humility, Time, Impact, etc.

Innovation = Knowledge, Making a Difference, Originality, Creativity, Intuition, Vision, Fun, etc.

Adventure = Courage, Individuality, Wonder, Risk Taking, Self Expression, Optimism, Playfulness, Travel, Learning, Leisure, Nature, Confidence, Challenge, Perseverance, etc.

Years from now I may look back and laugh that these were my values at this stage in my life; that also does not matter, these are mine right now and I embrace that.

I look forward to hearing about yours.

Core Values Exercise

Abundance
Acceptance
Accomplishment
Accountability
Accuracy
Achievement
Adaptability
Adventure
Advocacy
Alertness
Altruism
Ambition
Amusement
Assertiveness
Attentive
Awareness
Authenticity
Balance
Beauty
Being the best
Belonging
Boldness
Bravery
Brilliance
Calm
Candor
Capable
Career
Careful
Caring
Certainty
Challenge
Charity
Clarity
Cleanliness
Cleverness
Collaboration
Comfort
Commitment
Common sense
Communication
Community
Compassion
Competence
Competition
Concentration
Confidence
Connection
Consciousness
Consistency
Contentment
Contribution
Control
Conviction
Cooperation
Courage
Courtesy
Creation
Creativity
Credibility
Curiosity
Decisiveness
Dedication
Dependability
Determination
Development
Devotion
Dignity
Diligence
Discipline
Discovery
Diversity
Drive
Effectiveness
Efficiency
Empathy
Empowerment
Endurance
Energy
Enjoyment
Enthusiasm
Entrepreneurship
Environment
Equality
Ethics
Excellence
Experience

Exploration
Expressive
Fairness
Faith
Family
Famous
Fearless
Feelings
Ferocious
Fidelity
Financial stability
Focus
Foresight
Forgiveness
Fortitude
Freedom
Friendship
Fun
Future generations
Generosity
Genius
Giving
Goodness
Grace
Gratitude
Greatness
Grit
Growth
Happiness
Hard work
Harmony
Health
Home
Honesty
Honor
Hope
Humility
Humor
Imagination
Impact
Improvement
Inclusion
Independence
Individuality
Initiative
Innovation
Inquisitive
Insightful
Inspiring
Integrity
Intelligence
Intensity
Intuition
Job security
Joy
Justice
Kindness
Knowledge
Lawful
Leadership
Learning
Legacy
Leisure
Liberty
Logic
Love
Loyalty
Making a difference
Mastery
Maturity
Meaning
Mindfulness
Moderation
Motivation
Nature
Openness
Optimism
Order
Organization
Originality
Parenting
Passion
Patience
Patriotism
Peace
Performance
Perseverance
Persistence
Personal fulfillment
Playfulness
Poise
Potential
Power

Present	Sensitivity	Thoughtful
Pride	Serenity	Thrift
Prestige	Service	Time
Productivity	Sharing	Timeliness
Professionalism	Significance	Tolerance
Prosperity	Silence	Toughness
Purpose	Simplicity	Tradition
Quality	Sincerity	Tranquility
Realistic	Skill	Transparency
Reason	Skillfulness	Travel
Recognition	Smart	Trust
Recreation	Solitude	Trustworthy
Reflective	Spirit	Truth
Reliability	Spirituality	Understanding
Resourcefulness	Spontaneous	Uniqueness
Respect	Sportsmanship	Unity
Responsibility	Stability	Usefulness
Restraint	Status	Valor
Results oriented	Stewardship	Victory
Reverence	Strength	Vigor
Rigor	Structure	Vision
Risk-taking	Success	Vitality
Safety	Support	Vulnerability
Satisfaction	Surprise	Wealth
Security	Sustainability	Welcoming
Self-discipline	Talent	Well-being
Self-expression	Teamwork	Winning
Self-reliance	Temperance	Wholeheartedness
Self-respect	Thankful	Wisdom
Selfless	Thorough	Wonder

Mission | Vision

"He who knows the why, can withstand almost any how."

—Adapted from Friedrich Nietzsche

Now that you've identified your core values, it's time to take the next step toward living a life of purpose: defining your personal vision and mission.

I've always found the core values exercise to be challenging—but fun. Narrowing down a list feels manageable. You're reacting, noticing patterns, eliminating what doesn't fit. It's structured. It has edges.

Defining a personal vision and mission, on the other hand, felt much harder for me.

There's no list to pare down. No obvious starting point. You're trying to create something meaningful out of thin air—and that can feel intimidating. If you struggle with this part of the chapter, you're not alone.

Often, I find it easier to write down my goals first and then come back to refine my vision and mission. Goals feel concrete. They give shape to the future. Vision and mission take more imagination—and more honesty.

So if this section feels sticky, that's okay. You can always move forward to the goal-setting chapter and return here with more clarity. This work is iterative, not linear.

If you've spent time in the military, you're already familiar with vision and mission statements at the organizational level. Units define their mission and vision to align with higher headquarters and provide clarity of purpose. What most people haven't done is apply those same principles to their personal lives.

Let's clarify the difference.

Your **vision statement** is a long-term forecast. It describes the future you're working toward—the life you hope to build someday.

It's aspirational. It's directional. It answers why you're doing what you're doing.

Your **mission statement** is more practical. It describes how you show up in the world right now. What you do. How you do it. The value you provide along the way. It answers how you move toward your vision.

Your vision is your **Why**.

Your mission is your **How**.

Both should align with the core values you identified earlier in this chapter, and both should support the goals you'll set later. When they're aligned, decisions become easier. When they're not, friction shows up.

Creating Your Personal Vision Statement

Start by asking yourself: *Who do I aspire to Be, what do I want to Do, and what do I want to Have?*

A vision statement is typically short—one or two sentences—but it should be powerful. It should describe what you want most out of life.

As you write, consider these questions:

- What does success look like to you?
- What do you want your life to look like in 20 or 30 years?
- What do you stand for?
- What positive impact do you want to have on the world?
- When you imagine your ideal future, where are you, who is with you, and what are you doing?
- What is so important to you that you would change your life over it?

I often start with free-writing—either by hand or using talk-to-text—describing the life I want to live without worrying about structure or polish. Only after I've captured my own thoughts do I use AI to help synthesize them into something concise. I don't recommend starting with AI. Start with your ideas first. Then use tools to refine them.

If you're still stuck, keep it simple. Try this framework:

I am ____.

I work as ____.

I have ____.

I am happy because ________________________________.

During this process, your inner critic will probably show up. Mine always does. That's normal. This is your vision for your life. Set aside judgment—much of which you likely inherited from parents, family, or society—and write what you actually want.

No one else has to read this. Dream as big as you want. It's your life to live—or not.

My Personal Vision Statement:

____

____

____

____

____

Creating Your Personal Mission Statement

Your mission statement defines how you move toward your vision.

While the vision is aspirational, the mission is operational. It describes your approach to life. How you show up. How you create value. How you intend to pursue the future you've imagined.

Write one or two sentences that describe how you are going to live out your vision on a daily basis.

My Personal Mission Statement:

____

____

____

____

____

Action Steps:

1. **Finish the outputs—today.**

   Write down your **three core values**, a **one- or two-sentence vision**, and a **one- or two-sentence mission**. Don't leave this chapter with blanks on the page. Drafts are allowed. Avoidance is not.

2. **Turn values into a filter.**

   Pick one decision you're facing right now—money, career, relationship, health—and run it through your values. Ask: *Does this choice move me toward my vision, or away from it?* If you don't use your values, they're just words on paper.

3. **Make it visible and revisit it on purpose.**

   Put your values where you'll see them daily (phone, planner, mirror). Then schedule a recurring check-in—quarterly or annually—to review and update them. Life changes. You change. This work should evolve with you.

Chapter 6

Goal Setting

"We are what we repeatedly do. Excellence, then, is not an act, but a habit."

—Will Durant (often attributed to Aristotle)

Nothing dramatic happened that day.

No emergencies. No adrenaline spike. No moment where I walked away thinking, *That was the sortie where everything finally clicked.*

It was just another training day.

I was early in an upgrade—deep enough to know what "right" looked like, but not consistent enough to produce it on demand. The schedule was full of repetition. Similar profiles. Same airspace. Same objectives. Brief, fly, debrief. Over and over.

The sorties weren't glamorous. There were no big tactical wins to celebrate. Mostly just small corrections. Slightly late here. A little fast there. Scan discipline drifting. Sight picture off by a few degrees. Nothing unsafe. Nothing catastrophic. Just not quite right.

The kind of flying that tests your patience.

During the debrief, the feedback was familiar. A sentence here. A note there. *Fix this next time.*

I nodded, wrote it down, and moved on. Again.

If I'm being honest, that phase of training can feel discouraging. You're working hard, but progress is subtle. You don't feel "better" from one day to the next. There's no clear finish line in sight. Just a long series of average days stacked back-to-back.

And that day was no different.

I didn't walk away proud. I didn't walk away frustrated. I just walked away tired.

Weeks later—maybe months—I realized something had changed.

The corrections that used to dominate the debrief weren't coming up anymore. My scan had tightened without me consciously thinking about it. Timing improved. Sight pictures stabilized. Decisions came faster, with less effort. The jet felt quieter.

I hadn't had a breakthrough.

I had accumulated one.

Looking back, I can't point to a single sortie where it all came together. There was no defining moment. No dramatic leap forward. Just a slow, steady narrowing of gaps that used to feel permanent.

That unremarkable training day—the one where nothing happened—wasn't insignificant at all.

It was foundational.

In aviation, we don't build capability through heroic moments. We build it through repetition. Through showing up on days that feel average. Through fixing small things consistently until they're no longer things you have to fix.

That's how competence is earned.

It's also how most people miss progress.

We tend to overvalue big moves and undervalue steady ones. We look for motivation instead of systems. We wait for a surge of clarity or confidence before we act instead of trusting that clarity comes after consistent action.

But the truth is, the days that don't feel like much are often the ones doing the most work.

You don't notice them while they're happening.

You notice them later—when something that used to be hard suddenly isn't.

And that is what this chapter is about.

That day didn't feel important at the time because it wasn't exciting. There was no finish line, no applause, no immediate payoff. Just small corrections, applied consistently, with the expectation that they would compound over time.

That's how meaningful progress actually works.

Big outcomes rarely come from big moves. They come from ordinary actions repeated long enough for them to matter. The hard part isn't knowing what to do—it's trusting that showing up, day after day, is enough even when the results aren't obvious yet.

Goal setting exists to make that process visible—and repeatable. It takes an abstract future and turns it into something you can work on today. It replaces motivation with structure. And it gives you a way to measure progress on days that feel unremarkable—because those are usually the days doing the most work.

Now that your purpose is defined and you know where you are, it is time to determine where you are going. Goal setting is a crucial part of success—not because it guarantees outcomes, but because it gives effort a direction. Very few people achieve success in their life without having a goal that they are working toward—**because when you aim for nothing you will hit nothing**.

A former Chief of Staff of the Air Force once told me "Motor, if you don't have a plan, a timeline, and one person in charge, then you don't have anything, and it won't get done." I internalized that advice and to this day in nearly every situation I ask, "Who, Will do What, By When."

We are going to apply this framework to your life today. You are the who. There may be other "who's" in your life—people who support you, challenge you, and help you stay accountable. The What and the When come next. To define those, you will need to do a little reflection and deep work.

We will begin with an exercise that always feels a little uncomfortable to me—but consistently helps me reconnect with the aspirations I tend to bury under day-to-day life.

I remember doing this exercise as a cadet in the ROTC program; I wrote about how I was a decorated combat-tested fighter pilot who had done a lot of good in the world. Visualizing your future is one of the best ways to form a clear picture of what you want. Once you have a clear picture then you will be able to put it into concrete goals that you begin working toward. So, just like the exercise I did as an ROTC cadet, we are going to begin with a letter to yourself 20 years down the road.

On the next page, write a letter to your future self 20 years down the road—you can choose any timeline, but 20 years seems to be sufficiently far into the future to be aspirational. Write as if you are telling your younger self all about your life and accomplishments 20 years from now. If you are stuck, here are some prompts to help you:

You do not need to answer every question. Use them as guides, not requirements.

1. How old are you? Who is with you (family, friends, pets, etc.)?
2. What are you good at?
3. What is your financial situation?
4. Where do you live?
5. What season of life are you in?
6. What kind of leader, parent, friend are you?
7. What have you mastered?
8. What did you leave behind (habits, friends, places)?
9. What challenges have you overcome?
10. What perspectives have changed about your life?
11. What has stayed the same?
12. Who is no longer with you?
13. What is your health like?
14. What is your career like?
15. What matters the most to you? What no longer matters?
16. What business or investments are you in?
17. What has healed in your life?
18. What changes have you made?
19. What do you value?
20. What experiences and places have you encountered?

A 20-Year Letter to Myself

Who Do You Need to Become?

What does this person read, study, learn, know, etc.? Who does this person hang out with? Where do they vacation? What do they spend their free time on? Once you have defined what you want to Be, Do, and Have, you can define the person that you must become to achieve those things.

When I wanted to be an astronaut, I kept telling myself, "If I get picked, I am going to study astrophysics, orbital physics, etc., so hard before I am supposed to report for duty!" But the truth was, if I really desired to be an astronaut and if I really believed I was going to be one—then I would have already studied those things. When you have absolute faith and belief that you are going to achieve your goals, then it doesn't feel like a waste of time to start working on those things now. That was an eye-opening realization for me. It was when I determined that I *wanted* to go to space, but I did not *desire* to be an astronaut. As leadership expert John Maxwell once told my wife: "Many people want to be where I am, but very few want to do what I did to get here."

For this next section of your work, you are going to define the person who has achieved all these goals. You are going to start way out in the future, near the end of this great life of purpose that you designed and determine what attributes that person possesses.

The Be-Do-Have exercise uses your 20-year letter to consider these three core concepts that define who you are as a person. Spend a few minutes writing out answers to the following prompts:

1. Who do you want to Be: ______________________________

____

____

a. and who are you now? ______________________________

____

____

2. What do you want to Do: ______________________________

____

____

a. and what are you doing now? ________________________

____

____

3. What do you want to Have: ____________________________

____

____

a. and what do you have now? ___________________________

____

____

When you can answer both parts of each question you can build a roadmap to get there from where you are now. This is where the roadmap gets real. Now we turn aspirations into action steps.

Goal Setting: If you aim for nothing, you hit nothing.

A dream is vague. A goal is specific. We're going to make yours specific.

Goals act as checkpoints on your roadmap. Well-defined goals are not the end state, but signposts along the way—assuring us that we are still going in the right direction. Have you ever been driving somewhere new, following directions, and you have been driving on the same road for what feels like forever? You start to doubt yourself; maybe I missed a turn, or maybe I wasn't supposed to travel this far?

A good set of directions will give you updates along the way; things to look for so you know you are on the right track. That is what good goals do for you. Setting 10-year, 5-year, 1-year, monthly, and weekly goals allow you to take the next right step and know that you are headed toward your *Great Life of Purpose*.

A goal is not an aspirational idea like "someday I want to be a country music singer." A goal is a precise future desired result that you are committing to achieve. During my 20 years in the military, I was taught and always used the SMART principle for goal setting. This framework for goal setting was first defined by George T Doran in a 1981 article for the *Management Review,* but it was heavily influenced by the work of Peter Drucker.

For a goal to be well defined, it must be:

SPECIFIC—For a goal to be specific you should be able to answer Who, What, Why, Where, When, & How.

Instead of saying "be rich" say "have a net worth in the top 10% of the country."

MEASURABLE—How will you know if you made it if you can't measure it? A goal like "get rich" has no metrics associated with it, so you will not know whether you made it or not.

Instead of "net worth in the top 10%" say "have a net worth of more than $1.9 million."

ATTAINABLE—Is it realistic and attainable with your resources and skills.

Does anything in your life need to change to make this attainable? If you were born in an orphanage in a third world country, you may need to relocate for the goal of $1.9 million net worth to be attainable.

RELEVANT—Does this goal tie into my Core Values, my future self, and what I plan to Be, Do, and Have in my life?

If your list includes real estate investing, then maybe it is. "My goal is to have a net worth more than $1.9 million through real estate investing."

TIME-BOUND—Anyone can say "I want to be a millionaire" but until you create a plan and put a timeline against it, it is just a dream, not a goal.

"I am going to have a net worth of $1.9 million by the time I retire from the military in 20 years through sound financial principles and investing in real estate."

Big goals stop feeling impossible when you break them into the very next task that moves you forward. What feels unattainable becomes achievable the moment you stop staring at the finish line and focus on the very next step.

For the goal-setting activity, we begin by looking at these 6 key pillars of our life: Financial, Family and Friends, Personal, Professional, Health, and Spiritual. On a scale of 1 to 10, rate each area of your life. This is subjective, but you are the one determining how you feel you are doing in each of these categories.

If you are in the military, then it is likely you consider that your "job" category, but you may have separate goals for starting a business outside of the military—maybe that is professional. Or, perhaps,

"Professional" goals to you means getting your next promotion, finishing a degree, or learning a new skill.

There are no wrong answers here; this is YOUR life, and you get to decide. If you want to add or take away a category, go for it! These are the six that I use and I encourage you to categorize them in a way that meets your needs—maybe you want to separate Family from Friends into two separate categories, go for it.

This isn't a report card. It's a prioritization tool.

Financial	1	2	3	4	5	6	7	8	9	10
Family & Friends	1	2	3	4	5	6	7	8	9	10
Personal	1	2	3	4	5	6	7	8	9	10
Professional	1	2	3	4	5	6	7	8	9	10
Health	1	2	3	4	5	6	7	8	9	10
Spiritual	1	2	3	4	5	6	7	8	9	10

Now that you have ranked each category, I highly recommend focusing on one to three things for right now, then do this exercise again in a few months and see how things have changed. I typically focus on the three areas that scored the lowest unless you are comfortable with that score. If you have more than three priorities, then you really have no priorities—because if *everything* is a priority, then really, nothing is.

With your one to three categories chosen, we are going to move into the goal-setting phase. The first step of goal setting is to begin far out in the future with something you want to achieve someday.

You can call it the BHAG from earlier in this section; a Someday Goal; Strategic Goal; Ambition; North Star; Legacy Goal; or Main Objective. Whatever you choose to call it, it will become your guiding principle for the rest of your goal-setting journey. I prefer borrowing from the great Jim Collins and his book *Built to Last* and use the term BHAG—the Big Hairy Audacious Goal that you set for yourself in the future.

Your inspiration for your goal likely stems from your 20-year letter and your Be, Do, Have list in the previous section. If your goal does not significantly impact your life 20 years down the road then it likely isn't aggressive enough. Goal setting takes the same amount of effort whether we set small goals or big goals. But you don't want to be the person who achieves their goal only because you didn't set it high enough. Let's start by brainstorming those big goals. In the space below, list one to three big goals from what you have created so far.

This is where most people stop.

Don't.

Big Hairy Audacious Goal Brainstorming

First Goal: ______________________________

____

What Do I want to Be, Do, & Have?

How does this goal align with my Core Values?

Where do I see myself in 20 years in relation to this goal?

Second Goal: ______________________________

____

What Do I want to Be, Do, & Have?

How does this goal align with my Core Values?

Where do I see myself in 20 years in relation to this goal?

Third Goal: ______________________________

____

What Do I want to Be, Do, & Have?

How does this goal align with my Core Values?

Where do I see myself in 20 years in relation to this goal?

From Brainstorming to Planning

Next, choose 1 goal from the Brainstorming List per page.

GOAL: ____

____

Now, brainstorm everything that you could possibly do to achieve this goal in the next 5–10 years:

Using the Pareto Principle, circle the 20% of items above that would bring you closest to achieving your goal (one in every five). The Pareto Principle, known as the 80/20 rule, states that 80% of your outcomes will be the result of 20% of your actions. This principle helps us focus on effort on what really matters—lots of steps can take you closer to your goal, but you are not looking to get closer. You want the 20% that will help you *Achieve* your goal.

List the items you circled in order from most impactful toward your goal, to least impactful.

1. ____

2. ____

3. ____

4. ____

The top item on this list is your new five-year goal. Write your new five-year goal:

Now brainstorm everything that you could possibly do to achieve this goal in the next year:

5-Year Goal to *THIS YEAR* Goal

You now know how to correctly define a goal using the SMART principle; you know to look for the 20% of actions that will drive 80% of your results; and you know what the future vision of your life looks like. Let's drive it home.

Re-write your five-year goal using the SMART principle of goal setting:

Now, brainstorm everything that you will need to do in order to achieve this goal *within the next year.*

From this list, circle the top 20% of actions that will get you to your five-year goal.

Write the items you circled in order from most impactful toward your goal, to least impactful.

1. ____________________

2. ____________________

3. ____________________

The top item on this list is your new one-year goal. Write it using the SMART framework:

You now have a one-year goal defined using SMART goal-setting principles that will take you to your five-year goal, which will take you to your 10-year and 20-year goals. You have a vision for your future and clear goals to achieve. Now we move into the Action Steps associated with these goals—your mission.

You are not behind. You are building the system.

Take your goals one at a time. Do not set out by saying "someday I want to be rich and famous and have a private jet and mansions on the beach." That is probably 50 separate goals in one broad sentence. Get focused on one at a time. Redo these worksheets for each goal individually. Does it sound like a lot of work? Achieving big things in life IS a lot of work—but it is worth it to achieve the life of your dreams.

Consider the following questions and challenges for your new one-year goal:

1. Why do you want to achieve this goal? What will achieving it do for your life?

2. What will happen if you do not achieve it?

3. How are you going to measure success toward this goal?

   a. What are the key checkpoints along the way?

   b. How will you celebrate those checkpoints?

4. What changes do you need to make in your life?

   a. What do you need to say No to?

5. What is holding you back?

   a. How can you overcome these challenges?

6. Who will hold you accountable to this goal?

   a. Or how will you hold yourself accountable?

With these questions answered, you should have a solid understanding of why your goal matters, what will happen if you do not achieve it, and a rough outline of the plan to get there. The next step is to make a list of every step you need to take to achieve this goal. This is a brainstorm list so include everything that you believe you will need to accomplish.

Brainstorm every step to take this year to achieve your one-year goal:

Great job! Let's keep it going by adding specifics and deadlines to these tasks. In the space next to each item, or in the space below, write out the most basic task that is your LITERAL NEXT STEP (LNS) toward this task.

For instance, if your goal is to buy a rental property, and your tasks included "find a Realtor"—the LNS would be to conduct a search for a Realtor or ask friends for referrals. So next to "find a Realtor" you would write "conduct an online Realtor search" and "ask friends and family for a Realtor referral." Then you write the time it will take and when you will do it by.

If you get stuck, it's almost always because the next step isn't defined.

Task:	LITERAL NEXT STEP:	Time Commitment	When?
Find a Realtor	Conduct online search/ask friends	15 minutes	This afternoon

Task:	LNS:	Time:	When:

Task:	LNS:	Time:	When:

Action>Inaction.

> *"Watch your thoughts, they become your words; watch your words, they become your actions; watch your actions, they become your habits; watch your habits, they become your character; watch your character, it becomes your destiny."*
>
> —Lao Tzu

When I do this step of the exercise—breaking tasks into their Literal Next Step—I can usually accomplish some steps the very same day. For me I find that I often stop when I do not know my LNS—and I believe most people do that as well. They will dwell for weeks on the fact that they don't know any Realtors rather than simply doing an online search.

I also find that when I do this exercise I typically end up with a full page, single spaced, of LNSs. "Finding a Realtor" can be broken down to the LNS of doing an online search, but there are other steps as well. Once the online search is complete, my LNS would be "call 5–10 Realtors, explain what I want, see if they are value aligned." Those calls should last 20 minutes each so I will set aside two hours the next day for those calls and schedule them. Then, my LNS would be "meet my top two or three candidates for coffee and outline my plan." I would schedule those for this coming Saturday morning. Do you see where we are going with this?

The next key principle to understand for goal accomplishment is our *habits*. Like Lao Tzu said ". . .watch your actions, they become your habits. . ." For a deep dive into the power of habits, I highly recommend *Atomic Habits* by James Clear; *The Power of Habit* by Charles Duhigg; and *The ONE Thing* by Gary Keller and Jay Papasan. If you develop sound habits, they will propel you to your goals. And while quitting bad habits is known to be difficult, there is research to support the idea that replacing a habit is easier than stopping one.

For instance, when I quit drinking, I replaced my evening nightcap with tea and my can of beer with flavored sparkling water—I'm bougie like that. It was easier to substitute a can of water than it was to completely stop reaching for a beverage in the evening.

Feeling overwhelmed? I hope not; but if so, you are not alone. Stick with it and trust the process.

It may feel like writing out all these steps is a lot of work—and maybe it is. But so is holding a 9-to-5 job every day until you die just so you can make ends meet and never breaking out into the world of passive income. You have long-term goals broken down to annual goals, you have a list of steps you need to take to be on track, now let's organize these into monthly, weekly, and daily tasks for goal accomplishment. On the next page write out your tasks—both recurring and one-time tasks.

Using our brainstormed Literal Next Step List, write everything that you will do to achieve this one-year goal in the format "Who will do What by When?"

WHO:	will do WHAT:	by WHEN:

WHO:	will do WHAT:	by WHEN:

Goal Summary

If you have gone through this exercise a few times for the top areas that you want to work on, you are ready to write out your summary. I typically choose three goals to work through and break them down into monthly checkpoints so I know I am on the right track; weekly tasks to hit my checkpoints; and daily activities that will help me achieve my one-year goal. Remember, if every day is a *success*, then it is *impossible* NOT to achieve your goal!

1-Year Goals:

1.

2.

3.

Monthly Checkpoints:

1.	**5.**	**9.**
2.	**6.**	**10.**
3.	**7.**	**11.**
4.	**8.**	**12.**

Weekly Tasks:

1.

2.

3.

4.

5.

6.

Daily Activities:

1.

2.

3.

4.

5.

6.

GOAL—PLAN—ACTION (GPA)

Let's recap the goal planning that we have done so far on a fresh clean sheet:

1. Big Hairy Audacious Goal: Someday in my life I desire _____

____

____

2. Using my BHAG, the most productive thing I can do to move toward this goal in the NEXT FIVE YEARS is: ______________

____

____

3. To hit this five-year goal, the single best thing I can do IN THE NEXT YEAR is: ____________________________

____

____

4. To be on track for my one-year goal, I am going to hit these MONTHLY checkpoints: _________________________

____

____

5. To be on track for my monthly checkpoints, I am going to do these WEEKLY tasks: ______________________________

____

____

6. To accomplish my weekly tasks, I am going to do these DAILY activities: ______________________________

____

____

7. To consistently perform my daily activities, I am going to begin this new habit or process in my life: ______________

____

____

You might look at this list and think "that seems too simple, there must be more to it." Well, there could be if you want to add more detail. But the research shows that breaking long-term goals down into simple daily action steps is the most effective way to achieve your goal.

There are many ways to achieve your goal—most goals have more than one road to get there. The key to this exercise is to PICK ONE path that you believe will be the most effective to drive you toward your goal. There is an ancient proverb that applies here: "If you chase two rabbits, you will catch neither." Your objective for this exercise is to choose the single action that you can take that will most effectively move you toward the line above it. Here is an example of a goal-setting worksheet that I completed when I was at the 17-year mark of my military career.

BHAG: Someday I want to own a portfolio of real estate that makes me more than $1,000,000 per year in passive income.

5-Year Goal: To be on track for this, within 5 years I want to own 10 "doors"—cash-flowing rental unit.

1-Year Goal: To be on track for this I want to find, negotiate, and purchase my first multifamily deal within 1 year.

Monthly Checkpoint: Find at least 3 potential deals and speak with at least 10 sellers or real estate professionals.

Weekly Tasks: Find 1 property that is a potential deal and call the seller.

Tomorrow's Activity: Conduct my first online search.

Process: I am going to set aside 1 hour each day to study, learn, research, and absorb material related to real estate investing. I will do this every morning before work.

Habit: To get up early enough to have 1 extra hour, I will need to go to bed by 10pm. The biggest hurdle to me going to bed on time is looking at my phone late at night. *Therefore, the SINGLE thing that I can do to contribute to my future success is to turn my phone off by 9pm and read instead. Starting today I am setting an alarm on my phone for 9pm and committing to turning it off at that time.*

Desired Outcome: By turning off my phone at 9 & reading, I get better sleep. With better sleep I am fresher in the morning and eager to study. The more I learn, the more I want to implement what I learned. The more 'swings of the bat' I get at trying to implement what I learn, the more likely I will be to succeed.

So, how did this work out? Well, about **5.5 months** after I began this process I negotiated and purchased my first multifamily real estate deal: after reading multiple books, listening to podcasts, searching properties, running the profitability numbers, learning about financing options, and calling many sellers. And, using what I learned in my study, I increased the profitability of this fourplex 10-fold in 3 months! If I started by simply telling you, "Turning my phone off at 9pm led me to buying a multifamily property," you would probably look at me like I was crazy. But that is what happened. Trust the process.

Obstacles and Accountability

What was the last New Year's Resolution that you made? How long did you stick to it? The second Friday in January is colloquially known as "quitters' day." The day when up to 88% of all people give up on their recently made New Year's Resolutions. Yes, you read that correctly; nearly 9 out of 10 people quit their resolutions within two weeks. That statistic is mind-boggling. So, how do we make sure that you are in the 12% that continues and sticks with the goal? According to Jane Hanson writing for *Forbes*, there are seven steps to take to give yourself the best chance of success: start small and be specific, tie your goals to your core values, plan for obstacles, find a support system, track your progress, show yourself grace, and focus on habits not outcomes.[1] We have covered most of those seven tips so far, now let's look at the final two steps of our goal-setting formula: Obstacles & Accountability.

Obstacles present themselves in many forms—it could be a crying baby who keeps you up at night, absolutely crushing your sleep and thus your productivity the next morning. . .I had twins first, so I feel you. It could be other commitments that seem to eat up all your "free" time. The best place to start is to look at your calendar and compare how you planned to spend versus how you did spend your time. Then, wipe your calendar clean and start by putting in the "big rocks" first—the important things, the must-do items. Once you have those filled in you can add the next most important items, and so on. Lastly you can add all those little tasks that tend to eat up your time. There is an excellent example of this in a YouTube video where a professor fills a jar with rocks, sand, and water. If you start with the water, then add sand, there is no room left for the rocks. In this example, the rocks represent the most important things in your life—your family time, your goal achievement tasks, your health and wellness, etc. If, however, you start by filling the jar with the rocks, the jar appears full but there is still room. You can then add the sand, and the sand fills in the cracks between the rocks. And then there is still time for the water—the fluid things in life that can be worked into any small space. Life works in a similar way to the jar. If you start with the water and sand, you will have no time for the big rocks that meant the most to you.

The second aspect of addressing obstacles to your goals is the idea of saying "No" to more things. We always have enough time, every day, for the things that we choose to spend our time on. Every time that you say yes to one thing, you are saying no to something else. It might be that you just need to go sit in a park and reflect on life, but you feel guilty and so you agree to help a friend with something. By saying yes to the friend, you are saying no to yourself. It is okay to take time for yourself and do nothing. My best ideas, moments of clarity, and aha moments have been quiet moments alone while out running, hiking, or just enjoying nature.

Time-blocking is the solution for most obstacles. Become absolutely zealous about your calendar. The first thing that I add to my calendar every year is time to plan the following year. Every November I set aside a day, out of office, where I plan out my next year. Then, I add time to plan my next quarter, every quarter. Then I add time to plan my next month, every month. Once my planning time is locked in and written in stone (or ink anyway), then I start to add my top priorities for my life: rest time for me, monthly date nights with my spouse, monthly outings with my kids, time for health activities like running, biking, hiking, or going to the gym. If you are still on active duty, block your work hours, they are a commitment that you will keep—but you may be able to work some other priorities into your work schedule. Maybe your unit's morning Physical Training (PT) aligns with your health goals and activities anyway.

After all the big rocks are added, I find that I still have quite a bit of time left over. I make sure that I have time blocked for rest and then I add some things that just need to get taken care of—laundry, groceries, etc. But, if I really want to read this new book, I will listen to it while doing laundry. With a well-managed and planned calendar, you will find that you have much more time to achieve your goals than you probably realized.

Your goals are set, calendar prepped, you've said No to things that no longer serve your values and goals—so what else is there? Accountability. How are you going to hold yourself accountable when you just don't feel like doing something, when things get tough, when it feels like you are not making any progress. James Clear said, "you do not rise to the level of your goals you fall to the level of your systems." This is where habit forming and tracking comes into play. With a good system (habits) you will have a foundation to fall back on. After that, an accountability partner can be an excellent way to keep up with your goals—especially if you do regular check-ins.

Years ago, my wife and I started doing weekly business meetings—like a staff meeting in the military. We sit together every Sunday morning over a cup of coffee and talk about the details of our week. What went well last week, what we are striving for this coming week, and importantly—how can we help each other achieve our goals this week. For me, that has been the secret sauce. When my spouse and I are aligned on our goals, she knows mine and I know hers, we are in sync with each other even if we have different goals. We can then look for little ways to support each other if we know the why behind the late night at the office or the early morning alarm clock. Once we have our week mapped out and aligned (kid pickups, date nights, etc.), we can look further out into the future and plan fun things like vacations, trips, and shows we want to see. Our weekly business meeting has had a huge positive impact on our relationship, our business, our growth, and our success. Here is our business meeting worksheet, which I hope can help you like it helped me.

WEEKLY BUSINESS MEETING

If you do nothing else from this chapter, do this once a week

- What were your top three priorities last week? Did you achieve them?
  - What worked and what didn't?
  - What were the challenges you had?
  - How do you feel at the end of the week?
- What did we learn from last week that we can apply going forward?
- What are your top three priorities this coming week?
  - What is the #1 thing you want to accomplish?
  - Why?
  - How can I support you in achieving that?
- How do our goals align with each other?
- Where do we have competing goals or interests?
- What is one thing you are saying No to this week?
- What are you excited for this week?
- What are you grateful for this week?

Confirm our weekly calendars are sync'd and no conflicts exist.

- What is a habit you are working on or need help with?
- How do our weekly tasks align with our monthly checkpoints?
- How are we progressing toward our goals?
  - How do our goals align with our values?

- How is our family doing toward our family goals?
- What should we KEEP DOING?
- What should we STOP DOING?

Action Steps:

1. **Pick one target and commit for 30 days.**

   Choose **one** one-year goal (not three). Write the SMART version. Then commit to working on it for 30 days before adding anything else. If you chase two rabbits, you will catch neither.

2. **Define your Literal Next Step and schedule it. Today.**

   Write your top three tasks for the goal, then write the LNS for each one. Put the first LNS on your calendar within the next 24 hours. Momentum isn't motivation—it's execution.

3. **Install one accountability rhythm.**

   Either do a weekly business meeting with your spouse/partner/friend—or schedule a 15-minute weekly check-in with yourself. Review your monthly checkpoint, weekly tasks, and daily activities. If you track it, it grows. If you don't, it drifts.

Chapter 7

Living the Dream

"There is no way to happiness. Happiness is the way."

—Thich Nhat Hanh

The radio was quiet.

Not "something's wrong" quiet—just calm. The kind of quiet you only get in the middle of a long transit when your formation is stable, weather is smooth, and everyone has settled into the rhythm of the sortie.

We were high. High enough that the horizon looks curved if you stare at it long enough. The air was thin, the jet was trimmed, and the fuel flow was steady. The autopilot wasn't flying the jet—I was—it felt like the jet and I had made an agreement. Hands light on the controls. No wrestling. Just small inputs and steady correction.

The sun was off to my right, low enough to throw long shadows across the tops of clouds that looked like an endless ocean. Everything up there always looks clean. Too clean. Like somebody wiped the world down and reset it. The sky was darkening into that deep blue that makes you feel like you're not in the atmosphere anymore—you're on the edge of something bigger.

My wingman was tucked in close; close enough that I could see the shimmer of exhaust and the little changes in attitude as he made tiny corrections to stay locked in. Formation at altitude is a strange kind of intimacy. You don't talk much. You don't need to. You're paying attention, constantly, but not in a frantic way. More like a steady scan—jet, position, horizon, fuel, back to jet. It's discipline, but it's quiet discipline.

For a few minutes, nobody said anything.

No admin calls. No jokes. No "check left." No one was asking for anything. We were just . . . there. In the air. Together. Doing the thing.

And that's when it hit me.

Not like a lightning bolt. More like a thought that slipped in between breaths.

This is it.

This is what younger me wrote about. This is what I pictured when I was a kid staring at fighter jets overhead; when I was a teenager reading about aviation and pretending I had it all figured out; when I was a cadet grinding through training and telling myself it would all be worth it.

I used to think the dream would feel louder.

I assumed it would come with a soundtrack. A big moment. Some clear marker that said, Congratulations. You made it. Enjoy this now.

But up there, in that quiet blue space, it didn't announce itself at all.

It was just a normal day at work.

A transit. A stable formation. A trimmed jet. A steady fuel flow. A sun angle that made the world look like a painting.

And a fleeting awareness that I was living inside a chapter my younger self had only imagined.

The moment didn't last long.

The radio came alive again. An update from the radar controller. A reminder that the mission was still a mission, and we still had a job to do. I acknowledged, made a small correction, checked fuel, adjusted my scan, and kept moving.

But something had shifted.

Not externally. Internally.

Because once you notice a moment like that, you can't unknow it. You realize how easy it would have been to fly right through it while mentally rehearsing the next task, the next upgrade, the next goal, the next promotion, the next milestone.

You realize how many "dream" moments are probably happening all the time—and how often we miss them because we're waiting for the next one.

The dream doesn't announce itself.

It doesn't tap you on the shoulder and tell you to look around. It shows up quietly, disguised as an ordinary day, and it keeps moving whether you're paying attention or not.

And that's what this chapter is about.

That moment stayed with me—not because it was rare, but because it was easy to miss.

For most of my life, I believed the point was always somewhere ahead. The next milestone. The next qualification. The next promotion. The next goal. I treated the present like a hallway—something you move through quickly so you can get to the room that actually matters.

But up there, in that quiet stretch of sky, I realized something uncomfortable: if I didn't learn how to notice moments like that, I could achieve everything I set out to do and still feel like I was always chasing life instead of living it.

That realization forced me to look at the beliefs I had been carrying for decades—beliefs about sacrifice, service, money, and what it meant to want more. Many of those beliefs were honorable. Some were inherited. And a few were quietly costing me more than I realized.

That's where this chapter really begins.

The point is presence with alignment. Money is just the tool we use. Mindset is the gateway. And time is our currency.

The problem wasn't that I couldn't achieve the dream. It was that I didn't always feel allowed to enjoy it.

You took an oath "to support and defend the Constitution of the United States, against all enemies foreign and domestic. To bear true faith and allegiance to the same." You made a sacrifice.

The concept of sacrifice is deeply ingrained in the culture of the military—and in most militaries throughout history—because without brave young men and women willing to step up, take the oath, and put service before self, we would not be able to thrive as the greatest nation on Earth during a time of unprecedented prosperity.

Sacrifice is honorable.

It is also a mindset.

The military encourages sacrifice, lionizes those who paid the ultimate price in service to a greater purpose, and enshrines "service before self" in its core values. Standing shoulder to shoulder with our brothers and sisters in arms acts as the glue that holds us together and allows us to provide for the common defense and form a more perfect union.

I refer to this way of thinking as the "doctrine of sacrifice"—a necessary and honorable framework for serving one's country, but a very dangerous one when applied to personal finance.

For many of us, this doctrine was learned early and reinforced over decades of honorable service. Please don't misunderstand me:

I hold the utmost respect for service and for those who, like me, took the oath and dedicated themselves to a higher purpose.

But the doctrine of sacrifice does not belong in our financial lives.

That mindset helps in combat. It hurts in finance.

We should harbor no shame or guilt around wealth or the pursuit of wealth. If we can serve our country with honor and also build wealth through disciplined, sound investing, then we should.

Service before self is a value. Poverty is not a virtue.

I grew up believing that wanting more was a bad thing. Rich people were usually the villains in the story. Growing up in the Catholic school and church system, I learned in three places—Matthew, Mark, and Luke—that "it is easier for a camel to go through the eye of a needle than for a rich man to enter the kingdom of God."

But why is that? Why do we villainize the wealthy? We cheer for people on the way up, then make them the enemy once they arrive.

If church taught me that being rich was inherently evil, I was confused when I also learned that "all good things come from God." If God gives you gifts and talents with the intent for you to use them, would it not be a greater disservice to ignore those gifts?

If you were given creativity, drive, or vision—and the ability to build something that improves the world—would letting that potential go to waste really be the more virtuous choice?

Here is a simple example that makes the point:

If I make $30,000 per year and give 50% of it to charity, living well below the poverty line, I would contribute $15,000 a year for my working life and then likely rely on the welfare system afterward.

If I live up to my full potential, make $30,000,000 per year, give half to charity, and use the other half to continue building wealth and opportunity, then over a 40-year career I would have contributed $600,000,000 to charity.

Why, in the eyes of so many, is the first example often considered noble while the second is labeled greedy or evil? Who actually did more good over their lifetime?

The answer remains: it depends.

What matters most is doing good where you can while living up to your full potential—not blindly subscribing to the doctrine of sacrifice.

Looking back, what I didn't understand for most of my life was how these beliefs took root so deeply. The doctrine of sacrifice, the suspicion of wealth, the guilt around wanting more—none of it felt like a conscious choice at the time. It simply felt like "the way things are."

That's because these ideas live at the level of mindset. They are formed early, reinforced often, and rarely questioned. And until I learned to examine my own mindset, I had no idea how much it was shaping my decisions, my finances, and the limits I placed on myself.

Mindset

My personal journey with mindset began later in life. It was 2018, I was a 37-year-old Major in the US Air Force, and I was well set in my ways.

When my wife opened her first business, she hired a business coach. I was skeptical—another adult was going to come into her life and "coach" her on things she was already doing day to day? Suspect, right?

As usual, she was right.

What I came to appreciate about coaching—any kind of coaching—is how much we can benefit from the experience and perspective of others. Every Olympian has a coach. Every professional athlete has a coach. Why did I assume I wouldn't benefit from one?

The honest answer is that I wasn't humble enough to see it.

Once my eyes were opened, I looked back and shook my head at my old stubborn self, convinced I was too cool for "all that coaching nonsense."

It was through coaching that I was first introduced to the idea of intentionally growing and expanding my mindset. I acknowledged the benefits fairly quickly—albeit grudgingly, especially when my wife reminds me it was her idea.

Coaching made sense; this "mindset" stuff, on the other hand, felt a little too mushy for my fighter pilot brand of masculinity. Still skeptical, I waded cautiously into the ocean of personal development literature and ideas and was quickly overwhelmed by how much adopting a growth mindset could change the way I approached my life.

What I came to realize is that mindset is not something most of us consciously choose. We are born into environments we do not control and handed a set of values and beliefs from the people who raise us—what I think of as our early "agreements" about how the world works.

We absorb them before we are old enough to question them, and for many of us they remain intact in the subconscious for decades, quietly shaping our decisions without ever being examined.

When I finally started questioning my own agreements later in life, it was unsettling. I still find myself uncovering beliefs I didn't even realize I was living by. Something will happen, I'll react, and then I'll pause and think, *why did I respond that way?*

More often than not, I'm unpacking a 40-year-old agreement I inherited as a child—one that sat buried under layers of habit, time, and years of unhealthy coping mechanisms.

One of the most common and consequential places these early agreements show up is in our money mindset. This is why it's important to talk about money in a chapter on mindset—because this is where I personally got it wrong for a long time, and in many ways still struggle today.

For the average American, our early agreements reflect what Steve Siebold calls a *middle-class mindset* in *How Rich People Think*: trading time for money, the feeling that there is never quite enough, the belief that resources are limited, and the idea that a safe, comfortable job is better than taking the risks required to build real wealth.

These beliefs are taught early, reinforced often, and eventually accepted as truth.

For me, those beliefs were shaped by school friends, neighbors, parents, extended family, television—by the small, offhand comments that add up over time.

Things like, "Did you hear about so-and-so? I can't believe they bought that house."

Or family sayings like, "Close the refrigerator—do you think I'm paying to cool the whole neighborhood?"

Or hearing, "Sorry honey, we can't afford that," or "When you pay the bills, you can leave the lights on all you want."

None of this is inherently bad advice. We shouldn't be wasteful or reckless.

The problem is the underlying message: a worldview rooted in lack. A scarcity mindset, rather than one of abundance.

When your earliest experiences are shaped by scarcity, it takes intentional effort as an adult to undo those patterns.

A mindset of abundance flips the script. It starts from the belief that you can *be, do, and have* what you want in this life—not magically or without effort, but deliberately.

You still need a clear goal, a plan to reach that goal, and consistent action over time. Simply becoming aware of scarcity thinking when it shows up is often the first step. That awareness creates space for a different choice—and a different outcome.

What ultimately captured me about mindset was the realization that everything we see in the world that was created by humans began as a thought in someone's mind.

Where do thoughts arise from? Consciousness, perhaps—but where does that come from? There are countless hypotheses, ranging from the scientific to the metaphysical, and the truth is we still don't fully know.

Starting from a position of not knowing, however, doesn't stop us from making progress.

If everything created by humans began as a thought, it stands to reason that our thoughts have the power to shape our lives and bring new realities into existence.

In *Think and Grow Rich*, Napoleon Hill followed Andrew Carnegie and his close "mastermind" group for decades. His central takeaway was that we all possess the ability to use what he called "thinking substance" to bring our vision for our lives into reality.

In earlier chapters, we defined our Mission, Vision, and Values to give direction to the future we want to create. Now the work becomes more practical: learning how to recognize, shape, and direct our thoughts so they can be intentionally transmuted into reality.

If mindset is about deciding where you want to go, then awareness is about understanding where you actually are.

Setting goals gives direction to a future that is not yet fixed, but direction alone is not enough if you are unaware of the thoughts, habits, and reactions shaping your decisions in the present.

For most of my life, I believed discipline and drive were sufficient—that if I simply worked harder and stayed focused on the objective, everything else would take care of itself.

What I eventually realized was that much of my internal world was running unchecked, influenced by stress, assumptions, and emotional responses I had never slowed down enough to notice.

Before we can consistently execute the next right step toward our goals, we must first learn to pay attention to what is happening in our own minds.

That practice is called mindfulness.

Mindfulness

> *"No man ever steps in the same river twice, for it is not the same river, and he is not the same man."*
>
> —Heraclitus

The past has already happened, and the future has not yet been created. The only thing that truly exists is this moment, right now.

This is not a contradiction to goal setting—it is the very reason goal-setting matters. I do not believe the future is fixed. Instead, it is shaped moment-by-moment through the thoughts we think, the decisions we make, and the actions we take in the present.

Mindfulness is the practice that anchors us in that present moment, where real change actually occurs.

At its core, mindfulness is a form of meditation focused on being aware of your thoughts, feelings, and sensations without judgment or interpretation. It has been practiced for thousands of years, so to say it is tried and true would be an understatement.

You may be wondering where mindfulness fits into a discussion on financial freedom in the military.

As a fighter pilot, mindfulness was what allowed me to tune out everything that did not matter in the moment and focus on the most important task—what we called "the nearest alligator to the boat."

By adding a mindfulness practice to your life, you gain the ability to quiet the noise and focus on what actually matters. This is especially valuable in your financial life.

Whether you are sticking to your How I Spend My Money Plan, evaluating a real estate purchase, or making long-term investment decisions, the ability to stay grounded in the present moment prevents you from getting ahead of yourself emotionally or mentally.

Mindfulness has been shown to reduce stress and anxiety, lower blood pressure, and improve sleep. Do any of those sound like things people struggle with when money becomes a source of stress? Finances consistently rank among the top stressors in people's lives, and mindfulness serves as a powerful counterbalance.

It improves focus and concentration, reduces negative thinking, and enhances self-awareness and emotional regulation—skills that are critical when emotions threaten to derail good financial decisions.

Mindfulness also improves decision-making, enhances problem-solving, and increases productivity.

I once found a property my wife and I desperately wanted to buy, but it was well outside our budget and initially seemed impossible. Instead of reacting emotionally or forcing a bad decision, we slowed down.

Through deep thought—enhanced by a regular mindfulness practice—we identified a solution that allowed us to buy the new property, pull equity from our existing home, and keep that original property as a rental in our portfolio.

What initially felt like an insurmountable obstacle became a solvable problem once we created space to think clearly.

If you're not sure where to begin, start simple. Download a free app and take one of their introductory courses. Let them guide you.

Treat mindfulness like any other daily habit—something as routine as brushing your teeth—and over time the benefits will compound.

Just as small, consistent actions move you toward your financial goals, small moments of presence help you make better decisions along the way.

"Work-Life Balance" . . . and Other Lies We Tell Ourselves

I have always hated the phrase *work-life balance*. For me, it immediately brings to mind a set of scales, with work on one side and "life" on the other, and the goal is supposedly to find balance between the two.

In that framework, life is split into two categories—work and everything else—and you are constantly trying to keep them even. That picture has never reflected my reality, or the reality of most people I know.

In reality, life is made up of many important areas, often with competing priorities, all pulling for your time and attention in different ways. Work is only one of those areas—not half of your life.

Earlier, in the goal-setting chapter, we broke life into six important categories, because that is much closer to the truth.

You don't need *work-life balance*. You need *life balance*.

You've already done the hard work of identifying what you value and what your Why is. Now it's time to put that into practice with how you spend your time.

Just like the How I Spend My Money Plan, I advocate for creating a How I Spend My Time Plan. By writing down—ahead of time—what you will spend your time on, you are far more likely to follow through, and far more likely to stay aligned with your goals.

Time is one of your most precious resources, and one of the few things you can never get more of. Treat it like an investment account you get to spend from every single day.

Closely related to the idea of work-life balance is another concept I've always hated: time management.

You can't manage time. Time doesn't care about your to-do list. You can only choose how to use the time you've been given.

For that reason, I prefer the phrase *leveraging time*.

Every human being has exactly 24 hours in a day. No more, no less. Some people—like many successful businesspeople—have leveraged those 24 hours to build multi-billion-dollar (and soon trillion-dollar) companies. Others live in their parents' basement, play video games, and smoke weed.

We all get the same amount of time; the difference is how we choose to use it.

Highly effective people don't "manage time." They leverage it by focusing on the most important tasks and doing those first.

Nothing made this clearer to me than watching my wife during one of the most demanding seasons of our lives. When she had our third child in Korea, our twins were just 21 months old. We suddenly had three kids under the age of two, in a foreign country, with no real support network outside of the military. Shortly after, I deployed.

Her 24-hour days looked very different from our lives just two years earlier. She is a rockstar, and this is a huge shoutout to her.

During that same period, she was taking pro-bono immigration cases through the US Court of Appeals for the Ninth Circuit—and won the American Bar Association's Pro-Bono Attorney of the Year award while working out of a cubicle in the base library.

That is what prioritizing your 24 hours actually looks like.

Which brings me to another lie we tell ourselves that goes hand-in-hand with "time management": "*I don't have the time.*"

You have the same amount of time as those billionaire businesspeople. You always have enough time. The real issue is not time—it's priority.

Refer back to the goal-setting action steps you created earlier and act on the Literal Next Step (LNS) required to move you forward.

Progress doesn't require massive blocks of free time; it requires intentional use of the time you already have.

The most important word you can add to your vocabulary is the word *No*.

Say no to things that do not further your purpose and your goals. Say no to family expectations, work demands, social obligations, and societal pressures that don't align with what you've decided actually matters.

Start saying no—respectfully—and you'll discover something interesting: you suddenly have enough time for all the important things in your life.

The things you "don't have time for" are simply not priorities. Replace "I don't have time" with "that is not a priority for my time," and a lot becomes clearer.

Another lie we tell ourselves—especially relevant for those who serve—is the idea that your service to your country should take precedence over all else, at all times.

When you are 100 years old and on your deathbed, the military will not be there holding your hand.

Give the military your very best when you are on the clock. But the rest of your time is yours to invest. Invest it in your purpose. Invest it in your goals.

If you don't know what those are, go back and do the work to define them. Do not expect anyone else to hand you your values or your purpose. Only you can do that.

The longer you avoid it, the more likely you are to wake up one day feeling lost and rudderless.

The next lie is the idea that learning stops after high school or college.

Keep learning. Take an investing or real estate class. Use tuition assistance. Use the GI Bill. Take free classes on base. Read. Study. Grow. If you aren't growing, you are dying.

At the time of this writing, the average person spends two hours and twenty-four minutes per day on social media and more than five hours per day on their phone—every single day.

If you find yourself saying, "I don't have time to learn something new," I want you to reread the paragraph on why "I don't have time" is a lie.

It may be true that in this season of your life, learning a new skill is not a priority—and that's fine—as long as that decision is deliberate and not just the result of letting life happen to you.

The final "lie" is around societal norms and expectations: alcohol, consumerism, parenting expectations, and other nonsense that does not align with your personal Why.

Ask yourself one simple question: *Is this serving me?* Is this bringing me closer to my goals and furthering my purpose?

If the answer is no, stop doing it.

If a person in your life is not helping you live your great life of purpose, then that person does not get a seat at your table anymore.

This part is controversial, but if you truly want to live up to your full potential, it is unlikely that everyone currently in your life is going with you into the future—and that's okay.

People come into our lives for a reason, and many come only for a season.

You are the average of the five people you spend the most time with. If you want to uplevel your life, you will need to uplevel your friend group.

We all have financial set points, much like a thermostat in your house. You can add a space heater to a cold room, but once it gets warm enough, the air conditioning kicks on and brings the temperature back down.

You can make a little extra money, but your environment—often your friend group—will unconsciously work to pull you back to their level. Not because they are bad people, but because of a normal human response called cognitive dissonance.

If you start earning more and becoming more successful, it forces others to confront the uncomfortable idea that they could be doing more too. Knocking you back down justifies them staying where they are.

I lived this.

Imagine you're living in base housing, surrounded by other E-7s with kids. You start earning extra money through real estate investing and decide to buy a nice new car.

You pull into the neighborhood and hear, "Oooohhh, look at Mr. Moneybags," or "Didn't know you could make that much on the side," or "Enjoy it while it lasts—this market could turn," usually followed by, "I'm just messing with you," so they don't sound like a complete jerk.

But there's truth underneath those comments. Very few people will genuinely say, "Hey, congratulations—I'm really happy for you."

Isn't that strange? They're supposed to be your friends.

They aren't bad people. They're just reacting to their own financial set point and dealing with their own cognitive dissonance.

As you continue to grow, it's likely you'll leave some people behind.

If this section felt uncomfortable, that's intentional. Letting go of deeply held beliefs always is uncomfortable.

But removing what doesn't serve you isn't the end goal—it's just clearing the space.

Once you strip away the BS, what's left is the space and opportunity to be deliberate about how you actually want to live.

Living your best life isn't about optimizing every minute or squeezing productivity out of everything you do.

It's about aligning your time, your values, and your presence with what matters most to you.

And for me, some of the clearest examples of living my best life have nothing to do with money at all.

Remember, this chapter is about being awake while you build your dream life.

"Daddy Dragon"

I cannot write a chapter on living your best life without including some of the moments that have made me feel like I am living the best version of my life. For me, that is best illustrated by a game I started playing with my kids when they were very little.

I honestly don't remember where it came from, but I remember my twins being small and giggling with joy every time we played it.

The rules were simple. Step one: walk into the house. Step two: roar as loud as you can like a dragon.

The kids would immediately drop whatever they were doing and scatter, looking for places to hide. Once caught, they were tickled and then locked in the dragon's lair (the couch) until the rest were captured.

By the time I had four kids, this became a regular event in our house. The game eventually evolved to include the occasional full-clothing toss into the pool. My wife even got caught by the dragon once and thrown in. Once.

These memories will live forever in my mind—and they cost nothing.

Looking back, the lesson for me is the importance of being present with my family (what I value), and spending my time on moments like this as deliberately as I spend my money.

Reflecting on games like Daddy Dragon made me more intentional with how I chose to spend my time as my kids grew older. They don't know it yet, but I fully plan to continue Daddy Dragon well into adulthood, and I am already looking forward to sending their first boyfriends for a swim.

Time is such a precious resource that it deserves an entire book of its own. If we are going to talk about financial freedom, then we have to talk about *why* we want it in the first place.

For most people, financial freedom is simply a means to live the life of their dreams.

There is no sense in spending your entire life squeezing every dollar out of every minute, only to reach the end and realize that life passed you by while you were busy saving for it.

This might sound like I am saying, "Now that we know how to become a millionaire, forget about money altogether." That is not what I'm saying at all.

Time freedom and financial freedom are two sides of the same coin. Having one without the other is useless.

Don't spend your life chasing dollars and miss out on playing Daddy Dragon.

We only get about 15 to 20 Christmases with our kids. The same number of birthdays, Thanksgivings, and Easters. Once your child turns twelve, you have already spent roughly 75% of the total time you will ever spend together.

In 2024, Pew Research found that most adults see their parents about once per month. Each year of adulthood is roughly equivalent to one week of childhood.

There is not an elderly billionaire alive who wouldn't trade places with you—for most, if not all, of their fortune.

Spend your time as purposefully as you spend your money.

Health

If you live to be 110 years old but the last 40 years are painful, bed-ridden, and miserable, are you really winning?

On the other hand, if you are the healthiest human on Earth but you die at 40, you aren't winning either.

This is the idea of aligning your health-span with your life-span. You cannot live your life to its fullest potential if your physical and mental health are neglected.

I like to break health into two components: physical health and mental health.

Physical health is easy to talk about. No one feels uncomfortable when you mention going to the gym or working on your physique.

But bring up mental health, and suddenly people start shifting in their chairs.

There is still a stigma around mental health that I think we should be embarrassed by as a society, and work to move past like grown adults. Your mental health is just as important—often more important—than your physical health. Treat them with equal seriousness, and you will live a more balanced life.

I'm not suggesting everyone needs to find a therapist today (though maybe they do—I'm not a therapist).

Improving your mental health can be as simple as five minutes of meditation in the morning. It can mean journaling and reflecting. It can mean cutting negative social media feeds and filling your mind with positive inputs instead.

There are hundreds of ways to work on mental health, just like there are hundreds of exercises in the gym. The key is consistency.

Doing arm curls once won't change anything. Showing up regularly, increasing the load over time, and following a structured plan absolutely will. The same is true for your mind.

And for anyone reading this thinking they are "too cool" for mental health work—go read the book *To Be a Man*. Chances are, you were lied to, just like I was.

Coaching and Relationships

Since we're already talking about uncomfortable topics, let's talk about coaching.

When I first heard the word "coach," I immediately pictured the old Saturday Night Live skits with Stuart Smalley repeating affirmations into a mirror. It turns out coaching is nothing like that.

After multiple experiences with coaching, I cannot recommend it enough.

When Michael Jordan was at the peak of his career, he had multiple coaches helping him perform at the highest level. Coaching isn't about weakness—it's about leverage.

If hiring a coach isn't for you, find a mentor. The concept is the same: learn from someone who has already done what you're trying to do.

As men, the only experience I can personally speak to, we tend to struggle with friendships as we get older. Men are very transactional.

When we were younger, friendships came naturally through school, sports, or organized activities. Later, they often came through work.

As you move into the next phase of life, relationships require intentional effort.

Not every friend needs to provide you with something, but they should be aligned with your values and genuinely happy to see you succeed.

Your relationships create your environment, and your environment plays a massive role in your long-term health, happiness, and fulfillment.

That's why it makes sense to end this section on purpose by talking about the people you choose to surround yourself with.

Earlier in the book, I said that you are the average of the five people you spend the most time with. If that's true—and I believe it is—then choosing your relationships may be one of the most important decisions you make in living your best life.

Living the Dream Happens Now

Living the life of your dreams is not a someday destination or a reward you earn after decades of sacrifice.

It is built in the small, deliberate choices you make every day—how you spend your time, what you pay attention to, and who you allow to influence your life.

Financial freedom matters, but not as an end in itself. It is a tool that gives you the ability to be present, to say no, and to invest your time where it matters most.

When you align your values with your actions, challenge the beliefs that no longer serve you, and focus on health, relationships, and purpose, you stop living by default and start living intentionally.

That is what it means to live the dream.

If you only take one thing from this chapter, let it be this: the dream doesn't announce itself. You have to notice it.

Action Steps:

1. **Identify your "living the dream" moments.**

   Write three moments from the past year where you felt truly aligned with your core values, present, and fulfilled. Don't overthink it. Then use these as a guide for your goal setting.

2. **Eliminate one time suck from your life.**

   Choose one habit, activity, or commitment that is not serving you and helping you move toward your goals. Then say *no* to it—respectfully. Replace it with something from your living the dream moments above.

3. **Align one relationship.**

   Identify a relationship in your life that furthers your purpose, values, and goals. Then be deliberate about cultivating that relationship in your time planning.

This concludes Part II: Purpose.

Purpose is not something you stumble upon; it is something you choose and then reinforce through how you think, how you spend your time, and who you allow into your life.

In this section, we defined what matters to you, challenged the beliefs that quietly limit you, and reframed money, time, and success through the lens of alignment rather than sacrifice.

Living your best life is not about perfection or optimization—it is about presence, intention, and consistency.

When your values are clear, your goals have direction, and your awareness is sharpened, you create the conditions to live deliberately instead of by default.

Purpose is the foundation.

Everything that follows builds on it.

Purpose without action, however, quickly turns into frustration.

Clarity must be followed by movement.

With your purpose clearly defined and your foundation in place, the next step is growth.

Growth is where intention turns into capability, and where goals stop being ideas and start becoming reality.

In the next section, we'll focus on the skills, habits, and systems required to expand what you are capable of—financially, professionally, and personally—so you can sustain a life of purpose with financial freedom and build something that is not only meaningful, but resilient and scalable.

Part III

Growth

"The man who moves a mountain begins by carrying away small stones."

—Confucius

The first Red Flag I ever flew in, I was a wingman.

Not completely brand new, I had earned my spot. I could fly the jet, execute the mission, hit my timing, and stay where I was supposed to be. I knew the procedures. I knew the rules. I knew enough to not get myself—or anyone else—killed.

And I felt ready for more.

Red Flag is the most realistic air war training environment in the world. It's loud, complex, unforgiving, and deliberately overwhelming. Dozens of aircraft. Multiple nations. Real bombs. Real consequences. It's where everything you've learned gets tested at once.

On my first sortie, my job was simple: stay in position, execute as briefed, and bring one airplane home safely.

Then, in the middle of the fight, my flight lead's radio failed. No warning. No discussion. Just a visual signal I wasn't expecting.

You have the lead.

In an instant, the responsibility changed. I wasn't just flying my jet anymore—I was responsible for getting us home. Fuel. Timing. Deconfliction. Landing sequence. All of it. With hundreds of airplanes in the sky and zero margin for confusion.

It wasn't flashy. It wasn't dramatic. But it mattered.

I did okay. We landed safely. The mission was successful.

And afterward, part of me thought: *If I can do that, why not move straight into flight lead upgrade*?

But here's the truth I didn't understand yet:

Safely bringing one airplane home is not the same as being responsible for all aspects of a formation inside a complex fight.

At Red Flag, competence is expected. Reliability is required. Judgment is earned slowly.

The instructors didn't care about that one moment. They cared about what came next.

Did I fly correctly every sortie?

Did I show good judgment when nothing was happening?

Did I make conservative calls when the picture was unclear?

Did I stick to the plan?

Did I communicate clearly?

Did I do the boring things right—again and again?

Growth at this stage didn't come from a single impressive sortie. It came from dozens of unremarkable ones.

I was no longer learning how to fly. I was learning how to *lead under pressure*. How to make correct decisions when no one was watching. How to be predictable, dependable, and disciplined. How to resist the urge to rush the upgrade just because I felt ready.

That phase felt slow.

It was supposed to.

Because this is where trust is built—not granted.

Years later, I'd look back and realize something important: this is the phase where most people quit.

Not because they're failing—but because growth stops feeling exciting. The gains are quiet. The feedback is subtle. The progress is measured in consistency, not breakthroughs.

But this phase is where real capability is forged.

Part III of this book is about that phase.

You've defined your purpose. You know why you're doing this. Now comes the work—steady, patient, sometimes boring work that compounds over time.

Growth is not a leap.

It's a long series of correct decisions made when no one is applauding.

Trust the process.

We have come a long way in preparing your financial future. You've probably noticed how heavily I rely on mindset when building any long-term plan—because everything ultimately comes back to how you approach your own life.

In Chapter 1, you built your *How I Spend My Money Plan*. In Chapter 2, you started your retirement investment accounts with your Roth TSP—matching contributions first—followed by your Roth IRA. Chapter 3 helped you manage debt. Chapter 4 exposed the money traps that keep so many people stuck. In Part II, you stepped back and did the deeper work: defining your purpose and what your ideal life actually looks like.

By now, you should know your core values. You should have personal mission and vision statements. You should have goals defined for yourself. If you skipped the worksheets on goal setting, go back and do them now. No one is going to do this for you. Only you can take charge of your own life.

Up to this point, the work has been foundational. Necessary. Sometimes uncomfortable. But essential.

Now comes growth . . . and growth feels different.

This is the phase where things slow down—not because you're behind, but because the work changes. You're no longer just learning *what* to do. You're learning how to execute consistently, patiently, and correctly over time. This is where discipline replaces motivation, and where progress is measured in inches instead of leaps.

Now that you are on the road to financial freedom and living the life you've intentionally designed, it's time to get into the practical work—what to actually do with the money you've started setting aside.

First, understand this: money is not a single weapon to be fired and forgotten. It's a system. Your arsenal consists of cash, TSP, index funds, Roth advantages, taxable accounts—and each of them does a different job. The goal is not to use everything at once, but to pair the right tool to the right target so your resources work in alignment with your mission.

This section—and the remaining chapters in the book—will move away from the abstract and into the concrete. We're going to talk about investing, real estate, math, and strategy. But don't mistake "concrete" for "simple." This phase rewards patience, repetition, and restraint far more than excitement or speed.

The concepts from the earlier chapters still apply here. In fact, they matter more now than ever. When you apply your personal mission statement to *everything* you do—including your investments—you stop chasing outcomes and start building alignment. Where applicable, I'll refer you back to the early chapters and your why, because that foundation is what keeps you steady when progress feels slow.

If you adopt a true growth mindset, you'll begin to understand something most people miss: there is no fixed ceiling on your future—personally or financially—even if your income feels fixed today. Compounding doesn't care where you start. It only cares that you stay in the game.

That's what this section is about.

Not getting rich quickly.

Not shortcuts.

Not hacks.

Growth earned over time—by trusting the process.

Chapter 8

The Long Game | Compounding

"The stock market is a device for transferring money from the impatient to the patient."

—Warren Buffett

There was no single sortie where I suddenly felt like an instructor pilot. Maybe that's what surprised me the most.

When I first started flying, every flight felt different. Everything was loud, fast, and demanding. My scan was deliberate. My hands were stiff on the controls. I was thinking through every switch movement, every radio call, every formation correction. Flying an F-16 was not yet instinct—it was effort.

As the hours accumulated, the sorties began to blur together. Same jet. Same brief. Same airspace. Same basic problems. I remember thinking, *"This feels repetitive. Am I actually getting better, or just doing the same thing over and over?"*

The logbook filled slowly. One sortie at a time. One hour here. Two hours there. Nothing dramatic. No cinematic breakthroughs. Just showing up, briefing thoroughly, flying the plan, debriefing honestly, and doing it again the next day.

Instructor pilot upgrades don't come from one great flight. They come from consistency. From discipline in the small things—prepping the brief even when you already "know" it, tightening your scan even when no one is watching, correcting a habit that's good enough but not quite right.

At the time, it didn't feel like progress. It felt like maintenance.

Then one day, everything changed—and nothing did.

We were flying a complex sortie. Multiple aircraft. Weather deteriorating. Timeline compressed. Radios busy. The kind of scenario that used to spike my heart rate and narrow my attention.

Only this time, it didn't.

My hands moved without urgency. My scan widened instead of tightening. I anticipated problems before they announced themselves. When something deviated from the plan, I didn't rush to fix it—I calmly adjusted.

I remember thinking, *When did this get easy?*

The truth is, it didn't. It got earned.

All those identical feeling sorties had been stacking quietly in the background. The repetition had rewired my judgment. The small habits had compounded into confidence. The discipline I practiced when it didn't feel important became capability when it mattered most.

Nothing magical happened in that moment. No one tapped me on the shoulder and said, *Congratulations, you're better now*.

I just realized I was operating at a completely different level than I used to be.

That's how compounding works.

It doesn't announce itself while it's happening. It feels slow. Almost boring. Sometimes discouraging. But one day, you look back and realize the gap between who you were and who you've become is enormous.

This chapter is about that gap.

Not about big moves or lucky breaks—but about the quiet, relentless accumulation of small, correct decisions over time. The kind that don't feel powerful today, but change everything tomorrow.

Because whether you're flying fighter jets or building wealth, the long game always wins.

And the people who succeed are the ones who trust it long before the results are visible.

What that instructor upgrade taught me—long before I ever thought about money—was that real progress rarely feels dramatic while it's happening.

The hours didn't matter because of any single flight. They mattered because they stacked. Quietly. Predictably. Relentlessly. The discipline I practiced when no one was grading me became judgment when it counted. And the capability I built slowly showed up all at once when the situation demanded it.

Money works the same way.

Most people never give compounding a chance to do its job because they're looking for visible progress too soon. They want a big win. A breakthrough. Proof that it's working. But just like flying, wealth is built in the background—through small, consistent decisions that don't feel powerful today but dramatically shape your future.

The military gives us something incredibly rare in the civilian world: time, stability, and structure. When those are paired with patience and sound decision-making, the results compound faster than most people realize.

That's what this chapter is about.

Not chasing returns. Not getting rich quick. But understanding how to let time, consistency, and smart risk do the heavy lifting—so one day you look back and realize you're operating at a completely different financial level than you used to be.

As a military member, you have access to something most people never get: **a steady paycheck for decades and a powerful set of built-in advantages** if you choose to use them well.

Healthcare. Tuition assistance. VA loans. The GI Bill. SCRA protections. The Blended Retirement System. The TSP. Those are not small benefits. When you understand how they work together—and you have a clear picture of your finances over the next 20 years—your path to financial freedom stops being mysterious. It becomes a math problem.

This section is about learning how to **leverage your military pay, benefits, and experience** to build long-term, generational wealth.

And it starts with risk.

Risk

As the commander of a fighter squadron, I used to ask my team a simple question: "**Are you playing to win—or are you playing not to lose?**"

That question applies just as much to investing as it does to combat. Growth requires risk. The key is taking it **intentionally**, not emotionally.

Fighter pilots don't blindly fly into the middle of a fight without situational awareness. And you shouldn't blindly throw your money into an investment just because your friend's cousin's boyfriend made a killing on it last year. Everything involves risk. The goal is not to avoid it—it's to decide **where** to take it and **how much** you're willing to accept at different stages of your life.

In aviation, every mission starts with guidance from the commander defining the *Acceptable Level of Risk (ALR)*.

When ALR is high, we may accept losses to achieve mission success—perhaps striking a decisive blow against a hostile regime. When ALR is low, we prioritize the survival of people and assets over the objective.

In your financial life, **you are the commander**.

Only you get to define your personal ALR.

Most financial advisors agree on one general principle: take more risk when you're young, when you have time to recover from losses, and gradually reduce risk as you approach retirement, when you'll need to rely on the wealth you've built.

I can't define your risk tolerance for you—but I can give you the framework so you can choose intentionally.

Choosing Your Risk Profile

If your mindset sounds like this:

> *I'm buying ownership in companies and indexes, not price tags. If the market drops 50–70%, I don't panic—I wait. I don't need this money tomorrow, and I believe in the long-term value of what I own.*

Then you'll likely be comfortable with **higher-risk, higher-reward portfolios** that include a larger allocation to stocks. If, instead, your mindset sounds more like this:

> *I may need this money in the next few years. I can't afford a major drawdown, and I don't trust that I'll be emotionally steady during a crash.*

Then a **lower-risk** profile may be more appropriate—accepting a lower upside in exchange for a smaller downside.

Neither approach is right or wrong. The mistake is choosing one **by default**, instead of by design.

One of the financial institutions I invest with, Charles Schwab, breaks investor risk profiles into six broad categories, shown in Table 8.1.[1]

Compound Interest

Compound interest is interest earned not just on the money you invest—the principal—but also on the interest that money has already earned.

In other words, you start earning **interest on interest**.

That one shift changes everything. It causes your money to grow faster over time, even if the rate of return never changes. The dollars you earn in the future become much larger than the dollars you earn today—not because you're doing anything different, but because time is doing the work for you.

The problem is that compound interest doesn't feel powerful at first.

For years—sometimes close to a decade—it can feel slow and unimpressive. Your account grows, but not enough to be exciting.

Table 8.1 Investor Risk Profiles

Risk Profile	Stock Allocation (%)	Description
Conservative	20	Focused on defensive assets like treasury bonds and cash; moderate amount of stocks
Moderately Conservative	29–37	Emphasis is on less volatile investments like treasury bonds but still have some stocks for higher yields
Moderate	42–50	Slightly more stocks than treasury bonds; balanced portfolio for risk versus growth
Moderate Growth	58–66	Sizeable stock allocation, bond allocation includes high-yield bonds, emerging markets bonds
Growth	72–81	Large allocation to stocks and volatile assets, REITs, emerging markets; some cash and treasury bonds for stability
Aggressive Growth	88–94	Heavily invested in stocks and volatile assets; minimal defensive assets like cash

Then, almost without warning, it starts to take off. The curve steepens. The same contributions suddenly produce much larger results.

That's compounding.

This is what separates compound interest from simple interest, which is only earned on your original principal. We covered simple interest in Chapter 1. Compound interest is different—and it is the secret sauce behind every successful long-term investment strategy.

Start early. Stay consistent. Let time do the heavy lifting.

How Compounding Works

Let's make this concrete.

If you invest $100 and earn 10% interest per year, at the end of year one you'll have $110.

In year two, you're no longer earning 10% on $100—you're earning it on $110. That gives you $11 in interest, and now you have $121.

Nothing dramatic happened. But something important did.

You earned interest on interest.

Over time, that effect compounds and accelerates.

A quick way to estimate how long it takes to double your money is the **Rule of 72**. Divide 72 by your average annual return, and you'll get the approximate number of years it takes to double your investment.

- At 10% return: $72 \div 10 = 7.2\,\text{years}$
- At 9% return: $72 \div 9 = 8\,\text{years}$

You can also use this rule in reverse—to estimate how long it takes for **debt** to double, or to determine what rate of return you need to double your money within a certain timeframe.

Is it perfect? No. If you run the exact math in a spreadsheet, the answer at 10% is closer to 7.27 years. But for decision-making purposes, the Rule of 72 is more than sufficient.

Why Time Matters More than You Think

Let's walk through a hypothetical scenario.

Airman Jones starts investing at age 20. He puts away $100 per month for 10 years, then stops at age 30 when life gets busy—marriage, kids, a house. He never invests another dollar. His investments average 8% per year. His total principal invested: **$12,000**.

Sergeant Smith waits. He doesn't start investing until his mid-30s, after the same life milestones. Money is tight, but he scrapes together $100 per month and invests consistently at the same 8% return. His total principal invested: **$36,000**.

Who do you think ends up with more money at age 65?

It's Airman Jones.

At age 65, Jones has **$270,492**.

Smith has **$149,036**.

Let that sink in.

Smith invested **$24,000** more than Jones and did it for **22 additional years**—yet he ended up with almost **half as much money**.

That difference isn't discipline. It isn't intelligence. It isn't luck.

It's time.

Jones's money grew slowly at first. But later, it started earning interest on decades of accumulated interest. Like a snowball rolling downhill, it picked up speed and momentum until it was nearly impossible to stop.

That's compounding.

It starts slow—like turning a heavy flywheel—but once it's moving, it's powerful and hard to slow down.

Why Starting Early Changes Everything

When you start early, your money works while you sleep. Then the interest it earns goes to work too. The growth curve becomes exponential.

In this example, Jones and Smith invested the same amount per month, earned the same return, and invested in the same type of vehicle. The only meaningful difference was time—and that difference was decisive.

That's why early consistency beats late intensity almost every time.

Jet Fuel for the Equation

Want to throw jet fuel on this?

Invest 5% of your salary in the Roth TSP from day one—and don't stop.

We covered this in Chapter 2, but it's worth reinforcing.

If you start at age 18 as an E-1 and contribute 5% of your base pay, the government automatically contributes 1% after 60 days. After two years of service, they match an additional 4%—giving you a full 5% match.

If you maintain that contribution for a 20-year career and earn an average of 8%, you'll have roughly **$260,000** in your TSP at retirement at age 38.

Then here's the key part: you stop contributing—but the money keeps working.

At the same 8% return, that balance grows to approximately **$2.2 million by age 65**.

All from starting early. All from consistency. All from letting compounding do its job.

Nothing flashy. Nothing dramatic.

Just time, discipline, and patience working together (Table 8.2).

What I want you to take away from this is simple: **compound interest makes early action exponentially more valuable than later action.**

This is not an opinion. It's math.

Table 8.2 Side-by-Side comparison of Jones Versus Smith

Airman Jones			Sergeant Smith		
Age	**Year #**	**EOY Balance**	**Age**	**Year #**	**EOY Balance**
21	1	$ 1,244.99	21	0	$—
22	2	$ 2,593.32	22	0	$—
23	3	$ 4,053.56	23	0	$—
24	4	$ 5,634.99	24	0	$—
25	5	$ 7,347.69	25	0	$—
26	6	$ 9,202.53	26	0	$—
27	7	$ 11,211.33	27	0	$—
28	8	$ 13,386.86	28	0	$—
29	9	$ 15,742.95	29	0	$—
30	10	$ 18,294.60	30	0	$—
31	11	$ 19,758.17	31	0	$—
32	12	$ 21,338.83	32	0	$—
33	13	$ 23,045.93	33	0	$—
34	14	$ 24,889.61	34	0	$—
35	15	$ 26,880.77	35	0	$—
36	16	$ 29,031.24	36	1	$ 1,244.99
37	17	$ 31,353.74	37	2	$ 2,593.32
38	18	$ 33,862.03	38	3	$ 4,053.56
39	19	$ 36,571.00	39	4	$ 5,634.99
40	20	$ 39,496.68	40	5	$ 7,347.69
41	21	$ 42,656.41	41	6	$ 9,202.53
42	22	$ 46,068.92	42	7	$ 11,211.33

(continued)

Table 8.2 (*continued*)

Airman Jones			Sergeant Smith		
Age	Year #	EOY Balance	Age	Year #	EOY Balance
43	23	$ 49,754.44	43	8	$ 13,386.86
44	24	$ 53,734.79	44	9	$ 15,742.95
45	25	$ 58,033.58	45	10	$ 18,294.60
46	26	$ 62,676.26	46	11	$ 21,058.04
47	27	$ 67,690.36	47	12	$ 24,050.84
48	28	$ 73,105.59	48	13	$ 27,292.04
49	29	$ 78,954.04	49	14	$ 30,802.26
50	30	$ 85,270.36	50	15	$ 34,603.82
51	31	$ 92,091.99	51	16	$ 38,720.91
52	32	$ 99,459.35	52	17	$ 43,179.72
53	33	$ 107,416.10	53	18	$ 48,008.61
54	34	$ 116,009.39	54	19	$ 53,238.30
55	35	$ 125,290.14	55	20	$ 58,902.04
56	36	$ 135,313.35	56	21	$ 65,035.87
57	37	$ 146,138.42	57	22	$ 71,678.81
58	38	$ 157,829.49	58	23	$ 78,873.11
59	39	$ 170,455.85	59	24	$ 86,664.53
60	40	$ 184,092.32	60	25	$ 95,102.64
61	41	$ 198,819.70	61	26	$104,241.10
62	42	$ 214,725.28	62	27	$114,138.06
63	43	$ 231,903.30	63	28	$124,856.45
64	44	$ 250,455.57	64	29	$136,464.47

Table 8.2 *(continued)*

Airman Jones			Sergeant Smith		
Age	**Year #**	**EOY Balance**	**Age**	**Year #**	**EOY Balance**
65	45	$ 270,492.01	65	30	$ 149,035.94
	Balance	**$ 270,492.01**		**Balance**	**$ 149,035.94**

No market return is ever guaranteed, but history gives us a very clear signal. Over the long term, the US stock market has averaged roughly a 10% nominal annual return. More importantly, when you look at rolling 20-year periods, **more than half of them delivered returns greater than 10%.**[2] Individual decades vary. Individual years can be ugly. But time smooths the noise.

When I invest in the market, I am not trying to pick winners and losers among individual stocks. I'm not betting on a company—I'm betting on the system. I put my money into the overall market and trust that the US economy will continue to grow, innovate, and create value over time.

If you don't believe in the long-term staying power of the United States, this strategy isn't for you. But you also probably made the wrong career choice joining the US military.

For service members with steady income, **time in the market consistently beats timing the market**. The market has grown reliably for more than a century—but that growth has never been smooth. There have been recessions, crashes, wars, bubbles, pandemics, and political chaos. And yet, over time, the trajectory has remained upward.

Trying to jump in and out based on headlines is a losing game. In fact, if you had missed just the **20 best trading days over the last 20 years**, you would have missed out on most of the market's total growth. The problem is those best days often come immediately after the worst ones—when fear is highest and people are most likely to sit on the sidelines.

This is why timing the market is such a bad play.

The data backs this up. Over a 20-year period, roughly **92% of US large-cap active funds underperformed the S&P 500** (SPIVA).[3] These funds are managed by teams of highly educated, highly paid professionals whose entire job is to beat the market. And yet, the overwhelming majority of them fail to do it consistently.

What does that tell us?

That even the world's best investors—Warren Buffett, Ray Dalio, and everyone in between—cannot reliably predict the future. If they can't do it with teams, algorithms, and inside access, you and I probably aren't going to pull it off between PT and staff meetings.

The takeaway isn't that investing is risky.

The takeaway is that **simplicity, consistency, and patience win**.

Compounding rewards people who stay in the fight, keep contributing, and resist the urge to outsmart the system. Trust the process. Stay the course. Let time do what it does best.

In the example of Airman Jones and Sergeant Smith, the primary difference was **starting date**—not income level, special pays, bonuses, or investment performance.

Both followed similar career paths. Similar promotions. Similar final rank. The only real variable was **when they started**.

That's the lesson: **timing beats earning power**.

An E-1 who starts investing on day one of her military career and stays consistent will outperform an O-5 who waits until he "has enough money" to invest—every single time. And I chose *her* intentionally.

Multiple studies, including a 2018 Warwick Business School report and a 2021 Fidelity Investments study, have shown that women tend to be better investors than men.[4] Not because they're smarter or luckier—but because they're more disciplined. Men, on average, overestimate their ability to predict or time the market.[5] Women are more likely to trust the process, invest steadily, and leave their money alone.

Slow. Boring. Effective.

That's compounding in real life.

At this point, you might be wondering: *What if Airman Jones had simply kept investing after those first ten years? What if he never stopped?*

Table 8.3 answers that question. It shows the impact of investing just **$100 per month from age 20 through age 65**, earning an average annual return of 8%.

The results aren't flashy at the beginning. For years, the account grows quietly, almost unnoticeably. But over time, the curve bends. And once it does, it's hard to stop.

That's the power of compounding—not intensity, not brilliance, not perfect timing. Just **early action, consistency, and patience**.

You can build this entire model yourself in an Excel spreadsheet and run the numbers. I highly recommend it.

Anytime I'm debating whether it's worth tucking away a little extra money this month, I pull up my long-range plan and remind myself what that small decision today becomes over time. Seeing the math laid out makes the discipline easier. It turns sacrifice into intention.

Once you build the spreadsheet, you can start adjusting the variables—monthly contribution, years invested, or rate of return—and immediately see how your future changes. For example, at an 8% annual return, investing $190 per month for 45 years gets you to roughly $1 million. Increase the return to 10%, and you get there in about 38 years.

Those are just numbers on a page, but the lesson is real: **consistency matters more than intensity**, and time is the most powerful variable you control.

Table 8.3 Investing $100/Month at 8% for 45 Years

Airman Neverquit		
Age	**Year #**	**EOY Balance**
21	1	$ 1,244.99
22	2	$ 2,593.32
23	3	$ 4,053.56
24	4	$ 5,634.99
25	5	$ 7,347.69
26	6	$ 9,202.53
27	7	$ 11,211.33
28	8	$ 13,386.86
29	9	$ 15,742.95
30	10	$ 18,294.60
31	11	$ 21,058.04
32	12	$ 24,050.84
33	13	$ 27,292.04
34	14	$ 30,802.26
35	15	$ 34,603.82
36	16	$ 38,720.91
37	17	$ 43,179.72
38	18	$ 48,008.61
39	19	$ 53,238.30
40	20	$ 58,902.04
41	21	$ 65,035.87
42	22	$ 71,678.81

Table 8.3 *(continued)*

Airman Neverquit		
Age	**Year #**	**EOY Balance**
43	23	$ 78,873.11
44	24	$ 86,664.53
45	25	$ 95,102.64
46	26	$ 104,241.10
47	27	$ 114,138.06
48	28	$ 124,856.45
49	29	$ 136,464.47
50	30	$ 149,035.94
51	31	$ 162,650.85
52	32	$ 177,395.78
53	33	$ 193,364.53
54	34	$ 210,658.69
55	35	$ 229,388.25
56	36	$ 249,672.35
57	37	$ 271,640.03
58	38	$ 295,431.01
59	39	$ 321,196.63
60	40	$ 349,100.78
61	41	$ 379,320.97
62	42	$ 412,049.41
63	43	$ 447,494.31

(continued)

Table 8.3 *(continued)*

Airman Neverquit		
Age	**Year #**	**EOY Balance**
64	44	$ 485,881.10
65	45	$ 527,453.99
Retirement Balance		**$ 527,453.99**

There are a lot of "what-ifs" in investing, but this part is not up for debate. Start early. Stay invested. Let compound interest do the heavy lifting. That is not speculation—that is math.

Up to this point, we've focused on why the long game works and why patience matters. In the next chapter, we'll get practical and talk about how to invest—what these vehicles actually are, how they work, and how to use them correctly without trying to be smarter than the market.

Before we do that, lock in the foundation.

Action Steps:

1. **Build your compounding model**.

   Create a simple spreadsheet that shows your current investments, monthly contributions, expected rate of return, and long-term outcome. Seeing the math makes discipline easier and turns abstract goals into something real.

2. **Commit to consistency, not perfection**.

   Pick a contribution amount you can sustain—even if it feels small—and automate it. Compounding only works if you stay in the game. Boring and consistent beats clever and inconsistent every time.

3. **Decide to play the long game**.

   Write down—explicitly—that this money is not for next year, or five years from now. It is for future you. This decision will protect you from panic, second-guessing, and emotional reactions when markets inevitably fluctuate.

Next, we'll zoom in on the actual tools—stocks, bonds, index funds, and accounts—and break down what they are, how they work, and how to use them without overcomplicating the process. This is where strategy replaces theory.

The long game only works if you understand the pieces.

Chapter 9

Investing 101

"Slow is smooth. And smooth is fast."

—Fighter Pilot Axiom

The first time you learn to fly formation, you think the job is about control and precision.

You stare at the jet in front of you. You lock your eyes on an external aircraft panel or a fuel door and try to hold it perfectly still. The moment it moves—even a fraction—you react. A little stick. A little throttle. A bigger correction. Then another.

Before long, the jet starts to feel unstable. You're working hard, but things are getting worse, not better. The sight picture oscillates. Your scan narrows. You're behind the jet.

And then the instructor says something that feels completely backward.

"Relax your shoulders."

Sometimes they'll add, "Wiggle your fingers and toes."

It sounds ridiculous. You're flying a fighter jet at hundreds of knots, a few feet from another aircraft, and the advice is to loosen up and wiggle your toes?

But the moment you do, everything changes.

When you stop overcontrolling, the jet settles down. Small inputs replace big ones. Trim starts doing the work it was designed to do. Instead of chasing perfection, you allow the airplane to fly.

That's when formation becomes smooth.

New pilots overcontrol. They think more effort equals better results. Experienced pilots know the opposite is true. The goal isn't activity—it's stability. Not tension, but discipline. Small corrections.

Air refueling teaches the same lesson. If you try to force the jet into position, you'll never stay connected. The pilots who struggle the most are the ones making the biggest corrections. The pilots who look effortless are barely moving at all.

They're not passive. They're precise.

They trust the systems. They trust the aerodynamics. And most importantly, they trust time.

Investing works the same way.

Most people think investing should feel like something. Exciting. Active. Responsive. They want to be doing something—making moves, adjusting, reacting. When the market moves, they feel the urge to move with it.

That instinct is exactly what causes instability.

Just like formation flying, investing rewards small, deliberate inputs applied consistently over time. Big swings create oscillations. Emotional reactions introduce error. Overcorrection destroys position.

The best investors don't fight the system. They set it up correctly, trim it, and then let it work.

This chapter is not about hot tips or flashy trades. It's about learning how to stop overcontrolling your financial future. About choosing the right tools, matching them to the mission, and executing with discipline.

Because in both flying and investing, the goal is the same:

Stay in position.

Stay consistent.

And don't interfere with what's already working.

In flying as well as investing, mistakes usually don't come from not knowing enough—they come from doing too much.

Once the jet is trimmed and stable, your job is no longer to constantly correct it. Your job is to monitor, make small inputs when necessary, and avoid introducing unnecessary instability. Investing works the same way. The hardest part isn't picking the perfect fund or timing the perfect entry. It's resisting the urge to overcontrol something that is already designed to work.

Up to this point, you've done the hard setup work. You've clarified your goals, aligned your purpose, automated your savings, and learned why time and compounding matter more than intensity. The foundation is in place.

Now the question becomes practical, not emotional: *where should the money actually go?*

What Investing Actually Is: A Mental Model

So, what is an investment?

At its most basic, an investment is an asset you buy with the expectation that it will make you money over time—by generating income, increasing in value, or creating profit. It's a way to earn money on money you have.

When you put your money into a bank, you earn interest. Typical checking account interest rates are tiny. Savings accounts are only slightly better. Some institutions offer a high-yield savings account (HYSA), and those can be decent in certain seasons.

But here's the real point: the bank isn't paying you out of kindness. They take your money, lend it to other people, charge those people interest, and then give you a small percentage.

Investing is simply you stepping into the role the bank has been playing all along—putting your money to work instead of letting it sit still.

And one important clarification: **investing is not the same thing as trading**.

Investing is building wealth with systems, discipline, and time. Trading is trying to outsmart the market in the short term. This book is about financial freedom and generational wealth, not casino behavior dressed up as confidence.

Reality Check: Your Bank Is Not Your Friend (and That's Okay)

A savings account is not an investment strategy. It's a parking spot.

It's useful for emergency funds and short-term needs, but over the long run, keeping large sums of money in low-interest accounts quietly works against you. Inflation does the damage slowly, which makes it easy to ignore—but the math never forgets.

When you put your money into a bank, you earn interest. Typical interest rates for checking accounts are very low—around **0.07%**—and savings accounts are only slightly higher, often around **0.4%**.[1] Some institutions offer a *high-yield savings account* (HYSA) with interest rates as high as **4–5%**, but most people will find them in the high-2% to low-3% range depending on market conditions.[2]

Banks are great for liquidity and safety.

But investments are how you build wealth.

The Most Important Rules

There are a few almost-universal principles that matter more than any hot tip.

1. **Don't put all your eggs in one basket**

   Diversification matters. If every dollar you owned was in the stock market in 1929, you likely lost most of your portfolio value. Same for the dot-com crash or the housing crash. But if you had a balanced portfolio, you still took a haircut—but you probably didn't lose your shirt.

2. **Take more risk early, less risk later**

   A common approach is to take more risk when you're young and dial it back as you get closer to retirement. You'll see portfolios that look like:

   - **20s:** 80/20 stocks-to-bonds
   - **30s:** 70/30
   - **40s:** 60/40
   - **50s:** 50/50
   - **60s:** 40/60
   - **Retirement and beyond:** 20/80

There are too many variables to prescribe a perfect ratio in a book like this, but here's good news: almost every base has a Military & Family Readiness Center (the office name might vary) with a financial advisor on staff.

Your civilian friends are paying good money for financial advice. You can get it for free. Before you turn this page, search for the number of your local office and set a calendar reminder to call them first thing in the morning—phone number in the event details.

That's your **Literal Next Step**.

Nothing will change if you don't act.

The Building Blocks: Stocks, Index Funds, Mutual Funds, Bonds

Stocks: Owning a Piece of a Company

Stocks are a type of security that represent a share of ownership of a company. When you buy a stock, you become a partial owner. You may get voting rights, and you may get dividends depending on the company.

One key concept: **share price alone is not the value of the company**. Market cap matters.

Market cap = share price × number of shares.

A company at $50 per share could be worth far more than a company at $100 per share depending on how many shares exist.

In the United States, there are roughly 4,000 publicly traded companies that anyone can buy a piece of. Most of them trade on two major exchanges: NYSE or NASDAQ.

Indexes: "Buying a Share of America"

When people talk about "the market," they're usually referring to indexes—groups of companies tracked together to measure performance. Two you've heard of:

- **Dow Jones:** tracks 30 large, established US companies
- **S&P 500:** tracks 500 of the largest US companies by market cap

If you don't have a specific company you want to bet on, and your belief is basically: "Hey Motor, I'm new to this, but I think the US economy will continue to grow over the long term . . ."

. . . then you probably want an **index fund** that tracks the market.

You're not betting on one company. You're betting on long-term economic growth. And historically, that's been a very good bet.

It's like buying a share of America.

Mutual Funds Versus Index Funds: Simple Beats Sexy

You'll hear people say, "I'll just put my money in a safe mutual fund earning around 7% per year."

I hear this *all the time*. It sounds reasonable. Responsible, even.

But what most people don't realize is that there are **nearly twice as many mutual funds as there are companies** to invest in—more than 7,000 mutual funds at last count.[3] And most of them are actively managed, meaning a team of professionals is constantly trying to pick which stocks will outperform the market.

That sounds great . . . until you look at the data.

Over a 20-year period, about **92% of large-cap actively managed funds underperformed the S&P 500**. Let that sink in. These funds are run by highly educated, well-resourced professionals whose full-time job is to beat the market—and **nearly all of them** fail to do it over time.

Not because they're dumb. Not because they're lazy. But because *predicting the future consistently is impossible.*

Now layer fees on top of that.

Most mutual funds charge around 0.6% per year, and some charge as much as 2%. That may not sound like much, but fees compound against you the same way returns compound for you.

Compare that to a low-cost index fund like Vanguard's VOO, which tracks the S&P 500 and charges about 0.03%. Over the last 30 years, the S&P 500 has averaged around 10% nominal returns, despite multiple crashes, recessions, and political swings.[4]

So when someone says, "I don't want to take risks, I'll just do a mutual fund," what they usually mean is:

"I'm going to pay higher fees for a product that has a high probability of underperforming the market."

That's not "safe." That's just expensive.

"Sounds cool—how do I buy an index fund?"

Pretty easy.

Open a brokerage account at a bank or brokerage (I recommend shopping around for low or no fees). I'm not sponsored by anyone, but I've used **Schwab** for years.

Transfer money from savings into that brokerage account.

Search the fund (like VOO).

Click **Buy**.

That's it.

If you had $10,000 sitting in a savings account earning 0.4%, you'd make $40 in a year. That same $10,000 invested in an S&P 500 index fund in an average year during the last 30 years would have made about $1,000. And had you been in a mutual fund, there is a 92% chance that you would have made less money than simply investing in an index fund. No guarantees—but the math heavily favors the index fund over time.

That's why I like low-cost index funds. Not because they're exciting—because they work. If you're investing for financial freedom, boring is your friend.

"But what if the market crashes?"

If the market drops, your account value drops. That risk is real, and not everyone is emotionally built for it.

But here's a different way to think about it:

If I buy shares of a company I believe will be around for decades—like Coca-Cola—and the stock drops, I still own the same number of shares. The price tag changed. My ownership didn't.

A correction might be around 10%. A bear market is often thought of as around 20%. And yes, crashes happen. But the long-term growth of the market includes those downturns. That's the deal.

The chart only goes up over time because the economy grows over time.

This book is not a get-rich-quick scheme. We are playing the long game.

If you still have faith in the United States of America—and I'm guessing you do, since you joined the military—then you can understand this simple idea:

Long-term investing is betting that America keeps building.

Bonds: Lending Money for Stability

Bonds are loans to a government or corporation. Treasury bonds carry the full faith and credit of the US government. Corporate bonds can offer higher yields but usually come with higher risk as they are backed by a corporation.

Bonds are often considered "safer" than stocks, and many people use them for stability, especially as they get closer to retirement or when they want less volatility.

If you want to buy US Treasury Bonds directly, you can use TreasuryDirect.gov.

I recommend trying it once just to learn the process and connect your accounts.

I once bought a 13-week bond for $10,000. The bond cost me about $9,866, and 13 weeks later I got $10,000 back. Stable. Predictable. Not sexy. Useful.

The downside is obvious: your money is tied up for the term of the bond.

Behavior: Buying, Selling, and Not Losing Your Mind

You can purchase shares through many brokers with different fee structures. I've used JPMorgan, Robinhood, and Charles Schwab, and I also have managed money invested in index funds.

When I buy individual companies, I do it with a specific mindset: I buy things I trust and believe in.

And then I treat myself like a firefighter—metaphorically speaking—running toward the fire when a great company is "burning."

Nike is a good example. I believe in Nike. I believe it's a staple of America. When it has a bad day or a bad month, my first thought is not panic.

My first thought is: "*Awesome. Nike stock is on sale.*"

If the shoe store had a huge sale on Air Jordans, you'd be tempted to grab a pair (I know I would). Same concept for stocks.

Now—important caveat: I don't buy random companies just because they're tanking. Some companies go out of business. You can lose your money.

But if you build a list of companies you believe in, learn how to read basic info, and then buy when they're discounted, you'll already be ahead of most people. Usually when I buy, I've been watching for a while. I've done some research. I've formed my own opinion.

It's not always right—but it's a whole lot better than firing in the dark and hoping you hit a winner.

Now Apply It: The TSP Simplified

Now let's talk about the most important investing platform for military members: the Thrift Savings Plan.

Congratulations—you've waited 60 days, the DoD has begun contributing the automatic 1% of your base pay, and you decide to contribute 5% immediately. You set up your online account at TSP.gov and then go to myPay to set your allotments.

So what happens when your money hits the TSP?

By default, it goes into an **L Fund** (Lifecycle Fund) based on your age.[5] If you do nothing, it stays there until you withdraw it.

Lifecycle Funds are built around a simple principle: **take more risk when you're young and reduce risk as you approach retirement**. The allocation is adjusted over time. It's basically a countdown clock to your withdrawal date with less-and-less risk as you get closer.

When the fund reaches the target date, it rolls into the **L Income Fund**.

Here's what I recommend for most people:

Stay in your Lifecycle Fund until you understand investing well enough to build your own mix.

There is no shortage of people on social media selling their "perfect blend" of TSP funds. Exercise extreme caution. No one can predict the future. The "perfect blend" from last year might be the biggest loser this year.

The L Funds aren't random. They're managed and updated quarterly by professionals who do this for a living.

If you eventually want to adjust your allocation yourself:

- Go to the Investments tab on TSP.gov
- Select Change Investments
- You'll see options like changing future contributions versus moving existing money

There's also a Mutual Fund Window option that allows more flexibility, but it comes with higher fees and requires a certain balance. I don't recommend it early. More options are not always better. Sometimes it's just more ways to overcontrol.

This information is always available on the TSP website and should be reviewed regularly to make sure that your retirement investment is aligned with your retirement goals.[6]

HOW TO CHANGE YOUR TSP ALLOCATION (2-MINUTE GUIDE)

- Log in to the TSP website, www.TSP.gov
- Go to the Investments tab and select *Change Investments*.
- That will take you to three options:
  - Change Your Investment Mix,
  - Move Money Between Funds, and
  - Set Up a Mutual Fund Window Account.
- If you want to change the way all your future money gets allocated, then select the first option—Change Your Investment Mix.
- If you want to simply move around some of the money already in the account, then select the second option—Move Money Between Funds.
- Simply follow the steps for each of these, choose the money to move, then choose the new allocation. It is a simple process.

The Five Core TSP Funds (Simple Overview)

- G Fund: Special US Treasury securities (principal guaranteed). Low risk. Great for stability. Long-run returns may trail inflation.
- F Fund: US investment-grade bonds. Low to moderate risk. Helps diversify. Can get hurt when rates rise.
- C Fund: Large US stocks (S&P 500). Higher risk. Growth engine long term. Big drawdowns in bear markets.

- S Fund: US small/mid stocks not in S&P 500. Higher volatility. Complements C to cover more of the US market.
- I Fund: Developed international stocks. Diversifies beyond US currency swings and different market behavior.

Bottom line: the TSP gives you a clean, low-fee way to invest. Don't make it complicated.

Trim the jet. Then let it fly.

Simple Beats Sexy

There are far too many variables to call any one portfolio "the right one."

If you want a deeper understanding of investing, read *Money: Master the Game* by Tony Robbins. This chapter barely scratches the surface, and that's all it's meant to do. This is Investing 101—a framework you can build on.

Treat your financial intelligence as a lifelong learning journey and you will surely find success.

And remember the opening lesson:

Most people don't fail because they don't know enough. They fail because they do too much.

Set up the system. Make small, correct inputs. And don't interfere with what's already working.

Action Steps:

1. **Research brokerage accounts and choose one that suits your needs**.

   Robinhood is easy and user friendly. Schwab has been solid for me. Many institutions offer good options—compare fees and simplicity.

2. **Open a brokerage account and fund it with the minimum amount** (usually around $100).

   Start small. The goal is motion.

3. **Every time you skip a Big-Dumb-Coffee-Cup (or any other vice), move that money into your investment account.**

   Train the habit. Let it compound.

Investing in stocks and index funds is one of the cleanest paths to long-term wealth: liquid, scalable, and mostly passive once you automate it.

Real estate is different. Real estate is leverage, sweat, and strategy. It can build wealth faster—but it's not passive, and it's not forgiving if you overcontrol the wrong variable.

Same principles. Different weapon system.

Let's talk about it next.

Chapter 10

Real Estate

"Give me a lever long enough and a fulcrum on which to place it, and I shall move the world."

—Archimedes

The first time I truly understood the difference between *executing inside constraints* and *designing the battlespace* wasn't in a classroom. It was in the air, during a large force exercise sortie where everything was happening at once—radios barking, threats popping up, timelines compressing, and jets seemingly everywhere.

I was the mission commander, and I was supposed to execute the plan.

We had stepped to the jets on-time, pushed into the fight on-time, but almost immediately problems started cascading. Not "oh no, we're all going to die" problems—but the kind that turns a clean plan into a sloppy one. The kind that forces you to react instead of lead.

Our package was supposed to flow through a specific corridor in the airspace, hit our target, and then egress. But the enemy didn't read our slides. Their timeline didn't care about our timeline. Red air showed up in a place they "weren't supposed to be," and suddenly half the force package was making decisions in the moment. Small course changes. Small altitude changes. Small delays.

Those small changes started stacking.

The strike package commander called to say they were behind the timeline. The SEAD jets were already squeezed for gas and playtime. Escort had to choose between committing against long-range threats or staying in cover on the strikers. It felt like we were doing a lot—moving, reacting, working hard—yet somehow, we were losing control.

Then the escort commander came up on the radio, calm as if he was ordering lunch.

"Strikers lean north. Take the three block. Escort commit in the four block."

No drama. No panic. Just a decision. I had flown with him before, and he was as respected a fighter pilot as I had ever met. It was the right call and we went with it.

We shifted the flow, sanitized the airspace, and the entire sortie changed. The threats didn't disappear. The enemy didn't get nicer. But now we controlled the geometry. Now we controlled the timeline. Now we weren't begging the fight to go our way—we were shaping it.

And here's the part that hit me later after the debrief:

We didn't win because we flew better in the moment.

We won because we controlled something that controlled everything else.

That's what ownership does.

When you're a wingman, you can absolutely perform. You can be sharp. You can execute. But you're still operating inside boundaries that someone else set—altitude blocks, timelines, routing, fuel plans, rules of engagement. You can do everything right and still be limited.

Ownership is different.

Ownership is leverage.

It's the difference between renting a piece of sky for fifteen minutes... and having the authority to move the whole package because you control the space everyone has to pass through.

Most people look at real estate the way a brand-new lieutenant looks at a four-ship: too big, too expensive, too complicated, too risky.

But real estate isn't magic.

It's battlespace.

And when you learn how it works—mortgages, tenants, cash flow, appreciation, tax advantages—you realize this isn't about being reckless. It's about gaining control over an asset that can pay you for decades.

You're not buying a house.

You're buying leverage.

And once you learn how to use it, you stop reacting to your financial life... and you start designing it.

To attempt to cover Real Estate in a single chapter does not do justice to the field. But it *is* a critical topic when it comes to building generational wealth and achieving financial freedom.

Real estate is one of the most common wealth-building tools on earth. It has also ruined people who jumped in too fast, used the wrong loan, underestimated repairs, or trusted the wrong tenant.

But both things can be true.

That's why this chapter is not a hype piece. It's not "real estate is easy, bro." It's a framework so you can understand the game, avoid the common landmines, and build a plan that fits your life.

Many books have been written on building wealth through real estate, and if you are interested in this, you absolutely should go deeper than this chapter. Here are my top books that everyone should read to get started in real estate:

- Robert Kiyosaki, *Rich Dad Poor Dad* and *Cash Flow Quadrant*
- Brandon Turner, *The Book on Rental Property Investing* and *The Multifamily Millionaire* with Brian Murray
- Gary Keller, *The Millionaire Real Estate Investor* and *The ONE Thing* with Jay Papasan (this one is for goal setting but is an absolute must read)

This chapter is your **Investing 101** version of real estate: a framework you can build on.

The Game You're Actually Playing

Assets Versus Liabilities (The First Mindset Shift)

Let's begin with the concept of assets versus liabilities. Assets put money into your bank account and liabilities take money out of your account. Simplified:

- An **asset** is anything that **makes you money**.
- A **liability** is anything that **costs you money**.

With that in mind, the home you live in is not an asset unless you rent part of it out or move out and turn it into a rental property. This is one of the most common misconceptions among new real estate investors.

That statement makes people emotional because we were taught the opposite.

Many of us grew up with the middle-class mindset of: "Your home is your biggest asset." Well. . . turns out that is often false.

In fact, for most people, your home is likely your biggest liability: mortgage, taxes, insurance, repairs, upgrades you didn't budget for, and that one HVAC system that decides to die in July out of spite.

If you live in it and it costs you money every month, it's a liability. It might become a great asset later. But while you're living there and paying for it, it behaves like a liability.

And that matters because the goal of *real estate investing* is not "owning a house." The goal is owning **income-producing property**. That is: to make money.

The Purpose of Investing in Real Estate: Cash Flow

When you invest in real estate, the purpose is simple: find assets that make you money every month. That monthly profit is called cash flow.

Cash flow is the amount of money you take home after all expenses have been paid. And it matters because if a property is cash flow negative, then it will cost you money to own it. That's not investing. And many people's cautionary tales about real estate could have been avoided if they had calculated cash flow before they invested.

Real Estate Tax Advantages

In addition to cash flow, real estate offers major tax advantages through **depreciation, write-offs, and deferred capital gains**.

Depreciation is essentially reducing the value of the property each year by a small amount because of wear and tear. On a typical depreciation schedule, you reduce the value of the property over 27.5 years. So if your cost basis is $275,000, you get to write off about $10,000 per year in depreciation for 27.5 years.

Your **cost basis** is what you paid for the property (including acquisition costs), minus the value of the land.

And at the end of that depreciation schedule—after you've depreciated the structure down to $0 tax basis—if you sell the property, you can defer (i.e. not pay them now) capital gains taxes as long as you reinvest in another rental property.

You can repeat this process indefinitely, upgrading to larger properties and deferring the taxes. These 1031 exchanges have specific IRS timelines (45 days to identify a property, 180 days to close) and rules (like-kind property, qualified intermediary), so make sure to work with a professional when performing this type of transaction.

Why 27.5 years? I have no idea, and it's not worth the headache you'll get trying to rationalize it. It is what it is.

Also: the inner workings of the tax code are far more complex than this. Consult your CPA or tax advisor. But for the big picture, this is the basic idea.

Decide early whether you are building for income, appreciation, or eventual exit. This will help map your long-term strategy. With a properly structured estate plan you can eliminate most of the taxes at your passing and give your future generations income-producing real estate without a tax burden.

Depreciation Isn't Just the Building

In addition to depreciating the property itself, you can also depreciate individual items on the property, like:

- Appliances, furniture, carpet (often over five years)
- Improvements like driveways, fences, landscaping (often over 15 years)

Under recent tax law changes, you can also claim what's called **Bonus Depreciation**, where you can take full depreciation on items that would normally be depreciated over 15 years.

This is often done through a **cost segregation analysis**—a professional creates a depreciation schedule for a fee. Most companies will give you an estimate before charging you.

On a recent cost segregation I did, the company charged me about $5,000 and was able to produce almost $1,000,000 in bonus depreciation for me to use to offset my taxes. Since I pay taxes in a higher bracket, that $5,000 cost segregation investment paid for itself at more than 70 times what I paid for it.

Not every deal does this. But it should show you why real estate is more than "rent minus mortgage."

Reality Check, Risk, and. . .Gratitude

Real estate is not a magic bullet. Not every property will cash flow. Not every deal is a good one. Many people lose money in real estate, and not everyone gets wealthy this way.

Despite what some will have you believe, real estate is not without risk.

But everything has risk. Even leaving your house in the morning. Or staying in your house for that matter.

What we have to decide is what risk we're willing to take, how much we're comfortable with, and what path makes sense for our life.

For me, I look at investments on a 100-year horizon. That doesn't mean there's no risk. It means there's strong evidence that this has been a solid long-term strategy over time. I also diversify risk by investing in multiple revenue streams—and real estate is one of them.

I love the story of the turkey that gets fed and cared for by the farmer for 150 days. It believes it has security because it has never once had a bad day. Its confidence grows from June through November. It thinks it has a guaranteed future because there is no reason to think otherwise; everything has been safe and secure until now. Then it wakes up on Thanksgiving morning. . .

You get the point.

Looking at historical averages—whether it's the stock market, real estate, or anything else—does not guarantee success tomorrow. So, decide for yourself where you'll place your assets and what risk you can live with.

And start every day with gratitude. Tomorrow isn't guaranteed. If you live each day to its fullest, you'll be ready when the time does come.

Real Estate by the Numbers (So You Don't Get Fooled)

If ownership is leverage, then these numbers are the geometry of the fight.

Let's walk through a simple example to make this practical.

Consider a duplex that costs $300,000 to purchase and makes $30,000 per year in rental income ($1,250 per unit per month). You will pay for insurance, management fees, and taxes—combined cost of about $6,000 per year ($500 per month).

To determine if this is an investment you want to make, you need a few basic metrics:

- NOI (Net Operating Income)
- OpEx (Operating Expenses)
- CapEx (Capital Expenditures)
- Cap Rate (Capitalization Rate)
- Cash Flow
- Cash-on-Cash Return
- IRR (Internal Rate of Return)

Let's break these down.

NOI, OpEx, and CapEx (the Foundation)

Net Operating Income (NOI) is a key metric. It tells you how the property performs before financing.

To calculate NOI: NOI = Operating Income–Operating Expenses

Operating income is all the money the property makes: rent, coin laundry, parking passes, storage fees, etc. You also need to account for vacancies and turnover, because real life happens. Assume 5–10% vacancy in your projections unless you have strong and accurate data.

Operating expenses (OpEx) are what you pay to run the property: maintenance, property management, landscaping, pool service, utilities, insurance, property taxes.

If the tenant pays certain utilities, those don't count against your OpEx.

Important note: **mortgage payments are not operating expenses**. CapEx is also not OpEx. A common mistake is to include the mortgage in OpEx. The mortgage affects cash flow, not NOI.

$$\text{In our duplex example}: \$30{,}000 \text{ income} - \$6{,}000 \text{ expenses} = \$24{,}000 \text{ NOI per year}$$

Now let's talk about CapEx.

CapEx are the big expenses that improve the value or extend the life of the property: roof replacement, HVAC, plumbing, major repairs, structural work, driveway, fences, etc.

CapEx are not the routine costs of running the property. They're the "this is going to hurt" costs. You will have them. Budget for them.

Cap Rate (How Investors Price Deals)

The Cap Rate measures the potential return you'd get on a property based on NOI. Cap Rate = NOI ÷ Purchase Price

$$\text{For our duplex}: \$24{,}000 \div \$300{,}000 = 0.08 = 8\%$$

Cap rates vary by property type, location, timing, and market conditions.

In 2025, the average cap rate for a multifamily investment in Phoenix is about 6.1%. A year earlier it was 5.4%. One driver was demand weakening, which pushed prices down. Before that, a driver was rents rising across the city.

These numbers will move, but they give you a benchmark.

Also: smaller properties—single family, duplexes, up to fourplex—can sometimes have higher cap rates than large commercial deals, because commercial pricing is driven heavily by cap rate, while smaller properties are often driven by appraisals and local comps.

And here's the fun part: sometimes you can't move the purchase price much, but you can influence NOI.

For example, on one of my properties I switched one unit to a mid-term rental and rented it to traveling nurses for $75/night. That unit brought in an average of $2,250 per month, but the previous owner was only getting $900 per month as a long-term one-bedroom rental.

That one decision changed the NOI, which changed the cap rate, which changed the value. And while I added the upfront costs of furnishing and regulatory compliance, as well as the risk of vacancies, it has been much more profitable over time.

Once I had enough data to support the new income, I went back to the bank and renegotiated the loan terms—because in commercial property, the value is driven by income, not just appraisal vibes.

That new value allowed me to take money out of the property and invest in another one.

This is leverage. This is why learning cap rate matters.

Location Is More than a Zip Code

Every property sits inside a larger system. And that system matters.

A duplex in Phoenix is not the same risk as a duplex in rural Ohio. A fourplex in Texas behaves differently than one in California. Laws, taxes, insurance costs, population growth, job markets, landlord-tenant rules, and even weather patterns all influence your outcome.

Some states are landlord-friendly. Some heavily favor tenants. Some cities impose rent control. Some insurance markets are stable. Others are exploding in cost due to severe weather risk. These variables directly affect your cash flow and your stress level.

You are not just investing in a property. You are investing in a jurisdiction.

Before buying, ask:

- Is the population growing or shrinking?
- Are jobs expanding or leaving?
- What are the eviction timelines?
- How volatile are property taxes?
- What is happening to insurance costs?

A good deal in a declining market can become a slow bleed. A decent deal in a growing market can outperform expectations.

Control the geometry. That includes where you choose to stand.

Cash Flow (The Number You Actually Feel)

Your cash flow statement is probably the most important number month to month. It's what you get to put in your pocket before personal income taxes.

Cash flow is like NOI, but now we include debt service and CapEx reserves.

For our duplex: Income \$30,000 – OpEx \$6,000 = NOI \$24,000

Now add the loan. Let's assume a traditional loan example: 20% down, 6% interest, 30-year mortgage.

Principal + interest payment is $1,438.92 per month, which is $17,267.04 per year.

So, if we ignored CapEx (which you should not), cash flow would be: $24,000–$17,267.04 = $6,732.96 per year. That's a little more than $560/month.

But there is always something that needs fixing—i.e. CapEx. So, the best strategy is to set aside part of every month's income into a separate account for future CapEx.

This is where investing looks boring and adulthood shows up.

There's a famous Stanford study called the marshmallow experiment. Kids were told they could eat one marshmallow now or wait 15 minutes and get two. The kids who could delay gratification were more likely to succeed later.

Real estate is one long marshmallow experiment.

The investor who spends every dollar of cash flow because it "feels good" usually gets wrecked by the first roof replacement. The investor who saves, reinvests, and plans gets the second marshmallow.

Leverage: The Force Multiplier—and the Amplifier

Leverage is powerful. It's also unforgiving.

When you borrow money to buy real estate, you are using the bank's capital to control a larger asset than you could on your own. That's a force multiplier. If the property appreciates, you benefit on the full value—not just your down payment. That's why real estate can accelerate wealth.

But leverage does not care which direction the market moves.

If rents drop, if vacancies spike, if interest rates rise, if insurance doubles, or if you miscalculated repairs—your debt payment does not adjust itself to your optimism. The bank still wants its money every month. Leverage amplifies gains, but it also amplifies mistakes.

This is why reserves matter. This is why conservative underwriting matters. This is why I do not count on appreciation to save a deal. I want a property that works on paper, in today's conditions, with *a safety margin* built in. Real estate rewards patience and discipline. It punishes ego and overextension.

Control the leverage—or the leverage will control you.

Cash-on-Cash Return (Simple Performance)

Cash-on-cash return shows how much cash you earn relative to the cash you invested.

Cash-on-cash = Annual Cash Flow ÷ Total Cash Invested

In our example: Annual cash flow: $6,732

Cash invested: $60,000 down payment + $10,000 closing/repairs = $70,000

$6,732 ÷ $70,000 = 9.6%

By all accounts, that's solid. The S&P 500 has averaged around 10% over long periods, but with much more visible volatility. Real estate has different risks, but this helps you compare apples to apples.

IRR (for the Longer Game)

IRR (Internal Rate of Return) is the long-term return on the investment over the period you hold it. It includes the initial investment, cash flows, operating expenses, improvements, and sale proceeds.

The easiest way to estimate IRR is to use an online calculator like the one on LoopNet, or the IRR function in Excel.[1]

Your initial investment is the first "cash flow" and it's negative. Then you list annual net cash flow (after debt service) for each year you plan to hold the property. Then list the net proceeds from the sale (sale price minus loan payoff and selling costs).

Benchmarks I use:

- 8–10% IRR for core, stable properties
- 12–18% IRR for value-add properties that need some love
- 20%+ IRR for opportunistic, higher-risk deals

If you're just getting started buying your first single-family rental, don't get lost in IRR spreadsheets. Start with cash flow. IRR becomes more predictable in larger multifamily investments where the value is driven by rental income.

Funding Your Property (the Scary Part)

For most of us, buying something that costs hundreds of thousands of dollars is the most intimidating part.

We hear horror stories about the uncle with the nightmare tenant. We imagine leaking roofs and lawsuits and debt. And we think, "Nope. Not doing that."

Fear is what holds most people back. It held me back in the beginning, and it still shows up every time I stretch to the next level.

So let's take it one step at a time. We are not signing on dotted lines yet. Let's get curious about how you might finance a property if you decide to go for it.

There are many loan products available. I recommend doing your own research and talking with multiple lending professionals. I still run into lenders who have never heard of products I've used elsewhere. Many lenders get good at a few loan types and never learn the rest.

To get approved for a loan, banks often look at your financial history, your taxes, and your Debt-to-Income (DTI) ratio—the ratio of your expenses to your income.

Now let's talk about the biggest advantage military members have.

VA Loan (One of Your Greatest Benefits)

The VA loan is guaranteed by the Department of Veterans Affairs, and it is one of the single greatest benefits you have as a service member.

A VA loan can allow eligible borrowers to buy a home with:

- no money down,
- no PMI,
- low closing costs and competitive rates.

Eligibility generally comes from serving on active duty, Guard/Reserve time, or time in a combat zone. With full eligibility, there's *no formal limit* to the loan amount if the bank will finance it—as long as you have full entitlement and the lender will underwrite (approve) the loan.

Imagine a 100-yard dash.

Most civilians start at the starting line. The VA loan is you starting at the 50-yard line.

For most civilians, the biggest barrier is the down payment—often 20%. If the median home price is $410,000, that's $82,000 down. For a young person saving $100 a month, even at 8% returns, that can take decades.

Being able to buy a home decades before your peers can often be the fastest path to financial freedom. According to Federal Housing Finance Agency data, in the last 25 years home values have increased approximately 160%. And while there is no guarantee that you will make money on a certain property, the average home appreciates in value over time while also giving you tax savings along the way. That is why real estate investing plays a role in many people's path to financial freedom (Figure 10.1).

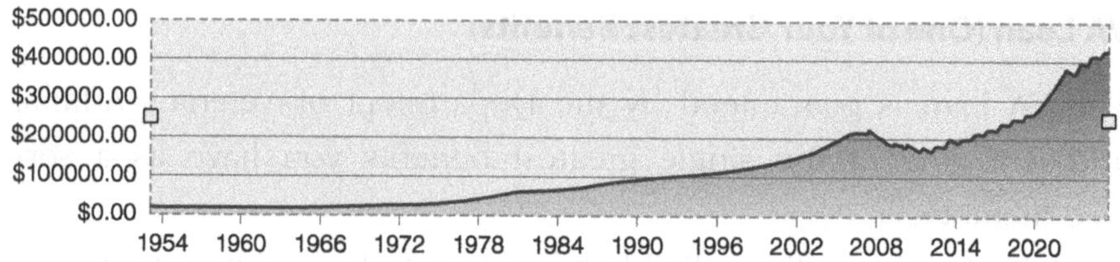

Figure 10.1 Median Home Prices in the US, 1954–2024[2]

Buying earlier can be a major path to financial freedom. Home values have generally climbed over long time horizons, and real estate can come with tax advantages along the way.

VA Loan Gotchas (Read This Twice)

There are cautions.

You cannot just buy a new home at every assignment, rent it out after you PCS, and stack VA loans forever. It's not designed for that.

To reinstate your entitlement after buying a house with a VA loan, you often must "dispose" of the property—which usually means sell it.

Some internet threads discuss "selling" your VA-loan house to an LLC to keep it and rent it. I advise against that. You are flirting dangerously close to mortgage fraud. It will never be worth it.

You can, one time in your career, refinance your VA loan into another loan type and restore your entitlement—called the **one-time restoration of entitlement**. I recommend preserving that for when you're ready to buy your forever home.

This has caught service member investors in the past when they learned that they will have to go back and sell multiple properties to restore their entitlement because they already used their "one-time restoration" (it was me, it happened to me).

There's also substitution of entitlement (another qualified service member assumes your VA loan), which can free up your entitlement—but understand the implications.

Example: you buy a home at your second duty station for $450,000 and decide to rent it out after you PCS. Then you refinance to reinstate entitlement and buy another home. Later you discover you must sell both properties to fully restore entitlement again. This clause has caught more than one service member off guard.

And no, paying off the VA loan doesn't automatically fix it. The same rules apply.

Crazy, I know.

Rental Property Loans (Conventional, HELOC, Cash-Out Refi)

Conventional rental property loans are similar to conventional primary residence loans, but usually with higher rates. They often require 15–30% down and a solid credit score.

After you have a few properties, you may be able to use tools like:

- HELOC (home equity line of credit)
- cash-out refinance

My first rental property appreciated over the first few years and I did a cash-out refinance. I got a lower rate and pulled nearly $100,000 out of the property. Because it's a loan, there's no tax on that cash.

I used that money to buy another rental property.

Eventually, when you sell, you may owe capital gains taxes on the gains—but the government also allows a tool called a 1031 exchange, where you can roll proceeds from one rental into another and defer taxes.

And this is one of the best advantages in real estate.

You can start with a small single-family rental, sell it later, roll the gains into a larger property, then larger again—eventually building your way up.

When you die and pass the property to your heirs, they may get a "step up in basis," meaning the property value resets to current market value, potentially reducing capital gains taxes if they sell.

Talk to an estate planning attorney. Have a will and trust. Do this the right way.

DSCR Loans (Property Qualifies Itself)

A Debt Service Coverage Ratio (DSCR) loan is a way to buy a rental property where the property's income does most of the talking.

If the property can show rent covers expenses plus a cushion (often around 20%), a bank may loan you the money with less emphasis on your personal income.

Roughly: if rent = 1.2×expenses, you're in the ballpark. More accurately: DSCR = NOI/debt service (it is NOI relative to debt payments). The bank wants to make sure that you can cover your mortgage with a little buffer.

Typical requirements: credit score often 620+, down payment 20–35%, appraisal, lease evidence, etc.

The "best kept secret": owner-occupied 2–4 unit loans (house hacking).

This is perhaps the best kept secret in real estate investing.

With this type of loan (often associated with Fannie Mae products), you can buy a 2–4-unit multifamily property with as little as 5% down.

If I could go back and do one thing over, it would be to use a 2–4-unit owner-occupied strategy at every duty station.

Imagine buying a duplex at your first duty station, living in one side, renting the other, and fixing it up over time. That concept is commonly called house hacking.

Example: duplex costs $300,000. 5% down is $15,000. Mortgage around $1,800. Rent around $1,200 per unit.

You rent one side for $1,200. You live in the other side. Your total rent stream is now $1,200 coming in monthly. You're still paying to live somewhere—but you're living with leverage.

Then you improve the unit you live in. When it's nice, you can rotate the upgrades and raise rents.

At the one-year mark you do it again. Buy another duplex. Move into it. Repeat.

Now the first duplex rents both sides. The second duplex starts the same cycle. And over time your "doors" (units) grow—duplex to triplex to fourplex to small apartment building.

Obviously not every deal works like this. But I promise you: someone is doing this right now.

And while it won't make you rich overnight, it can build a foundation of passive income that pays you for the rest of your life.

There are rules: you must live in one unit for at least a year. There are loan limits. You need reserves. You need insurance. And you need the discipline to treat this like a business.

For more detail, *The Multifamily Millionaire* by Brandon Turner and Brian Murray is a great place to start.

FHA and HUD Opportunity Zones (Options Worth Knowing)

FHA loans can be another strong option. Some FHA products allow 3.5% down if your credit score is above 580 and can include rehabilitation costs.

The big gotcha: you can typically only have one FHA loan in your name at a time. To buy another property, you may need to refinance into another loan type.

Opportunity Zones are meant to incentivize investors to improve properties in economically distressed areas. Many areas around military bases fall into this category.

HUD offers many options. Before finalizing a loan, it can be worth checking whether the property falls in an opportunity zone because that may open additional benefits.

Opportunity Zones (What They Actually Are)

Opportunity Zones were created to encourage long-term investment in economically distressed areas. The government designated specific census tracts across the country and said, in essence: if you invest capital gains into projects here and hold them long enough, we'll give you tax advantages.

The basic idea is this: if you sell an asset—stocks, business, real estate—and generate a capital gain, you can roll that gain into a Qualified Opportunity Fund that invests in one of these zones. In exchange for committing your capital for a set period of time, you may be able to defer—and potentially reduce—some of the taxes on that original gain.

This is not a beginner strategy. It requires strict timelines, specific fund structures, and professional guidance. But if you're already sitting on a large capital gain and looking at development or value-add projects in designated areas, it can be a powerful tool.

Like everything else in real estate, it's not magic. It's a lever. Use it intentionally.

Hard Money and Private Equity (Advanced Tools, Higher Risk)

If you are new to real estate, I recommend you avoid hard money and private equity until you understand them thoroughly.

These are often high-interest, short-term loans used for flipping or fast value-add projects.

Sometimes they're a great tool. Sometimes they are the fastest path to foreclosure if your timeline slips, your costs rise, or the market shifts.

They are not all bad. But they are not beginner-friendly.

Your Team: Realtors, Brokers, and Negotiation

Agent Versus Realtor Versus Broker (Quick Definitions)

A real estate agent is a licensed professional who can help buy, sell, or rent property.

A Realtor is an agent who is also a member of the National Association of Realtors.

Both Realtors and agents typically work under a licensed broker. A broker has a higher-level license and can operate independently and oversee transactions legally.

Finding a Rock Star (and Why It Matters)

If you've been investing for a while, you may take for granted that you have a great Realtor who finds deals that fit your needs. I know I do.

But I went through many real estate agents before finding one who aligned with my vision, mission, and goals. Once I found that person, it was like adding jet fuel to my real estate goals.

He and his team didn't just send me every house that hit the market. They learned what I was looking for and filtered 100 listings down to the best three to five.

Not all Realtors or real estate agents are the same.

Contracts, Pressure, and Remembering You're the Buyer

If you're working with an agent and you're not a raving fan, keep your options open.

In 2024 it became a nationwide requirement to enter into an agreement with a real estate agent before touring homes. That agreement outlines services, expectations, and fees.

Remember: these terms are negotiable.

You are the buyer. Not the agent.

If you don't like the contract, ask them to change it. One easy adjustment is shortening the contract length: one property, one month, whatever makes sense.

If they're great, they won't worry about it. If they pressure you, look elsewhere. There are tens of thousands of agents.

Don't Let the Seller's Agent Represent You

Do not allow the seller's agent to also represent you as the buyer. While legal in many states, it's a conflict of interest.

You want the lowest price. They want the highest price. The agent wants the deal to close. Those are competing interests.

I will not ever have the seller's agent represent me as the buyer—and I recommend the same to anyone asking.

Negotiation Matters (and Most Agents Aren't Trained for It)

Many agents are excellent at the rules, laws, and process of real estate. But many know little to nothing about negotiation.

Your agent will represent you to the seller. If they don't align with your style and your negotiation approach, you'll have a hard time.

Learn negotiation for yourself first. Two books I strongly recommend:

- Start with No by Jim Camp
- Never Split the Difference by Chris Voss

Negotiation is a life skill. The most frustrating thing I've encountered is negotiating through a middle person who doesn't understand negotiation and mischaracterizes what I'm saying.

I no longer work with that agent.

Closing: This Is Learnable—and Scalable

I am a big fan of real estate to grow your wealth.

You can start at almost any income level, learn the business as you go, and slowly grow your portfolio over your military career until you can retire and not need to work another day in your life—if you choose.

This is not a shortcut to wealth, effortless money, or a guaranteed win. It does not return money overnight. Set your expectations accordingly.

There are many ways to get started. All of them begin the same way: get curious and learn more. Read books. Listen to podcasts. Take a course. Then start.

If I could go back and restart my military career, I would try to purchase a small multifamily property at every duty station and leverage those into more properties.

In a way, Monopoly teaches the principles: buy properties, add houses to increase rent, upgrade to hotels, and the returns become exponential.

Nobody wins Monopoly without owning properties, houses, and hotels.

Action Steps:

1. **Choose your strategy and commit to mastering it.**

   Don't dabble. Decide whether you're buying a primary residence, house hacking a 2–4 unit, or purchasing your first true rental. Then go deep on that one path. Learn the loan products. Learn the risks. Learn the numbers. Clarity creates momentum. Momentum builds leverage.

2. **Learn to speak the language of the deal.**

   Run the numbers in this chapter until they're second nature. Calculate NOI. Understand CapEx. Know what drives cap rate. Build a simple spreadsheet and pressure test a few properties on Zillow just for practice. If you can't explain cash flow and cash-on-cash return without notes, you're not ready to deploy capital. This is a business—treat it like one.

3. **Build your team before you build your portfolio.**

   Have conversations with at least two lenders and two agents. Not because you're buying tomorrow—but because you're designing the battlespace. Ask better questions. Compare loan products. Negotiate contracts. Find professionals who align with your long-term vision, not your short-term emotions. The right team multiplies your leverage. The wrong team becomes friction.

Real estate rewards those who are prepared. Educate yourself. Get aligned. Then move forward with intention.

Chapter 11

To Side Hustle or Not to Side Hustle

"The successful warrior is the average man, with laser-like focus."

—Bruce Lee

There is a reason the F-16 has different loadouts.

Some days you take off clean and light, loaded with air-to-air missiles. Your job is escort, the air-to-air shield. Protect the strikers. Keep the air picture clean. Scan the radar. Manage timelines. Kill anything that threatens the package.

Other days you're loaded heavier with HARMs and targeting pods. You are SEAD. Suppression of Enemy Air Defenses. Your entire world is surface-to-air missile systems. You are listening for radar spikes, watching for search patterns, ready to shut down a threat before it shuts down one of your friends.

And then there are days when you are the striker. Two thousand pound bombs under the wings. Target coordinates burned into your kneeboard. Everything about that sortie is about one thing: put steel on target at the exact second required.

Each of those roles demands excellence.

Each demands focus.

The problem starts when someone looks at the jet and says, "Well. . . it can technically do all three."

And they're not wrong.

The F-16 is multirole. I can carry AMRAAMs, HARMs, and bombs on the same jet. I can defend myself, suppress threats, and strike a target.

But here's what they don't put on the brochure:

If you try to do all three at the same time, you kinda suck at all three.

I remember one sortie in particular. We were configured heavy—missiles, bombs, pods—a full combat loadout. The brief had us escorting part of the way in, then picking up a SEAD responsibility if a specific SAM came active, then transitioning to striker inside the IP.

On paper, it looked efficient. In our minds we would be the heroes "shwacking" all the baddies.

In reality, it was task saturation waiting to happen.

We ingressed toward the target area at medium altitude, radar sweeping, listening to the picture call, monitoring the datalink. As escort, my world was air-to-air. Red Doritos on the scope. Timeline to commit. Fuel state of the formation. Fight the nearest alligator to the boat.

Then the call came—a surface-to-air site lighting up twenty miles south of our route. Definitely a factor threat.

Now part of my brain switched hats. SEAD.

I'm thinking WEZ rings. HARM ranges. Is it tracking? Is it search? Is it a decoy? Do I have parameters? Who else is covering it? I'm cross-checking my HARM page while still monitoring the air picture.

And then, almost simultaneously, we're two minutes from the initial point.

Striker hat.

Dogfight switch center. Master mode air-to-ground. Confirm coordinates. Confirm laser. Confirm fusing. Confirm no errors. Confirm steering cue. Confirm time on target.

Most importantly, confirm that my formation is "capture" the right target.

Three missions. One cockpit. One brain.

Nothing was going catastrophically wrong. But I could feel the degradation.

My radar cross-check got slower.

My mental picture fuzzier.

My switchology less automatic.

I wasn't failing. I just wasn't sharp.

Then my backup SEAD arrived. "Panther has the south lane."

I could strike as fragged.

Just like that, half my brain was freed.

Air-to-air until the IP.

Air-to-ground inside the IP.

SEAD covered by someone else.

And it was immediate.

My SA bubble expanded. My comms cleaned up.

My attack run felt deliberate instead of rushed.

Here's the truth that fighter pilots learn early:

We do not multitask.

We switch tasks.

And every switch costs something.

If I'm escorting, I give escort my full attention.

If I'm striking, I give strike my full attention.

If I'm suppressing a SAM, *that* becomes the nearest alligator to the boat.

Could I be escort and striker on the same sortie? Absolutely. But only if they were time de-conflicted.

Escort on the way in.
Transition at the IP.
Strike with 100% focus.
Then switch back to air-to-air on egress.

Sequential excellence.
Not simultaneous mediocrity.

Not every pilot who flies more sorties gets better. Some just get tired.
And not every pilot who carries more weapons is more lethal. Sometimes he's just overloaded.

The jet can technically do everything.
The question is whether the mission requires it.
Because when it counts—when a weapon is about to leave the jet—focus is what gets you wins.

In aviation, we don't confuse capacity with priority.

Just because the jet can carry more doesn't mean it should. Just because I can do escort, SEAD, and strike on the same sortie doesn't mean that's how we design the mission. We decide what matters most, we allocate resources accordingly, and we execute with discipline.

Somewhere along the way, our culture forgot that lesson.

In today's world, if you're not running a business on the side, flipping something, launching something, trading something, posting something, building something—it can feel like you're falling behind.

But activity is not the same as progress.

And capacity is not the same as focus.

When I first started telling people that I was working on a book about financial freedom for military members, one of the first questions I almost always got from fellow service members was:

"What side hustle are you pushing?"

I didn't take offense. I used to think the same way.

If we are all on the same (or similar) pay structures: How can you possibly get wealthy if I am not? Unless you have some side hustle you are pushing.

Here is how I respond: a side hustle can be a tool. But it is not the foundation.

Your foundation is the set of habits that you build and stick to day in and day out. Your investments, your discipline, your long-term real estate plan. A side hustle is optional jet fuel—not the engine.

What to Do with Your Free Time First

I do not advocate making a side hustle your primary strategy for wealth creation.

But I also think many of us spend our free time on mind-numbing activities that do not move us any closer to our goals. If you don't have intention with your time, someone else will gladly rent it from you—social media, Netflix, video games, doomscrolling, whatever flavor of distraction you prefer.

Having purpose with how you spend your time gives you direction.

Just like compound interest grows your portfolio exponentially, doing a little bit every day compounds your personal growth.

So, the first thing I believe you should do with your free time is learn and get curious.

Spend a few minutes every day reading something that makes you better. Listen to audiobooks and podcasts in the car and at the gym. Replace social media doomscrolling with learning about real estate, tax strategies, investing, leadership, or anything that supports your mission.

Consider this an investment in your future.

Because one day you will wake up and realize you have something most people don't: options.

The Military Rules: Don't Get Yourself in Trouble

The rules for outside employment as a military member are well established.

Yes, it's possible to hold outside employment, but it's generally limited and can get you in trouble fast if you do it the wrong way. The military can only go so far in controlling what you do with your free time, but they can control conflicts of interest, time commitments, and anything that compromises readiness or violates ethics rules.

Here's a simple rule of thumb (and as always, consult your local legal office if you're unsure):

If you are an employee of another company, or you are beholden to anyone else under a contract, you're probably in "outside employment" territory.

So don't do that.

Your commander will not have any input if you decide to invest money into an index fund making a steady return, but will probably have a lot to say if you are caught working at a fast food drive through in the evenings.

Instead, look for passive investing opportunities—things that build wealth without creating a second boss. Real estate is a great example.

So Why Even Talk About Side Hustles?

Because not all "side hustles" are created equal.

There are plenty of ways to earn money in your free time that don't trigger the rules for outside employment—and honestly, you may already be doing things you could get paid for.

There's a growing company that pays people to walk with senior citizens and provide companionship. You'd be providing a heart-warming service, getting exercise, and getting paid.

There are companies paying freelancers to create beautiful PowerPoint presentations through apps like Fiverr. Becoming a PowerPoint wizard will help you in the military and can also pay you on the side.

Another great option is to spend time learning how to start and run a business—without starting one yet. If you spend your free time on active duty learning how businesses work, you'll be prepared when you retire or separate.

That's exactly what I did.

My Side Hustle Journey: I Tried a Lot. Most Didn't Work

I attended a business-planning workshop one weekend and learned a ton about how to build a business plan. Then I set a goal:

Find a business that would make me an extra $10,000 per month with only four hours of my time per week to run it. It seemed like a good BHAG.

My first idea: laser engraving.

I spent a week researching and building the plan—capacity, machine costs, lease options, staffing, startup costs, pricing, margins, overhead. I planned every detail that I could think of from employee benefits to how I would market the products.

After many iterations, I couldn't make it work. I could get to $10k a month but with a bigger time commitment than I was willing to give as an active-duty member.

Second idea: mobile car detailing.

Same process. Same conclusion. Time commitment too high.

Third idea: a patch-making company—lease sewing machines, hire help, produce squadron patches.

This one got the closest, mostly because I already knew people doing it and knew military spouses who wanted in. But even then, I decided not to pursue it.

Was I discouraged? Absolutely.

But I also remembered something that has served me my entire life: in all things, we either win or we learn.

Failure only happens when you quit.

So, I took a break, satisfied that the month of planning wasn't wasted—it was training.

Then I picked up a book on Airbnb.

And that's when things changed.

The Side Hustle That Worked: Airbnb (and Why It Worked)

I was fascinated with short-term rentals. I got curious. I read. I researched.

About a month later, I launched my first short-term rental using rental arbitrage: I rented a four-bedroom house for $2,400 per month, got permission from the landlord, furnished it, and listed it on Airbnb.

I furnished the entire house for a few thousand dollars using Facebook Marketplace, yard sales, PCS sales, thrift stores, and Goodwill. Here, I "hustled."

At the end of year one, that one property brought in $84,000 in revenue. It cost about $50,000 after rent, utilities, insurance, furnishings, and operating costs like cleanings.

I cleared around $30,000.

And while I was still a long way from $10,000 per month, after the initial setup I was spending less than two hours per week managing it.

Why?

Because I treated it like a system.

I set up automations for everything: messaging, cleaners, door codes, house manual, calendar management, pricing strategy—everything that could be systematized, I systematized.

In year two I added three more properties and hired a part-time college student to resupply the houses, check in on guests, respond to issues, and help set up furniture.

By the end of year three, I had fourteen units across Phoenix—and I was still spending less than four hours per week on them. That time was mostly higher-level work: bookkeeping, meeting landlords, managing the portfolio.

I also purchased a property, so I owned one unit and still used rental arbitrage in others.

Over time, the profit per unit started to decline as Airbnb became more popular and competition increased. That's how free markets work: excess profits get competed down toward the average.

So I adapted—moved some units to mid-term rentals for traveling nurses, closed others as regulations changed, and kept only the units that still made sense.

Some properties were awesome. I lost money on others.

Every time I lost money, I viewed it as tuition.

And I never risked more than I was willing to lose.

One more note: before I started, I took my plan to the base legal office. They analyzed it and gave me a written letter stating that because it was rental activity, it was acceptable.

Later, when I grew the company, I checked again. They approved it again.

I am not telling you that you're "cleared hot" to go do whatever you want.

I'm telling you that it's often easier than you think to outline your plan to the legal office and get clarity before you create a problem.

Speaking of Fear—This Part Matters

As I started building a portfolio of Airbnb's around my city, I caught pointed jokes from squadron members. Comments about being a "slum lord." Jokes about getting crushed in real estate. Little jabs disguised as humor.

They weren't really aimed at me.

They were aimed at what I represented.

Anytime you start doing something different—especially something that might work—people who haven't moved yet feel it. And if they don't have the courage to join you, the next easiest move is to mock you.

That's where fear shows up—not the fear of hard work, but the fear of being judged while you're still building. The fear of looking stupid before you look smart. The fear of being the guy who tried. . . and failed.

But here's what I noticed.

As momentum grew, the jokes changed.

Instead of making fun of my Goodwill-furnished short-term rentals, people started asking how I was doing it. They started asking if they could do it too. They started offering to buy me coffee to "pick my brain."

Same people. New tone.

I didn't build it overnight. I built it over months and years—slow growth, study, execution, and a willingness to keep moving even while people laughed.

That's the cost of doing anything worth doing: you have to be willing to endure the noise long enough to become undeniable.

The Real Lesson: Focus Before Hustle

Here's the part most people miss. The point of this chapter is not "don't side hustle." The point is: don't dilute your primary mission.

A side hustle is only useful if it does one of three things:

1. It increases your income without destroying your time.
2. It builds a skill that will compound for decades.
3. It creates leverage—systems, assets, or ownership.

If it doesn't do at least one of those, it's probably just noise. Some people "hustle" because they're building something meaningful. Other people hustle because they're afraid.

Afraid of being average.

Afraid of falling behind.

Afraid of missing out.

Afraid of what people will think if they're not grinding.

That kind of hustle is expensive.

It costs your energy. Your family. Your sleep. Your training. Your primary job performance. And the worst part?

You can do all that work and still not move the needle.

Focus is what gets you wins.

Not that you can't do other tasks at other times. You absolutely can. But when it counts, you need to concentrate your effort on the nearest alligator to the boat.

Sequential excellence. Not simultaneous mediocrity.

A Note for Military Spouses

The idea of a side hustle can also be powerful for military spouses.

After living overseas for multiple assignments, I truly believe the military spouse community is one of the most talented, resilient, and underleveraged communities I have ever encountered.

If you needed something done—and done right—overseas, you asked the military spouse network. No kidding.

If your spouse wants to put their talents toward a money-making venture, I'm cheering for them. There is real opportunity there.

If we combined the efforts of military spouses the world over, we could move mountains.

Treat Side Hustle Money Like Jet Fuel

If you do decide to earn extra money on the side—through real estate, investing, a business, or anything else—have a plan for the money before you begin.

First, don't treat it like normal income and inflate your lifestyle around it.

You can PCS. You can deploy. The market can shift. Regulations can change. If you build your life around side hustle income, that reliance can implode.

Instead, treat it like extra jet fuel in your financial freedom engine.

Use it to pay off debt faster. Build reserves. Fund investments. Buy back your future.

And if you structure things correctly, you may also unlock tax strategies that let you reinvest and keep more of what you earn.

Closing: You're One Action Step Away

There are so many opportunities right now for people willing to put in the work.

Every day, millionaires are being made across the world, and they all have one thing in common: they got started.

Most of us don't lack talent, knowledge, or capacity.

Most of us lack courage.

The courage to step into the unknown and risk looking foolish.

I was the same way.

When I retired and started making social media videos, I had no idea where it would lead. I just stopped caring what people thought and started taking action. That page took off and eventually led to this book.

You are one action step away from changing your entire life.

Action Steps:

1. **Define your primary mission.**

   Write down your number one financial objective for the next 12 months. Not five. Not three. One.

   Is it paying off debt? Building a six-month emergency fund? Buying your first rental property? Investing consistently? Growing a business?

   If everything is important, nothing is. Choose your primary mission and protect it.

2. **Audit your free time honestly.**

   For one week, track how you actually spend your discretionary time.

   - How many hours went to learning?
   - How many went to building?
   - How many went to scrolling?

   You don't need a side hustle. You need intentional use of time. Replace just 30 minutes a day of passive consumption with focused development and watch what compounds.

3. **Add only what supports the mission.**

   Before starting any side hustle, ask one question: Does this accelerate my primary mission—or distract from it?

   If it builds skill, cash flow, network, or leverage aligned with your long-term plan, proceed.

   If it feeds ego, comparison, or fear of missing out—abort.

   Sequential excellence. Not simultaneous mediocrity.

Chapter 12

Intro to Advanced Strategies

"The more you know, the more you realize you do not know."

—Aristotle

When you show up to your first fighter squadron, you think the coolest part of the jet is the advanced weapons and tactics.

The missiles. The bombs. The pods. The four-ship counterair missions.

You don't show up thinking about basic maneuvers.

But that's where it starts.

Before you ever employ an advanced weapon system, before you ever brief complex tactics, before you ever carry the heavy ordnance—you spend months learning how to fight the jet.

BFM. Basic Fighter Maneuvers.

One v one. No fancy sensors. No datalink. No formation. No distractions.

Just you, another jet, and the sky.

You've made it through pilot training. You survived the B-course. You're in an operational squadron now. And instead of flying large force exercises or employing advanced weapons, you're fighting another jet in a clean configuration like it's 1975.

You already passed this phase in the basic course. This feels like going backward.

I remember early in my flying career watching more senior pilots taxi out with a combat configuration—targeting pods, smart weapons, live ordnance—while I stepped to the jet with nothing but training rounds and a clean wing.

I wanted what they had.

I wanted the advanced tactics. The complex briefs. The "real" missions.

One day I asked my instructor why I couldn't fly the Defensive Counterair mission the next week.

He didn't laugh. He didn't lecture.

He just said, "Because you haven't mastered the jet yet."

At the time, that felt frustrating.

I could land the jet. I could refuel. I could fly formation. I passed all of my checkrides. What more did he want?

He wanted discipline. And instinct.

He wanted me to be able to fly the jet at the edge of its envelope without thinking about it. And safely.

Because advanced capability amplifies whatever is underneath it.

If the foundation is solid, advanced tactics make you lethal.

If the foundation is shaky, advanced weapons just make you dangerous.

There's a reason we don't drop a brand-new wingman into the most complex mission on day one.

Not because we're gatekeeping. And not because he doesn't have what it takes.

Because we're protecting him—and everyone flying with him.

Later in my career, when I was instructing in advanced tactics, techniques, and procedures—the upgraded weapons, the complex mission sets—I understood.

> Those tools come with weight.
>
> Responsibility. Consequence. Accountability.
>
> And if you skip the fundamentals, the jet has a way of exposing you.
>
> Advanced capability without foundational discipline is dangerous.
>
> That lesson never left me.

And it applies far beyond the cockpit.

When it comes to money, advanced strategies can look like those upgraded weapons and tactics—powerful, complex, and exciting. Tax arbitrage. Asset protection. Life insurance strategies. Leveraged investments. Layered trusts and LLCs. Things that sound like they belong in a hedge fund pitch deck.

It's tempting to want access to them immediately.

But just like in aviation, advanced capability amplifies whatever foundation you've built.

If your fundamentals are solid—disciplined spending, consistent investing, controlled debt, strong cash reserves—advanced strategies can accelerate your trajectory.

If your fundamentals are shaky, advanced strategies don't fix the problem.

They magnify it.

Some people reading this book may feel overwhelmed at the thought of committing even 5% of their salary to a retirement account they won't touch for 40 years. Every dollar already feels stretched. Debt may be creeping up. If that's you, I see you—and I've been there. Your mission right now is fundamentals. Meet with your base financial advisors. Build a simple How I Spend My Money Plan. Strengthen your foundation.

Others may be thinking, "Okay, tell me something I don't know."

Maybe you've been investing 5% into Roth TSP since day one. Maybe you opened a Roth IRA early and are now maxing it out. Maybe you even have a "fun investing" account where you drop in $9 every time you skip the Big-Dumb-Coffee-Cup.

You've built your foundation; your basic fighter maneuvers.

This chapter is for that person.

The one who has mastered the basics and is ready to responsibly explore what comes next.

This is not about shortcuts.

It's about earned tools.

In the pages ahead, we'll cover advanced tax strategies, leverage concepts, life insurance structures, and other vehicles that can expand your financial capability—if you're ready for them.

This chapter is meant to whet your appetite and heighten your curiosity about what lies beyond your current financial horizon.

And just like in aviation, we'll start with something that may feel "outside the box"—because sometimes the most overlooked strategic advantage is not a new weapon system. . .

It's where you choose to call home.

Advanced Strategy #1: Choose Your State of Residence on Purpose

Military members often have the advantage of moving around from state to state and they can typically choose which state they want to call home—within reason and rules, of course.

Over your career you can potentially save thousands, even tens of thousands. . .which can compound into millions. . .over the course of a 20-year service career by choosing the state that is right for you.

I've seen this concept utilized to great advantage and the strategy is sound.

But with anything, check your current state rules and analyze your own situation before making any major life changes.

Most states require that you register there within 10–90 days of moving. . .unless you are in the military and stationed there. You can keep your residency in another state while living where you are stationed.

Seems logical.

But most people don't view this as a wealth strategy, and it absolutely is.

I love every state I have visited—and I have been to all 50—for different reasons. I'm not throwing shade on any state, but here's a real-life example of how you might benefit from changing residency.

Let's say you were born in Washington DC and you join the military. Your first assignment is Tyndall AFB in Florida. You're excited to be near a beach and the ocean calls to you like Moana. I love it.

You have options:

Option A: Remain a DC resident, pay taxes, vote, register your vehicle, and keep your home of record there in case you want to move back there someday after retirement.

Option B: Change your residency to Florida.

What's the difference?

The District of Columbia has a graduated income tax rate. Florida does not have a state income tax.

Over a 20-year career-and then into retirement-that can be a six-figure lifetime swing depending on rank, income, and how you structure your life. For a full 20-year breakdown comparing state tax impact, see Appendix.

Now before you start hating on the District of Columbia: Georgia, Nebraska, Utah, Rhode Island, and Delaware are not exactly giving out hugs either. Most states impose at least some form of income tax.

If you decide to claim residency in a state, make sure you learn the rules, check with your local finance office, and mostly: do your own research.

Then, once those savings start rolling in, don't go spend it all on big dumb coffee cups—invest at least a portion of it to pour jet fuel into your investments.

Common Pitfalls

Here are some common areas where people find themselves in trouble-usually not intentionally, but the government and the numbers don't care if it was a mistake.

- Confusing Federal tax with State tax.
- Confusing Income tax with Sales tax.
- Assuming "my home state has no income tax, so none of my income is taxable anywhere."

A common trap: a military member is a resident of a no-income-tax state, PCSs to a state with income tax, and starts renting a home out in that new state. They assume they "don't pay state taxes," because that's been true for them personally.

Then they discover rental income can be taxed based on where the property is located, and now they have filing requirements they didn't plan for.

I'm not trying to scare you. I'm trying to save you.

This is why you verify. This is why you document. This is why you don't guess.

Advanced Strategy #2: Taxes—Stop Treating Them Like Weather

This is a fun topic. Truly, I think taxes are fascinating.

But I also think that no other word in the English language can make more eyes glaze over and people tune out faster than the word taxes.

As Benjamin Franklin said: "nothing in life is certain except death and taxes."

I get the premise, but I don't fully agree with the vibe.

Yes, taxes are part of life. But there are many things you can do to potentially affect your tax bill in a positive way. So, I prefer to approach taxes from a *proactive* rather than *reactive* point of view.

For most of my life I did what I was told to do: January through March I gathered receipts, W-2s, 1099s, dumped it into TurboTax, and crossed my fingers.

And when I got a fat refund check I felt like I won. Then I had the realization: "Wait. . .why am I getting money back?"

Because I overpaid.

Okay, so what did the government do with the money I overpaid? They used it. They sat on it. They did literally anything except invest it for me.

So I started asking: What if instead of overpaying them, I kept that money, invested it—even somewhere boring like a high-yield savings account—and then paid what I owed at the end?

Is that possible? Yep. To an extent anyway.

Here's the Mindset Shift

Most people do taxes in the past. At the end of the year they look backward and calculate what they owe the government. Then feel lucky if they get a refund because they *overpaid* the government during the year.

I want you to do taxes in the ***Future***.

Do your taxes in the future. "Wait, can you do that?"

Absolutely.

And it changes your behavior when you start to understand what is impacting your tax bill. You know your regular annual income with probably 99% accuracy. And you can estimate revenue from other sources with pretty close accuracy. Now, at the start of the year, do your taxes for the year ahead.

Calculate how much you will make and how much you will owe in taxes. Then set your withholding rate so you don't overpay. Then, take it to the next level and look for ways to cut down your taxes.

The Uncomfortable Truth About "Safe" Advice

I once asked a CPA: "I'm paying so much in taxes. Is there anything I can do to reduce the burden?"

He said, "Nope. That's just your tax bracket." I trusted him. And to this day I believe he believed it.

But it wasn't true. There are many ways to arrange your financial affairs to capitalize on opportunities that lawmakers put into the tax code.

Here's the more accurate statement:

Many tax pros are trained to be conservative. They'd rather you overpay than take a position they can't easily defend. That's not evil. It's just the "55 in the right lane" approach. My favorite analogy:

Your CPA says, "The speed limit is 65, so if we go 55 in the right lane, then we never have to worry about possible getting a ticket." This is true.

But the speed limit is 65. If you go 65, document it, and follow the rules, you can also never have to worry. So what does "65" look like?

It looks like using **well-defined tax benefits** the way they were intended.

Let me be crystal clear: do not ever cheat on your taxes. Period. That is stupid.

But paying more taxes than you are required to pay is also stupid, in my opinion. So, the goal becomes: pay exactly what you owe. Not a dollar more.

"Loopholes" Aren't Always Accidents

A lot of so-called loopholes are incentives. They exist on purpose to encourage certain behavior. Work with a tax professional to use those incentives to maximize the amount of money you put in your pocket every year.

A few examples:

- Short-term rental participation and deductions
- Augusta Rule (renting your home to your business for up to 14 days)
- Backdoor Roth contributions (Chapter 8)
- Home office use for your business
- Energy-related investments with incentives

This chapter is not an exhaustive tax manual. But it is a permission slip to stop being passive.

Advanced Strategy #3: Use Real Estate Tax Strategy (STR + Depreciation) Like Jet Fuel

We covered real estate earlier. Here's where you get to double down.

If you purchase a short-term rental property (Airbnb/VRBO), you can sometimes use depreciation strategies to reduce taxable income.

This is where people start calling it "unfair."

It's not unfair. It's the tax code.

The government wants more housing. It wants investment. It wants economic activity. So it built incentives.

Cost Segregation (How the Math Works in Real Life)

Example: you buy a property for $500,000.

The county estimates the land value at $100,000 (20%). That means the structure is roughly $400,000.

A cost segregation study identifies components—roof, flooring, fixtures, HVAC, appliances, furniture, etc.—and assigns depreciation schedules.

Let's say the study identifies $175,000 of components eligible for accelerated treatment.

Now you have a deduction tool you can potentially use to reduce taxable income—sometimes dramatically. You could use this to reset your military income to $0 for probably more than one year and pay essentially no taxes.

This is why real estate isn't just "rent minus mortgage."

It's an entire strategy stack.

The Gotchas (Read This Twice)

This is where I slow you down like an instructor pilot.

To use short-term rental losses to offset W-2 income, you have to follow specific rules. This is not "wing it" territory.

The STR must meet certain thresholds (like average stay), and you must meet material participation tests. Mixed use and house hacking can affect the eligible basis. Bonus depreciation percentages change with law and timing. Placed-in-service dates matter.

This is why documentation matters.

You don't need to memorize the tax code. But you do need to treat this like a real strategy, not a TikTok hack. Consult with a tax professional before you utilize any advanced tax strategies; they will pay for themselves in the long run.

The "Check in Your Hand" Visualization

Here's how I think about it:

At the end of the year, you write a big fat check for what you owe in taxes.

Once that check is written (and I encourage you to physically write it out), look at it, hold it in your hand, then decide who to hand it to.

Pretend that sitting across the table from you are two people—an IRS agent and a real estate agent.

One of them is getting your check.

If you give it to the real estate agent, they're going to find you a property that pays you cash flow for the rest of your life.

If you give it to the IRS agent, they're going to give you a receipt stamped "Paid."

Now you get to choose.

Advanced Strategy #4: Build Legal and Clean "Business Deductions" (Home Office + Augusta Rule)

Once you have real business activity in the eyes of the IRS, you can also take deductions related to that business.

If you have a home office, you can deduct it.

Don't make this stuff up. Document it well and take exactly what is authorized.

If your office is a repurposed closet that is 4 feet by 10 feet, then claim 40 square feet. It's better than nothing.

The Augusta Rule (One of My Favorites)

If you have events related to your business, you can host them at your house and rent your house back to your business for up to 14 days per year at a fair rental price.

That income can be excluded under the rule if done correctly.

Documentation is key.

Document what the meeting is about, who attends, agenda items, start/stop times, and outcomes. I treat it like a military TDY. I write an after-action report, and it lives in my tax file.

Think of it this way: you were going to rent a space anyway to host your annual strategic vision and planning meeting. Instead of paying premium rates at a local hotel conference center, you can rent your own house back to your business for that event at a fair market rate.

Call around, get quotes, document the fair rate.

Then invoice your business.

Your business gets the write-off. You get the check, potentially tax-free if structured correctly. If the going rate in your area is $1,000 for a commercial daily rental space, then you can be looking at writing 14 checks for $1,000 each for each event you host.

That is $14,000 that you get to receive tax-free because it is not considered rental income, and your business gets to deduct it from the top line revenue.

It's one of those "wait, you can do that?" things.

Yes. If you do it right.

Advanced Strategy #5: Life Insurance as a Wealth Protection Tool (and When It Becomes a Wealth Tool)

When it comes to life insurance, I've always liked the adage: "a little more than you think you need, a little earlier than you think you need it."

The military provides baseline coverage. I took advantage of it. Then when I got married and had kids, I added additional policies.

Each time I added a policy, I re-evaluated my needs and projected the "what-if" outcomes if something happened to me—and to my wife.

Here's the simple way I think about coverage:

1. I want this policy to pay off any debts.
2. I want this policy to replace the income that I would have made each year if I were still alive.

My personal equation for minimum life insurance was this: Debt payoff + (annual family spend ÷ 5%). I assumed that my family could live on 5% interest when invested wisely, without having to ever touch the principal amount.

Example:

- \$350,000 mortgage
- \$45,000 cars
- \$5,000 credit cards

Debt = \$400,000

If my family lives comfortably on \$100,000/year, then \$100,000 is 5% of \$2,000,000. So, my coverage target was \$2.4 M in life insurance.

Re-evaluate every few years. Life changes.

Term Versus Permanent (and the Honest Truth)

Term is simple. It covers you for a period, then goes away.

Permanent is more complex. Whole and universal categories. This is a world where you should consult a professional.

For most of my life I used term because it was easy.

Later, I learned more about whole life policies designed properly—and the idea of using them strategically.

That leads to the next advanced strategy.

Advanced Strategy #6: Infinite Banking Concept (IBC)—Advanced, Powerful, and Not a Shortcut

The Infinite Banking Concept (IBC) was introduced to me through the book *Becoming Your Own Banker* by Nelson Nash.

I can't do justice to that book in a few paragraphs. If this topic interests you—and it should—go read Nelson's book. But until I found his book I had no idea that this existed. A second resource is *What Would The Rockefellers Do?* By Garrett Gunderson and Michael Isom.

IBC is complex and simple at the same time. Confusing at first. Elegant once you understand the principles.

Here's the concept in normal language:

You put money into a properly structured whole life policy.

Over time, it builds cash value. You can borrow against that cash value. Then you pay it back—with interest—to your own "family bank."

And the key feature that makes people's eyebrows go up:

Your policy can continue to grow while you borrow against it, depending on structure. This is not "free money." It's a long-term system.

It requires patience. It requires commitment. It requires understanding.

Why It Matters

Money is not stationary. It's flowing. It's changing. And you're always paying interest—either explicitly, or through opportunity cost.

Buy a car with financing? You pay interest to a bank.

Buy a car with cash? You pay interest in what that money could've earned elsewhere.

IBC is a strategy to keep your money working, while also using it—and to recapture interest payments inside your own system.

The "I'm Not Selling You This" Section

This is not me telling you to go buy a policy tomorrow.

This is me telling you: this exists, it's used by high-net-worth families, and it can be a powerful tool for generational wealth if you learn it and implement it responsibly.

Most of these policies take time—often years—to mature before they become meaningfully useful.

This is BFM again. Go learn it. Then you earn it.

Advanced Strategy #7: Up-Leveling—Buying Back Time and Reducing Friction

I said it earlier: I do not believe most people will simply cut their way to millionaire status or financial freedom.

You must adopt the mindset of someone who lives financially free, make conscious decisions about how you use your money, and implement your plan with discipline.

Then something interesting happens.

You start to realize you're winning.

Maybe you're not fully there yet, but you're running the numbers and you can see the glidepath. If you continue this way, you'll be there in a few years.

So when do you start enjoying the fruits of your labor?

In my opinion: **throughout the journey**.

Financial freedom is a journey, not a destination.

I never woke up one morning and said, "Okay, there it is. I made it. I am now officially financially free."

And honestly, I'm glad. Because if my purpose was only to reach the destination, what would I do after?

Life is about purpose, meaning, and what we do with our time.

So, with that in mind, I recommend looking for your "pain points" and solving them through creative problem-solving.

The same proactive approach you're using financially can be applied to the things that bring stress, pain, annoyance, or fights with your spouse.

Which brings me to one of the funniest and most life-changing "advanced strategies" I've ever used.

The Dinner War

I was on a Zoom call with my wife and our marriage counselor.

We've been married for 20 years. She is my person. And I'm not too proud to say I did a lot of things wrong over the years. Getting help made a huge difference.

That day we were discussing what caused the most stress in our lives.

And I chuckle thinking about it now.

We were laser focused on: who's turn it is to make dinner.

Sounds silly. It wasn't.

With four children ages two to six and both of us working, it felt like there was never a spare moment.

Someone had to grocery shop. Someone had to plan meals. Someone had to cook. Because we weren't planning, we ended up ordering takeout or throwing something together last minute—usually not very healthy—and it was causing stress for everyone.

I get stressed remembering four cranky hungry kids while I'm trying to make the mac and cheese boil faster.

Our counselor asked, "How could you solve this differently?"

And something clicked.

"I guess we could hire someone to cook."

The words felt forced. My internal voice immediately started listing reasons it wouldn't work—mostly cost.

But I tried to keep an open mind.

How much money would I trade to remove one of the greatest stress points in our life?

So, like any decent CFO, I ran the numbers and came up with a plan.

"Honey, I'm going to put an ad on Care.com for someone to come over four to five hours per week for $100 total. They'll come Monday for three hours. Groceries delivered at the same time. They'll make four healthy family meals and salads for lunches. Then they come back Thursday for an hour or two and make two more meals and we'll get fresh produce for the weekend delivered then."

"Until now we've been spending $400 per week on groceries, wasting food, and planning like amateurs."

"And here's the kicker—I'm going to give them a grocery budget of $300."

My wife looked at me side-eyed. "Can you even feed us all for that much?"

"I don't know. But if she buys heads of lettuce and bags of carrots instead of pre-mix salads, we'll stop wasting money. If she buys a whole chicken and makes two to three meals out of it instead of packages of chicken breasts, it'll go further."

My wife smiled.

"I love it. Even if it costs a little more, I'm willing to pay someone to not have these fights anymore. I'll get to spend that time playing with the kids instead of stressing—I'm in."

That evening I ran the job ad and put my phone away.

The next day I had 42 applicants.

And our life changed.

We found a wonderful woman—an empty nester—who didn't need the money but loved the company and loved cooking in a busy kitchen with four little ones running around. She was ready to be the cool grandma before her kids had kids.

She fed our family healthier meals, helped us plan, reduced waste, and removed one of the biggest points of friction in our home.

And here's the punchline: we had essentially hired a chef for $0 above what we were already spending because we fixed the waste and the chaos.

We ate healthier. We fought less. We had more time. We felt peace.

To this day we still use this model.

Cooking healthy dinner for four small children may not be your pain point.

But whatever you're seeking to overcome, you are one decision away from living an entirely different life.

And you don't have to do it alone.

Action Steps:

1. **Confirm your foundation before you go "advanced."**

   Write down your current fundamentals scorecard:

   - Are you consistently investing?
   - Do you have cash reserves?
   - Is your debt controlled?
   - Do you have a working *How I Spend My Money* plan?

   If not, your advanced strategy is simple: build the base. No shame. That's wisdom.

2. **Pick one advanced strategy and go one layer deeper this week.**

   Not six. One.

   Choose the strategy that fits your season: home state residency, tax planning, STR strategy, deductions, life insurance coverage, or IBC.

   Your task: read for 30 minutes a day for seven days and write down the top 10 questions you need answered before you act.

3. **Solve one pain point with a "buy-back-time" experiment.**

   List the top three stressors in your life. Pick one.

   Design a 30-day experiment that reduces friction: meal planning, cleaning, childcare swaps, automations, outsourcing, systems.

   Your goal is not luxury. Your goal is leverage. More peace. More presence. More capacity.

Conclusion

"In the end, it is not the years in your life that count. It is the life in your years."

—Abraham Lincoln

It wasn't dramatic.

There were no emergency procedures.

No mayday calls.

No fireworks over enemy territory.

Just a normal sortie.

I had thousands of hours in the jet by then. I knew the cockpit so well I could reach every switch without looking. I could feel when the engine was slightly off before any gauge told me. The jet didn't intimidate me anymore. It felt. . . familiar.

Like an extension of my nervous system.

We briefed, stepped, taxied. I ran my hand across the canopy rail like I always did. The crew chief gave the same thumbs-up he'd given a hundred times before.

I remember thinking—almost casually—this will be the last time I do this.

Not because anything was wrong.

Just because seasons change.

The takeoff was smooth. Rotation at the exact airspeed. Positive rate. Gear up. We converged smoothly into formation without thought. I glanced over at my wingman—a young lieutenant with the same fire in his eyes I used to have.

I remembered being him.

Back then, I measured progress in qualifications.

Four-ship upgrade.

Instructor pilot.

Mission commander.

Deployments. Combat hours.

Each one felt like leveling up in a game.

But somewhere along the way, the scoreboard changed.

On that final sortie, I wasn't thinking about flight hours or awards. I wasn't calculating how many bombs I had dropped or how many sorties I had led.

I was thinking about alignment.

Did I live this deliberately?

Did I lead well?

Did I build something that lasts beyond me?

The jet felt effortless that day. The mechanics were automatic. The tactics were instinct.

What wasn't automatic was the awareness that it would end.

We climbed into the working area and ran through the tactical portion of the sortie. I listened to the younger pilots on the radio. Their voices carried the same edge I once had—a mix of adrenaline and ambition.

They were chasing milestones.

I smiled because I knew something they didn't yet.

The milestones matter. But not for the reasons you think.

It's not the prestige.
It's not the qualification.
It's not even the mission success.

It's the discipline you built getting there.
It's the character formed in the repetition.
It's the habits that followed you home.

On recovery, I flew a wide pattern and extended the downwind just a little longer than necessary. Not unsafe. Not dramatic. Just. . . intentional.

I wanted one more look.

As I turned base to final, the runway filled the HUD. The landing was smooth. Aerobrake. Nose down. Light tap on the brakes.

Taxi speed.

Clear the runway.

That was it.

No music. No ceremony. No dramatic soundtrack.

Just a jet cooling down on the ramp and a chapter closing quietly. My family waiting by the sunshade beaming at me with pride.

And here's what surprised me most:

When I shut the engine down for the last time, I didn't feel loss.

I felt gratitude.

Because I realized something important.

The scorecard had changed.

Early in my career, success meant flying fighters.
At the end, success meant living in a way that I would be proud of when I couldn't fly anymore.
The jet was never the point.
The discipline was.
The responsibility was.
The people were.
But most of all: the alignment between who I said I wanted to be. . . and who I actually became.

When I shut down the F-16 Fighting Falcon for the last time, I did not think about individual sorties.

I thought about patterns developed over an entire career. Preparation. Discipline. Execution. Debrief. Repeat.

This book was never about money. It was about alignment. Mindset matching the big vision for our lives and executing to bring that vision to life.

Here is what we built together.

Part I: Getting Started

Mission Planning for Your Financial Life

Before we ever talk about growth, we talk about control.

In **Chapter 1**, we started where all good missions start: awareness.

You learned that most financial problems are not math problems. They are attention problems. You gave every dollar orders. You replaced "budgeting" with "How I Spend My Money." You moved from passive spending to active command.

That's not financial strategy. That's identity shift.

In **Chapter 2**, we targeted backward. Retirement stopped being a vague future event and became a mission with defined roles: TSP, Roth IRA, matching contributions, automatic escalation. You learned that the government match is not a suggestion—it's a contract. And contracts matter.

You saw clearly that you cannot go back in time and reclaim missed contributions. In aviation terms: runway behind you is useless.

In **Chapter 3**, we confronted drift. Debt is rarely catastrophic at first. It's quiet deviation. Small rationalizations. Incremental compromise. You learned that discipline is not about never making mistakes—it's about catching deviation early and correcting before it compounds.

Aviate. Navigate. Communicate. Fly the jet first; know where you are going; then communicate it.

With debt: stop digging. Build the ladder. Climb steadily.

In **Chapter 4**, we talked about resilience. Taxes. Emergency funds. Setbacks. The "Spin." The reset.

You learned that emergency funds are not pessimism—they are professionalism. Taxes are not something to react to in April; they are something to plan in January.

You stopped being surprised by money and started anticipating it.

Part I wasn't flashy. It was foundational. Because advanced capability without discipline is dangerous.

A Letter to My 25-Year-Old-Self

Hey L-T Motor,

You think you are behind.

You won't say it out loud, but you feel it.

You are newly married. You are proud to wear the uniform. You are flying the jet that you dreamed about since you were a kid. And yet, underneath all of that, you are carrying something heavy.

Fifty thousand dollars in debt.

You smile when people talk about investing and retirement, but you quietly assume they are talking to someone else. Someone further ahead. Someone who started earlier. Someone who hasn't made the mistakes you think you made.

You smile because if there is one thing you hate it is feeling like you are clueless. Yet, in this financial stuff you mostly are. It is not your fault. You will get there.

Let me tell you something clearly: you are not behind. You are early.

Right now you think financial freedom is about money. But it's not.

It's about ownership. Ownership of your decisions. Ownership of your habits. And ownership of your future.

True financial freedom is being able to do whatever you want with your time, without having to stress about money or trade your time for someone else's money in order to get by.

You don't need a side hustle. You don't need a genius-level investing strategy. You don't need to impress anyone.

You need discipline.

Start small. Five percent. That's it.

Open the Roth TSP. Contribute consistently. Build a simple plan for how you spend your money. Stop pretending it will work itself out.

It won't.

But you will.

Start being proactive about your financial life like you are about your flying.

You and your new wife are going to learn together. More importantly, you are going to grow together. Not at the same rate, so don't expect that. But in your own time and in your own ways.

You're going to have conversations that feel uncomfortable at first. You'll realize that being aligned is more important than your income. You'll fight about things that don't matter and eventually learn how to fight for each other instead of against each other.

You're going to discover that stress isn't caused by a lack of money. It is caused by a lack of clarity.

Clarity gives you confidence. Confidence gives you momentum. Momentum changes your trajectory.

You are also going to wrestle with fear. Not tangible fears like flying, heights, or war.

Fear of looking foolish. Fear of starting something new. Fear of failing. Fear of people judging you.

Here's the truth: most of the people you're worried about are too busy worrying about themselves to matter to your long-term plan.

And the ones who do judge you? They are usually defending their own inaction.

Step out anyway.

You will start businesses that don't work. You will invest in things that tank. You will have ideas that fail.

None of that will define you.

What will define you is that you kept learning. You kept showing up.

You refused to stay average just because average was comfortable.

And listen carefully to this next part: success is not the size of your portfolio.

It is alignment between who you say you are and how you actually live your life.

At 25 you think the scorecard is the next promotion, the flight hours, the qualifications, and your income.

Later you will realize that the scorecard is different.

It's how you spent time with and treated your wife and family.

It is whether your kids feel safe around you.

It's whether you had the courage to live deliberately.

It's whether your money served your values—or replaced them.

You will make more money than you think. You will also realize money doesn't fix misalignment.

So, build your life in the right order: Character first. Marriage second. Discipline third. Money fourth.

If you get that order wrong, everything feels unstable—even when the numbers look good.

There will come a day when you sit quietly in the jet, late in your career, and realize how fast it all went.

You won't be thinking about debt. You won't be thinking about your net worth. You'll be thinking about whether you lived intentionally.

So, start now.

Not when the debt is gone.

Not when you make Major.

Not when the kids are older.

Not when the house is paid off.

Now.

You don't need to sprint. You need to commit. You are capable of more than you believe right now.

Not because you are extraordinary. But because you are willing to learn.

One more thing: be grateful earlier.

You are flying fighters.

You are married to a woman who believes in you.

You are healthy.

You are surrounded by people who would take a bullet for you. Don't wait until you're older to appreciate that.

Live it now.

I'm proud of you. You're going to be okay. Now go build something that matters.

—Shawn

Part II: Purpose

Why You're Building Any of This in the First Place

In **Chapter 5**, you defined Mission, Vision, and Core Values.

Money without direction creates drift.

Wealth without purpose creates emptiness.

You clarified who you are becoming—not just what you are accumulating.

In **Chapter 6**, you translated vision into goals. Not vague hopes. Not motivation. Systems. Calendar blocking. Anti-goals. Sequential excellence.

You learned that focus wins fights.

In **Chapter 7**, you confronted lifestyle. What does "living the dream" actually mean? Is it consumption? Or is it time autonomy? Is it status? Or is it alignment?

You began measuring success differently.

Not by what you show.

But by how you live.

Part II was about internal alignment. Because financial freedom without personal clarity just builds a bigger cage.

Part III: Growth

From Stability to Acceleration

In **Chapter 8**, we zoomed out. The Long Game. Compounding. Time as your greatest ally. You learned that small, disciplined actions—repeated—become exponential.

The Big-Dumb-Coffee-Cup wasn't about coffee.

It was about trajectory.

In **Chapter 9**, we broke down Investing 101. Risk. Volatility. Index funds. Asset allocation. You stopped fearing markets and started understanding them.

Because fear thrives in ignorance.

In **Chapter 10**, we entered real estate. Leverage. Risk. Location. Cash flow. Appreciation. Taxes. You learned that leverage is powerful—but unforgiving. You learned that location variables matter. You learned that real estate is not magic—it is math plus management.

In **Chapter 11**, we dismantled hustle culture.

You don't need to fly escort, SEAD, and strike simultaneously.

Sequential excellence. Not simultaneous mediocrity. Side hustles are not moral obligations. They are strategic tools. Focus remains king.

In **Chapter 12**, we talked advanced strategies.

BFM before escort. Advanced tools amplify whatever is underneath. If your fundamentals are weak, leverage magnifies weakness. If your foundation is strong, advanced strategy multiplies strength.

Part III was about controlled acceleration. Not hype. Not shortcuts. Not ego.

The Through-Line

From the first mission commander story to the last flight, the lesson stayed the same:

- Target backward.
- Give every dollar orders.
- Respect compounding.
- Debrief without ego.
- Build systems.
- Increase capacity slowly.
- Never confuse activity with alignment.

Financial freedom is not about becoming rich. It is about building a life where your time belongs to you.

And that is not achieved through intensity. It is achieved through consistency.

The Real Scorecard

At the beginning of your career, you measure progress by milestones such as rank, income, net worth, properties, or portfolio size.

At the end, the scorecard changes. It becomes so much more about the life you lived than the money you made: Did you live deliberately? Did you steward your resources well? Did you build margin instead of stress? Did you use money as a tool—or let it use you?

This book is not a get-rich manual. It is a discipline manual. It is a mission-planning guide for your financial life.

And if you execute it—not perfectly, but consistently—you will look up one day and realize you built something extraordinary without ever chasing extraordinary.

The Five Anchors

We have covered a lot of ground in this book: Tactics, Tools, Systems, Mindset, Advanced Strategies. If you still doubt the platform available to you, review Appendix and run your own numbers.

If you forget everything else, there are five anchor strategies I want you to take away. Five principles that, if executed consistently, will change your life.

First, win the 5% battle.

If you do nothing else, invest 5% of your base salary into a Roth TSP.

Not when you "feel ready." Not when the market looks safe. Not after you pay off everything.

Now.

The military matches your 5% after two years. That match is not generosity. It is leverage. It is acceleration.

If you start on day one and contribute 5% for 20 years, assuming an average 8% return, you will walk away from active duty with roughly $260,000.

Then leave it alone. Do not touch it. Do not panic. Do not get cute.

Let compounding do what it has done for centuries.

By age 65, that single disciplined habit can grow to more than $2 million. Not because you were brilliant. Because you were consistent.

Second, command your money.

Create your How I Spend My Money plan and stick to it.

Be disciplined and uncompromising with your goals.

Know your core values, vision, and mission for your life. That will be your true north when things are difficult, and things will be difficult at times.

Work on yourself first: personal growth precedes professional growth.

Third, build your Roth ladder.

When you are able, start contributing to a Roth IRA for yourself and eventually your spouse.

Increase this investment every year by the raise that you receive in January (historically around 2% average per year).

Continue to increase this investment annually and at every promotion until you have maxed it out the year's contribution limit.

Invest in low-cost index funds that give you average returns on the market and diversify your investments.

This is not sexy. But it is powerful.

Fourth, stay curious.

As you grow your knowledge through continuous self-improvement, get curious about what options may exist for you.

Learn about investing, real estate, and business. Learn about leadership and mindset.

Treat this knowledge like bricks you are putting into a wall. One day you will step back and have an entire building of knowledge that you built.

Use this knowledge to improve your quality of life and advance your goals.

Fifth, stay open to opportunity.

Once your foundation is solid, you earn the right to explore.

Real estate, business, advanced tax strategies, life insurance structures.

Your retirement base provides safety. Your knowledge, confidence. That combination allows you to move beyond survival and growth. Then beyond growth to impact.

Maslow called it self-actualization. I call it operating with a margin.

Borrow My Belief

If you made it this far, you already care.

And if you are still thinking, "This is great for you. . . but I don't know if it works for me," then let's address the real issue.

It's not knowledge.

It's belief.

Lacking belief is different than lacking ability. If that's where you are, then borrow mine.

I have seen ordinary military members build extraordinary lives through small, consistent decisions.

You do not need perfect timing. You do not need perfect income. You do not need a side hustle empire.

You need discipline. You need patience. And you need the courage to take the first step.

Leaving your comfort zone never becomes easy. But it does become familiar. And confidence is built through execution, not inspiration.

If you are finished living only the life that was expected of you—if you are ready to design your own trajectory—then consider this your official clearance.

Cleared hot.

I believe in you.

Now go build something that matters.

Appendix

20 Year Military Wealth Platform (Enlisted and Officer Examples)

Before we talk about advanced strategies, let's zoom out. There is a narrative floating around that you "can't build wealth in the military."

That narrative is wrong. Let's run the numbers.

An average Airman goes from E-1(Airman Basic) to E-3 (Airman 1st Class) in the first 16–24 months of their career.[1] The promotion from E-1 to E-2 (Airman) happens automatically upon successful completion of basic training. And the promotion to E-3 also happens automatically at the completion of technical training school. Promotion timelines vary widely between services, individuals, and career fields, so we will use some generalizations for this exercise.

Senior Airman (E-4) promotions are typically around three years' time-in-service (TIS) and the first Non-Commissioned Officer rank of E-5 (Staff Sergeant) can happen once the member has been an E-4 for at least six months, although the average promotion time is closer to 4.5-6 years. E-6 (Technical Sergeant) requires a minimum of five years but the average time to promotion for E-6 is about 12 years. E-7 is the first rank that is considered a Senior Non-Commissioned Officer or Senior NCO and is called Master Sergeant. The minimum for E-7 is eight years TIS and 2 years as an E-6, but the average promotion to E-7 happens at 17 years. E-8, Senior Master Sergeant, is a highly competitive rank and the average time to promotion to E-8 is around 19–20 years (the minimum requirement is 11 years

TIS and 20 months as E-7). And finally, E-9, or Chief Master Sergeant, is the highest grade one can achieve in the enlisted system and the average TIS to get promoted to E-9 is 22 years.

Much has been written about how to promote quicker through the military, so I will not delve deeply into this topic other than to offer a few observations from my 20+ years of service. The first piece of wisdom is to only worry about the things you can control. Too often I see military members stressed about some upcoming board but spending no time on the things within their control. I've always said that PT tests are free. They give you the test questions AND the answers ahead of time. And the test doesn't change, except to get a little easier as you age. If you are stressed about your next promotion, go out for a run, stop every half mile for some sit ups and push-ups. If you start two months before your test and do 10 push-ups and 10 sit ups in your workplace every single hour by setting an iPhone alarm, you will crush the test. The same applies for weight management. While there are many factors affecting weight, health, and physical fitness, nearly all of them are within your control. Fitness is free.

Invest in yourself. Read ahead. The military tells you what you need to do to be promoted. Instead of playing those extra few hours of Xbox, study and make 5-level as quickly as possible. Then get yourself to ALS and compete in WAPS. You may not get promoted right away, but at least you got yourself a seat at the promotion discussion by completing the eligibility requirements that are within your control. If you haven't figured it out yet, taking personal responsibility for your life and your career is one of the most profound steps that you can take in life, and a true step toward self-love.

Back to the good stuff—math. For this example, I am going to use the average promotion timeline outlined above. I understand that this is not universal, but it represents the average. Go ahead and fill in your own timeline if you would like. There are also some assumptions that I will be required to make, like annual pay increases, where I will use historical averages. While recent years have seen above average increases in basic pay, the historical (20 year) average as of 2024 is 2.6%. For BAH, I used Phoenix—my city—to calculate the rate. You can put your own city into a BAH rate calculator online to adjust the calculations.

Enlisted

For this example I will use these variables and controls:

1. They will begin in 2026 as an E-1 and promote on an average promotion timeline for 20 years.
    a. That means promote to E-2 at 6 months; E-3 at 18 months; E-4 at 36 months; E-5 at 7 years; E-6 at 12 years; E-7 at 17 years; E-8 at 20 years.
2. The government will give about a 2% raise to base pay every year.
3. They will be single and live in the dorms for the first three years.
4. They will move off base and rent years four to seven.
5. They will get married around year six and start having kids around year eight.
6. They will buy their first house around year 8–10.
7. They will receive BAS from the time they move off base.
8. They will receive BAH from the time they move off base, average for their rank and the nation.
9. They will receive a basic clothing allowance every year for uniforms.

TOTAL 20-YEAR COMPENSATION: $1,931,174
Breakdown by Component:

- **Base Pay (taxable):** $1,202,297
- **BAH (tax-free):** $600,361
- **BAS (tax-free):** $117,291
- **Clothing Allowance:** $11,225

Key Milestones:
Years 1–3 (Dorms, E-1 to E-3):

- Annual compensation: ~$31,000–$39,000
- No BAH/BAS (living in dorms, eating at chow hall)

Years 4–7 (Off-base single, E-4 to E-5):

- Annual compensation: ~$73,000–$93,000
- Start receiving BAH and BAS

Years 8–20 (Married with kids, E-5 to E-8):

- Annual compensation: ~$96,000–$145,000
- Higher BAH rate for dependents
- Peak earning years

Important Notes:

1. **Tax Advantages:** Of the $1.93M total, approximately $717,652 is **tax-free** (BAH + BAS + clothing), which is a huge benefit!

2. **This calculation DOES NOT include:**
    - Special duty pay
    - Hazardous duty pay
    - Deployment/combat pay
    - Bonuses (enlistment, re-enlistment, special skills)
    - Free healthcare value (~$10,000+/year for family)
    - GI Bill education benefits (~$100,000+ value)
    - Retirement pension after 20 years
3. **State Tax Impact:** If stationed in/from D.C. (10.75% tax) versus Florida (0% tax):
    - D.C. would pay ~$129,000 in state taxes on base pay over 20 years
    - **Florida saves $129,000**—which if invested could be worth **$500,000+** by retirement!

Bottom line: A 20-year enlisted career with average progression provides nearly $2 million in direct compensation, plus hundreds of thousands more in benefits—making the military one of the best total compensation packages available, especially when you factor in the tax advantages!

Officers

If you join the military as an O-1. . . Officer who starts as an O-1 with the following assumptions:

1. They will begin in 2026 as an O-1 and promote on an average promotion timeline for 20 years.
    - That means promote to O-2 at 2 years; O-3 at 4 years; O-4 at 10 years; O-5 at 15 years.

2. The government will give about a 2% raise to base pay every year.
3. They will be single and live in the dorms for the first one year.
4. They will move off base and rent years two to five.
5. They will get married around year six and start having kids around year eight.
6. They will buy their first house around year six.
7. They will receive BAS from the time they move off base.
8. They will receive BAH from the time they move off base, average for their rank and the nation.

TOTAL 20-YEAR OFFICER COMPENSATION: $3,349,916
Officer Breakdown by Component:

- **Base Pay (taxable):** $2,445,887
- **BAH (tax-free):** $816,894
- **BAS (tax-free):** $87,133

Key Milestones:
Year 1 (Dorms, O-1):

- Annual compensation: ~$48,000
- No BAH/BAS

Years 2-5 (Off-base single, O-1 to O-3):

- Annual compensation: ~$76,000–$121,000
- Rapid progression through junior officer ranks

Years 6-10 (Married, O-3):

- Annual compensation: ~$127,000–$158,000
- Company grade officer peak

Years 11-20 (Married with kids, O-4 to O-5):

- Annual compensation: ~$168,000–$261,000
- Field grade officer, top earning years

OFFICER VERSUS ENLISTED COMPARISON:

Category	Officer	Enlisted	Difference
Total 20-Year Comp	**$3,349,916**	**$1,931,174**	**+$1,418,742**
Base Pay	$2,445,887	$1,202,297	+$1,243,590
BAH	$816,894	$600,361	+$216,533
BAS	$87,133	$117,291	−$30,158
Tax-Free Portion	**$904,027**	**$717,652**	**+$186,375**

Key Insights:

1. **Officers earn 73.5% MORE** than enlisted over 20 years—nearly **$1.4 million more**!
2. **Tax advantage is HUGE:** Officers have $904,027 in tax-free compensation versus $717,652 for enlisted

3. **State Tax Impact (D.C. versus Florida):**
    - Officer in District of Columbia: ~$263,000 in state taxes on base pay
    - Officer in Florida: $0
    - **Savings: $263,000** (which invested could be worth **$1+ million** by retirement)
4. **Annual compensation in Year 20:**
    - Officer: $261,053
    - Enlisted: $145,360
    - Officer makes $115,693 more in the final year alone!
5. **College is worth it:** The ~$1.4 million difference more than pays for any college degree (even if you paid full price at a private university)

Important Notes:
This does NOT include:

- Flight pay, submarine pay, special duty pays (can add $10,000–$30,000+/year)
- Deployment/combat/hazardous duty pay
- Bonuses (retention bonuses for officers can be $35,000–$100,000+)
- Free healthcare (~$10,000–$15,000/year value for family)
- Post-9/11 GI Bill (can transfer to dependents)
- **Retirement pension:** Officers retiring as O-5 with 20 years get ~$50,000–$60,000/year for life!

Bottom Line: A 20-year officer career provides **$3.35 million in direct compensation** plus potentially $1-2 million more in benefits and retirement pay. Combined with tax advantages and the state residency decision, the total lifetime value easily exceeds **$5–6 million**!

Month-by-Month Example

5% invested in TSP; promotions on an average timeline; 2% approximate raise to base pay each year; and 8% return from your investments.

Month	Grade	YOS	Base Pay	Member Contrib	Agency Contrib	Balance
1	E-1	0.083	$2,407.12	$–	$–	$–
2	E-1	0.167	$2,407.12	$–	$–	$–
3	E-2	0.250	$2,697.97	$134.90	$26.98	$161.88
4	E-2	0.333	$2,697.97	$134.90	$26.98	$324.84
5	E-2	0.417	$2,697.97	$134.90	$26.98	$488.88
6	E-2	0.500	$2,697.97	$134.90	$26.98	$654.02
7	E-2	0.583	$2,697.97	$134.90	$26.98	$820.26
8	E-2	0.667	$2,697.97	$134.90	$26.98	$987.60
9	E-2	0.750	$2,697.97	$134.90	$26.98	$1,156.06
10	E-2	0.833	$2,697.97	$134.90	$26.98	$1,325.65
11	E-2	0.917	$2,697.97	$134.90	$26.98	$1,496.36
12	E-2	1.000	$2,697.97	$134.90	$26.98	$1,668.22
13	E-2	1.083	$2,751.93	$137.60	$27.52	$1,844.46
14	E-2	1.167	$2,751.93	$137.60	$27.52	$2,021.87
15	E-2	1.250	$2,751.93	$137.60	$27.52	$2,200.46
16	E-3	1.333	$2,893.59	$144.68	$28.94	$2,388.75
17	E-3	1.417	$2,893.59	$144.68	$28.94	$2,578.29
18	E-3	1.500	$2,893.59	$144.68	$28.94	$2,769.09
19	E-3	1.583	$2,893.59	$144.68	$28.94	$2,961.17
20	E-3	1.667	$2,893.59	$144.68	$28.94	$3,154.52

Month	Grade	YOS	Base Pay	Member Contrib	Agency Contrib	Balance
21	E-3	1.750	$2,893.59	$144.68	$28.94	$3,349.17
22	E-3	1.833	$2,893.59	$144.68	$28.94	$3,545.11
23	E-3	1.917	$2,893.59	$144.68	$28.94	$3,742.36
24	E-3	2.000	$3,075.27	$153.76	$30.75	$3,951.83
25	E-3	2.083	$3,136.77	$156.84	$156.84	$4,291.85
26	E-3	2.167	$3,136.77	$156.84	$156.84	$4,634.14
27	E-3	2.250	$3,136.77	$156.84	$156.84	$4,978.71
28	E-3	2.333	$3,136.77	$156.84	$156.84	$5,325.58
29	E-3	2.417	$3,136.77	$156.84	$156.84	$5,674.76
30	E-3	2.500	$3,136.77	$156.84	$156.84	$6,026.27
31	E-3	2.583	$3,136.77	$156.84	$156.84	$6,380.12
32	E-3	2.667	$3,136.77	$156.84	$156.84	$6,736.34
33	E-3	2.750	$3,136.77	$156.84	$156.84	$7,094.92
34	E-3	2.833	$3,136.77	$156.84	$156.84	$7,455.90
35	E-3	2.917	$3,136.77	$156.84	$156.84	$7,819.28
36	E-4	3.000	$3,623.08	$181.15	$181.15	$8,233.72
37	E-4	3.083	$3,695.54	$184.78	$184.78	$8,658.16
38	E-4	3.167	$3,695.54	$184.78	$184.78	$9,085.44
39	E-4	3.250	$3,695.54	$184.78	$184.78	$9,515.56
40	E-4	3.333	$3,695.54	$184.78	$184.78	$9,948.55
41	E-4	3.417	$3,695.54	$184.78	$184.78	$10,384.43
42	E-4	3.500	$3,695.54	$184.78	$184.78	$10,823.22
43	E-4	3.583	$3,695.54	$184.78	$184.78	$11,264.92

Month	Grade	YOS	Base Pay	Member Contrib	Agency Contrib	Balance
44	E-4	3.667	$3,695.54	$184.78	$184.78	$11,709.58
45	E-4	3.750	$3,695.54	$184.78	$184.78	$12,157.20
46	E-4	3.833	$3,695.54	$184.78	$184.78	$12,607.80
47	E-4	3.917	$3,695.54	$184.78	$184.78	$13,061.40
48	E-4	4.000	$3,882.58	$194.13	$194.13	$13,536.74
49	E-4	4.083	$3,960.23	$198.01	$198.01	$14,023.01
50	E-4	4.167	$3,960.23	$198.01	$198.01	$14,512.51
51	E-4	4.250	$3,960.23	$198.01	$198.01	$15,005.29
52	E-4	4.333	$3,960.23	$198.01	$198.01	$15,501.35
53	E-4	4.417	$3,960.23	$198.01	$198.01	$16,000.71
54	E-4	4.500	$3,960.23	$198.01	$198.01	$16,503.41
55	E-4	4.583	$3,960.23	$198.01	$198.01	$17,009.45
56	E-4	4.667	$3,960.23	$198.01	$198.01	$17,518.87
57	E-4	4.750	$3,960.23	$198.01	$198.01	$18,031.69
58	E-4	4.833	$3,960.23	$198.01	$198.01	$18,547.92
59	E-4	4.917	$3,960.23	$198.01	$198.01	$19,067.60
60	E-4	5.000	$3,960.23	$198.01	$198.01	$19,590.74
61	E-4	5.083	$4,039.43	$201.97	$201.97	$20,125.28
62	E-4	5.167	$4,039.43	$201.97	$201.97	$20,663.40
63	E-4	5.250	$4,039.43	$201.97	$201.97	$21,205.10
64	E-4	5.333	$4,039.43	$201.97	$201.97	$21,750.41
65	E-4	5.417	$4,039.43	$201.97	$201.97	$22,299.35
66	E-4	5.500	$4,039.43	$201.97	$201.97	$22,851.96

Month	Grade	YOS	Base Pay	Member Contrib	Agency Contrib	Balance
67	E-4	5.583	$4,039.43	$201.97	$201.97	$23,408.25
68	E-4	5.667	$4,039.43	$201.97	$201.97	$23,968.25
69	E-4	5.750	$4,039.43	$201.97	$201.97	$24,531.98
70	E-4	5.833	$4,039.43	$201.97	$201.97	$25,099.47
71	E-4	5.917	$4,039.43	$201.97	$201.97	$25,670.74
72	E-5	6.000	$4,537.62	$226.88	$226.88	$26,295.64
73	E-5	6.083	$4,628.37	$231.42	$231.42	$26,933.78
74	E-5	6.167	$4,628.37	$231.42	$231.42	$27,576.18
75	E-5	6.250	$4,628.37	$231.42	$231.42	$28,222.86
76	E-5	6.333	$4,628.37	$231.42	$231.42	$28,873.85
77	E-5	6.417	$4,628.37	$231.42	$231.42	$29,529.18
78	E-5	6.500	$4,628.37	$231.42	$231.42	$30,188.87
79	E-5	6.583	$4,628.37	$231.42	$231.42	$30,852.97
80	E-5	6.667	$4,628.37	$231.42	$231.42	$31,521.49
81	E-5	6.750	$4,628.37	$231.42	$231.42	$32,194.47
82	E-5	6.833	$4,628.37	$231.42	$231.42	$32,871.94
83	E-5	6.917	$4,628.37	$231.42	$231.42	$33,553.92
84	E-5	7.000	$4,628.37	$231.42	$231.42	$34,240.45
85	E-5	7.083	$4,720.94	$236.05	$236.05	$34,940.82
86	E-5	7.167	$4,720.94	$236.05	$236.05	$35,645.85
87	E-5	7.250	$4,720.94	$236.05	$236.05	$36,355.58
88	E-5	7.333	$4,720.94	$236.05	$236.05	$37,070.05
89	E-5	7.417	$4,720.94	$236.05	$236.05	$37,789.27

Month	Grade	YOS	Base Pay	Member Contrib	Agency Contrib	Balance
90	E-5	7.500	$4,720.94	$236.05	$236.05	$38,513.30
91	E-5	7.583	$4,720.94	$236.05	$236.05	$39,242.15
92	E-5	7.667	$4,720.94	$236.05	$236.05	$39,975.85
93	E-5	7.750	$4,720.94	$236.05	$236.05	$40,714.45
94	E-5	7.833	$4,720.94	$236.05	$236.05	$41,457.98
95	E-5	7.917	$4,720.94	$236.05	$236.05	$42,206.46
96	E-5	8.000	$4,917.67	$245.88	$245.88	$42,979.60
97	E-5	8.083	$5,016.03	$250.80	$250.80	$43,767.73
98	E-5	8.167	$5,016.03	$250.80	$250.80	$44,561.12
99	E-5	8.250	$5,016.03	$250.80	$250.80	$45,359.80
100	E-5	8.333	$5,016.03	$250.80	$250.80	$46,163.80
101	E-5	8.417	$5,016.03	$250.80	$250.80	$46,973.16
102	E-5	8.500	$5,016.03	$250.80	$250.80	$47,787.92
103	E-5	8.583	$5,016.03	$250.80	$250.80	$48,608.11
104	E-5	8.667	$5,016.03	$250.80	$250.80	$49,433.76
105	E-5	8.750	$5,016.03	$250.80	$250.80	$50,264.92
106	E-5	8.833	$5,016.03	$250.80	$250.80	$51,101.63
107	E-5	8.917	$5,016.03	$250.80	$250.80	$51,943.91
108	E-5	9.000	$5,016.03	$250.80	$250.80	$52,791.80
109	E-5	9.083	$5,116.35	$255.82	$255.82	$53,655.38
110	E-5	9.167	$5,116.35	$255.82	$255.82	$54,524.72
111	E-5	9.250	$5,116.35	$255.82	$255.82	$55,399.85
112	E-5	9.333	$5,116.35	$255.82	$255.82	$56,280.82

Month	Grade	YOS	Base Pay	Member Contrib	Agency Contrib	Balance
113	E-5	9.417	$5,116.35	$255.82	$255.82	$57,167.66
114	E-5	9.500	$5,116.35	$255.82	$255.82	$58,060.41
115	E-5	9.583	$5,116.35	$255.82	$255.82	$58,959.11
116	E-5	9.667	$5,116.35	$255.82	$255.82	$59,863.81
117	E-5	9.750	$5,116.35	$255.82	$255.82	$60,774.54
118	E-5	9.833	$5,116.35	$255.82	$255.82	$61,691.33
119	E-5	9.917	$5,116.35	$255.82	$255.82	$62,614.24
120	E-5	10.000	$5,252.92	$262.65	$262.65	$63,556.97
121	E-5	10.083	$5,357.98	$267.90	$267.90	$64,516.48
122	E-5	10.167	$5,357.98	$267.90	$267.90	$65,482.38
123	E-5	10.250	$5,357.98	$267.90	$267.90	$66,454.73
124	E-5	10.333	$5,357.98	$267.90	$267.90	$67,433.56
125	E-5	10.417	$5,357.98	$267.90	$267.90	$68,418.92
126	E-5	10.500	$5,357.98	$267.90	$267.90	$69,410.84
127	E-5	10.583	$5,357.98	$267.90	$267.90	$70,409.38
128	E-5	10.667	$5,357.98	$267.90	$267.90	$71,414.57
129	E-5	10.750	$5,357.98	$267.90	$267.90	$72,426.47
130	E-5	10.833	$5,357.98	$267.90	$267.90	$73,445.11
131	E-5	10.917	$5,357.98	$ 267.90	$267.90	$74,470.54
132	E-6	11.000	$5,801.73	$290.09	$290.09	$75,547.18
133	E-6	11.083	$5,917.77	$295.89	$295.89	$76,642.61
134	E-6	11.167	$5,917.77	$295.89	$295.89	$77,745.33
135	E-6	11.250	$5,917.77	$295.89	$295.89	$78,855.41

Month	Grade	YOS	Base Pay	Member Contrib	Agency Contrib	Balance
136	E-6	11.333	$5,917.77	$295.89	$295.89	$79,972.89
137	E-6	11.417	$5,917.77	$295.89	$295.89	$81,097.82
138	E-6	11.500	$5,917.77	$295.89	$295.89	$82,230.25
139	E-6	11.583	$5,917.77	$295.89	$295.89	$83,370.23
140	E-6	11.667	$5,917.77	$295.89	$295.89	$84,517.81
141	E-6	11.750	$5,917.77	$295.89	$295.89	$85,673.04
142	E-6	11.833	$5,917.77	$295.89	$295.89	$86,835.97
143	E-6	11.917	$5,917.77	$295.89	$295.89	$88,006.65
144	E-6	12.000	$5,917.77	$295.89	$295.89	$89,185.14
145	E-6	12.083	$6,036.12	$301.81	$301.81	$90,383.32
146	E-6	12.167	$6,036.12	$301.81	$301.81	$91,589.48
147	E-6	12.250	$6,036.12	$301.81	$301.81	$92,803.69
148	E-6	12.333	$6,036.12	$301.81	$301.81	$94,026.00
149	E-6	12.417	$6,036.12	$301.81	$301.81	$95,256.45
150	E-6	12.500	$6,036.12	$301.81	$301.81	$96,495.10
151	E-6	12.583	$6,036.12	$301.81	$301.81	$97,742.02
152	E-6	12.667	$6,036.12	$301.81	$301.81	$98,997.24
153	E-6	12.750	$6,036.12	$301.81	$301.81	$100,260.83
154	E-6	12.833	$6,036.12	$301.81	$301.81	$101,532.85
155	E-6	12.917	$6,036.12	$301.81	$301.81	$102,813.35
156	E-6	13.000	$6,036.12	$301.81	$301.81	$104,102.38
157	E-6	13.083	$6,156.84	$307.84	$307.84	$105,412.08
158	E-6	13.167	$6,156.84	$307.84	$307.84	$106,730.52

Month	Grade	YOS	Base Pay	Member Contrib	Agency Contrib	Balance
159	E-6	13.250	$6,156.84	$307.84	$307.84	$108,057.74
160	E-6	13.333	$6,156.84	$307.84	$307.84	$109,393.81
161	E-6	13.417	$6,156.84	$307.84	$307.84	$110,738.78
162	E-6	13.500	$6,156.84	$307.84	$307.84	$112,092.73
163	E-6	13.583	$6,156.84	$307.84	$307.84	$113,455.69
164	E-6	13.667	$6,156.84	$307.84	$307.84	$114,827.75
165	E-6	13.750	$6,156.84	$307.84	$307.84	$116,208.95
166	E-6	13.833	$6,156.84	$307.84	$307.84	$117,599.36
167	E-6	13.917	$6,156.84	$307.84	$307.84	$118,999.04
168	E-6	14.000	$6,156.84	$307.84	$307.84	$120,408.05
169	E-6	14.083	$6,279.98	$314.00	$314.00	$121,838.77
170	E-6	14.167	$6,279.98	$314.00	$314.00	$123,279.03
171	E-6	14.250	$6,279.98	$314.00	$314.00	$124,728.89
172	E-6	14.333	$6,279.98	$314.00	$314.00	$126,188.41
173	E-6	14.417	$6,279.98	$314.00	$314.00	$127,657.67
174	E-6	14.500	$6,279.98	$314.00	$314.00	$129,136.71
175	E-6	14.583	$6,279.98	$314.00	$314.00	$130,625.62
176	E-6	14.667	$6,279.98	$314.00	$314.00	$132,124.46
177	E-6	14.750	$6,279.98	$314.00	$314.00	$133,633.29
178	E-6	14.833	$6,279.98	$314.00	$314.00	$135,152.17
179	E-6	14.917	$6,279.98	$314.00	$314.00	$136,681.19
180	E-6	15.000	$6,279.98	$314.00	$314.00	$138,220.39
181	E-6	15.083	$6,405.58	$320.28	$320.28	$139,782.42

Month	Grade	YOS	Base Pay	Member Contrib	Agency Contrib	Balance
182	E-6	15.167	$6,405.58	$320.28	$320.28	$141,354.86
183	E-6	15.250	$6,405.58	$320.28	$320.28	$142,937.78
184	E-6	15.333	$6,405.58	$320.28	$320.28	$144,531.26
185	E-6	15.417	$6,405.58	$320.28	$320.28	$146,135.36
186	E-6	15.500	$6,405.58	$320.28	$320.28	$147,750.15
187	E-6	15.583	$6,405.58	$320.28	$320.28	$149,375.71
188	E-6	15.667	$6,405.58	$320.28	$320.28	$151,012.11
189	E-6	15.750	$6,405.58	$320.28	$320.28	$152,659.41
190	E-6	15.833	$6,405.58	$320.28	$320.28	$154,317.70
191	E-6	15.917	$6,405.58	$320.28	$320.28	$155,987.04
192	E-7	16.000	$7,133.56	$356.68	$356.68	$157,740.31
193	E-7	16.083	$7,276.23	$363.81	$363.81	$159,519.54
194	E-7	16.167	$7,276.23	$363.81	$363.81	$161,310.63
195	E-7	16.250	$7,276.23	$363.81	$363.81	$163,113.65
196	E-7	16.333	$7,276.23	$363.81	$363.81	$164,928.70
197	E-7	16.417	$7,276.23	$363.81	$363.81	$166,755.85
198	E-7	16.500	$7,276.23	$363.81	$363.81	$168,595.18
199	E-7	16.583	$7,276.23	$363.81	$363.81	$170,446.77
200	E-7	16.667	$7,276.23	$363.81	$363.81	$172,310.70
201	E-7	16.750	$7,276.23	$363.81	$363.81	$174,187.06
202	E-7	16.833	$7,276.23	$363.81	$363.81	$176,075.93
203	E-7	16.917	$7,276.23	$363.81	$363.81	$177,977.40
204	E-7	17.000	$7,276.23	$363.81	$363.81	$179,891.54

Month	Grade	YOS	Base Pay	Member Contrib	Agency Contrib	Balance
205	E-7	17.083	$7,421.76	$371.09	$371.09	$181,832.99
206	E-7	17.167	$7,421.76	$371.09	$371.09	$183,787.38
207	E-7	17.250	$7,421.76	$371.09	$371.09	$185,754.81
208	E-7	17.333	$7,421.76	$371.09	$371.09	$187,735.35
209	E-7	17.417	$7,421.76	$371.09	$371.09	$189,729.09
210	E-7	17.500	$7,421.76	$371.09	$371.09	$191,736.13
211	E-7	17.583	$7,421.76	$371.09	$371.09	$193,756.55
212	E-7	17.667	$7,421.76	$371.09	$371.09	$195,790.43
213	E-7	17.750	$7,421.76	$371.09	$371.09	$197,837.88
214	E-7	17.833	$7,421.76	$371.09	$371.09	$199,898.97
215	E-7	17.917	$7,421.76	$371.09	$371.09	$201,973.81
216	E-7	18.000	$7,421.76	$371.09	$371.09	$204,062.48
217	E-7	18.083	$7,570.19	$378.51	$378.51	$206,179.91
218	E-7	18.167	$7,570.19	$378.51	$378.51	$208,311.46
219	E-7	18.250	$7,570.19	$378.51	$378.51	$210,457.23
220	E-7	18.333	$7,570.19	$378.51	$378.51	$212,617.29
221	E-7	18.417	$7,570.19	$378.51	$378.51	$214,791.76
222	E-7	18.500	$7,570.19	$378.51	$378.51	$216,980.72
223	E-7	18.583	$7,570.19	$378.51	$378.51	$219,184.28
224	E-7	18.667	$7,570.19	$378.51	$378.51	$221,402.53
225	E-7	18.750	$7,570.19	$378.51	$378.51	$223,635.57
226	E-7	18.833	$7,570.19	$378.51	$378.51	$225,883.49
227	E-7	18.917	$7,570.19	$378.51	$378.51	$228,146.40

Month	Grade	YOS	Base Pay	Member Contrib	Agency Contrib	Balance
228	E-7	19.000	$7,570.19	$378.51	$378.51	$230,424.39
229	E-7	19.083	$7,721.59	$386.08	$386.08	$232,732.71
230	E-7	19.167	$7,721.59	$386.08	$386.08	$235,056.43
231	E-7	19.250	$7,721.59	$386.08	$386.08	$237,395.63
232	E-7	19.333	$7,721.59	$386.08	$386.08	$239,750.42
233	E-7	19.417	$7,721.59	$386.08	$386.08	$242,120.92
234	E-7	19.500	$7,721.59	$386.08	$386.08	$244,507.22
235	E-7	19.583	$7,721.59	$386.08	$386.08	$246,909.43
236	E-7	19.667	$7,721.59	$386.08	$386.08	$249,327.65
237	E-7	19.750	$7,721.59	$386.08	$386.08	$251,761.99
238	E-7	19.833	$7,721.59	$386.08	$386.08	$254,212.57
239	E-7	19.917	$7,721.59	$386.08	$386.08	$256,679.48
240	E-7	20.000	$7,721.59	$386.08	$386.08	$259,162.83

Reading List:

Personal Growth and Development

- *7 Habits of Highly Effective People* by Stephen Covey
- *Atomic Habits* by James Clear
- *21 Irrefutable Laws of Leadership* by John Maxwell
- *Think and Grow Rich* by Napoleon Hill

Real Estate

- *Rich Dad Poor Dad* by Robert Kiyosaki
- *The Multifamily Millionaire* by Brandon Turner and Brian Murray
- *Cash Flow Quadrant* by Robert Kiyosaki

Negotiating

- *Start with No* by Jim Camp
- *Never Split the Difference* by Chris Voss and Tahl Raz

Business

- *BE2.0 (Beyond Entrepreneurship 2.0)* by Jim Collins and Bill Lazier

Notes

Part I

1. slickcharts.com/sp500/returns
2 *Any references to investment returns in this book are based on historical data from the S&P 500. These figures are provided for educational purposes only and should not be interpreted as a guarantee of future investment performance.*

Chapter 1

1. https://www.lonestarlaw.net/study-shows-that-military-personnel-marry-at-younger-age/#:~:text=According%20to%20a%20Department%20of,before%20the%20age%20of%2030
2. https://www.militaryonesource.mil/data-research-and-statistics/survey-findings/spouse-voices/#:~:text=50%25%20of%20active%2Dduty%20members%20are%20married
3. James Clear, Atomic Habits.
4. https://militaryfamilies.com/money/top-financial-mistakes-enlisted-military-members-make/#:~:text=Financial%20mistakes%20aren't%20limited%20to%20enlisted%20service,without%20staying%20long%2Dterm%20(more%20than%203%2D5%20years)
5. https://www.bls.gov/opub/ted/2024/a-toast-to-the-new-year.htm#:~:text=In%202023%2C%20households%20in%20the%20United%20States,$147%20in%202020%20to%20$343%20in%202023

Chapter 2

1. https://www.tsp.gov/making-contributions/contribution-types/#:~:text=Agency/Service%20automatic%20(1%25),50%20cents%20on%20the%20dollar
2. The Ripple Effect of Automatic Enrollment, James Choi, Professor of Finance, Yale School of Management; https://www.youtube.com/watch?v=SWsilhlAw4o&t=13s
3. The Downside of Defaults, Jeffrey R Brown, University of Illinois at Urbana-Champaign and NBER; Anne M Farrell, Miami University; Scott J Weisbenner: chrome-extension://efaidnbmnnnibpcajpcglclefindmkaj/https://www.nber.org/sites/default/files/2020-08/orrc11-01.pdf
4. You put in 5%, they match 5%, a total of 10% of your base salary without any additional cost. This is an agency automatic 1% + up to 4% match policies depending on service time and can change.
5. *Any references to investment returns in this book are based on historical data from the S&P 500. These figures are provided for educational purposes only and should not be interpreted as a guarantee of future investment performance.*
6. https://www.tsp.gov/bulletins/20-u-1/#:~:text=All%20uniformed%20services%20members%20first,Beneficiary%20Participant%20Account%20(BPA)
7. https://www.tsp.gov/funds-lifecycle/

Chapter 3

1. My FICO Score: https://www.myfico.com/credit-education/whats-in-your-credit-score
2. Federal Reserve Education, Credit Score: https://www.federalreserveeducation.org/teaching-resources/personal-finance/managing-credit/how-a-fico-credit-score-is-determined
3. https://www.tsp.gov/tsp-loans/

Chapter 6

1. https://www.forbes.com/sites/janehanson/2025/01/10/why-millions-quit-their-resolutions-today-and-how-you-can-be-the-exception/

Chapter 8

1. https://www.schwab.com/learn/story/guide-to-risk-profiles
2. https://awealthofcommonsense.com/2023/02/deconstructing-10-20-30-year-stock-market-returns/?utm_source=chatgpt.com
3. chrome-extension://efaidnbmnnnibpcajpcglclefindmkaj/https://requisitecm.com/pdf/SPIVA-US-Scorecard-Year-End-2024.pdf
4. chrome-extension://efaidnbmnnnibpcajpcglclefindmkaj/https://www.fidelity.com/bin-public/060_www.fidelity.com/documents/about-fidelity/FidelityInvestmentsWomen&InvestingStudy2021.pdf
5. https://www.forbes.com/sites/timmaurer/2023/04/30/why-women-are-better-investors-than-men/

Chapter 9

1. NerdWallet. https://www.nerdwallet.com/banking/learn/average-rates-for-deposit-accounts#:~:text=The%20national%20average%20rate%20for%20checking%20accounts,much%20higher%20rates%20than%20the%20national%20average.
2. Investopedia. https://www.investopedia.com/high-yield-savings-accounts-4770633
3. https://www.statista.com/statistics/255590/number-of-mutual-fund-companies-in-the-united-states/
4. https://awealthofcommonsense.com/2023/02/deconstructing-10-20-30-year-stock-market-returns/?utm_source=chatgpt.com
5. https://www.tsp.gov/bulletins/20-u-1/#:~:text=All%20uniformed%20services%20members%20first,Beneficiary%20Participant%20Account%20(BPA).
6. https://www.tsp.gov/funds-lifecycle/

Chapter 10

1. https://www.loopnet.com/cre-explained/tools/irr-calculator/?gad_source=1&gad_campaignid=23461240511&gbraid=0AAAAAD_kiK5WwA0iod2C1eSC67OJCbqb1&gclid=Cj0KCQiA7fbLBhDJARIsAOAqhsfeU3OQMsUTLbozg23nAATzc6G8fUkmANnsWtjyC1HV7H48KI-5ADAaAqthEALw_wcB
2. https://dqydj.com/historical-home-prices/

Appendix

1. https://foreverwingman.com/how-quickly-can-you-rank-up-in-the-air-force/

Acknowledgments

There is a moment in every fighter pilot's career when they realize that no mission—not a single one—was ever truly flown alone. The debrief gets the glory, but the real work happened long before the jet ever left the ground. The planners. The crew chiefs. The controllers. The wingmen. Every one of them made the mission possible.

Writing this book was no different.

Hillary. Where do I even start?

You are the reason any of this exists. Not the book—the life. The actual life that inspired every word on these pages.

You have been my ride-or-die since this young lieutenant with more ambition than answers walked into your world and somehow convinced you to come along for the ride. Twenty years of marriage, four kids, a dozen duty stations, more deployments than either of us care to count, and somewhere in the middle of all of it—you became the best person I have ever known.

You have taught me more than any book, any mentor, any mission debrief ever could. You challenged me to be better on the days I thought I was already pretty good. You held a mirror up and showed me the version of myself I was capable of becoming—and then you stood there patiently while I figured out how to get there. That is not a small thing. That is everything.

You lifted me when I was low. You kept me grounded when I flew too high. You stood beside me in the seasons when I was winning as well as the seasons I was losing—and you never, not once, made me feel like one was more worthy of your presence than the other. That kind of love doesn't just support a person—it transforms them.

You are my best friend. My wingman. My home.

This book is as much yours as it is mine. Thank you for every hard conversation that made me a better writer, a better husband, and a better man. I love you more than I will ever be able to say—but I'll spend the rest of my life trying.

Ryan, Evie, Lucy, and Linc—you are the whole point. Everything I have built, every sacrifice I made, every early morning and late night—it was all so that you would inherit not just resources, but a model. A way of thinking. A belief that anything is possible if you show up, work hard, and never quit. Daddy Dragon loves you more than words. Don't let him catch you.

Mom and Dad, and sibs—thank you for the foundation. Growing up the way we did, in a house full of people who worked hard and loved each other even when times were tight, taught me more about gratitude, grit, and the value of a dollar than any financial textbook ever could. Mom and Dad—you gave me everything that mattered, even when you didn't have much to give. I never forgot that. I never will.

To everyone who sat down with me for a cup of coffee over the years, asked a hard question, or trusted me with their story—thank you. You are the reason I wrote this. You gave me a purpose worth putting on paper.

This one's for all of you.

About the Author

Shawn "Motor" Walsh is not going to tell you he was the best at anything.

He grew up in New Jersey—one of seven kids in a working-class family where the cable bill and the phone bill took turns getting paid. He played sports. He participated. He worked hard. He was not the star of the team, not the top of his class, not the kid anyone looked at and said, *that one's going to be something special.*

He earned an ROTC scholarship to study engineering at Embry-Riddle Aeronautical University in Florida—not because doors were opened for him, but because he found them and knocked. He graduated. Not at the top. But he graduated. He earned a pilot slot in the United States Air Force, went through pilot training, and repeated the same sequence he'd been running his whole life: show up, work hard, don't quit, and trust that the process eventually pays off.

It did.

Over a 20-year career, Shawn flew the F-16 Fighting Falcon, commanded a fighter squadron, deployed multiple times with different units, saw combat, and served alongside some of the finest men and women this country has ever produced. He lived and worked on multiple continents—from the American Southwest to South Korea to Europe—and came home from each assignment with a deeper appreciation for what it means to be a free people, governed by a Constitution worth defending.

He started his career $50,000 in debt with no idea what he was doing financially.

He retired from the Air Force with an eight-figure net worth and what he calls the only thing that actually matters: the freedom to do whatever he wants with his time.

But here is the part he most wants you to hear.

None of that happened because he was special. It happened because he refused to quit. He made more mistakes than he can count—financial mistakes, leadership mistakes, life mistakes—and every single one of them taught him something. He won or he learned. He never failed, because he never stopped.

Every day you wake up is either a success or a failure working toward your goal. If every day is a success—even a small one, even an unremarkable one—it is mathematically impossible not to reach your destination eventually.

That is not motivation. That is just math.

Shawn shares his story, his strategies, and his mistakes openly because he believes the most dangerous lie in personal finance is the idea that wealth building is reserved for people who started with advantages. He didn't. You don't have to either.

He lives in Phoenix, Arizona, with his wife Hillary and their four children.

He still makes his own coffee every morning.

Connect with Shawn on social media, where he shares content on fighter aviation, financial freedom, and the pursuit of a life well lived. @realshawnwalsh Facebook, Instagram, TikTok, YouTube.

Index